ERUERA

ERUERA
THE TEACHINGS
OF A MAORI ELDER

ERUERA STIRLING as told to ANNE SALMOND

OXFORD UNIVERSITY PRESS
WELLINGTON

Oxford University Press
OXFORD   LONDON   GLASGOW
NEW YORK   TORONTO   MELBOURNE   WELLINGTON
KUALA LUMPUR   SINGAPORE   HONG KONG   TOKYO
NAIROBI   DAR ES SALAAM   CAPE TOWN
DELHI   BOMBAY   CALCUTTA   MADRAS   KARACHI

ISBN 0 19 558069 9   CLOTH
      0 19 558070 2   PAPER

Designed by Publication Graphics Ltd.
Photoset in Baskerville and
printed by Whitcoulls Ltd, Christchurch
Published by Oxford University Press
222-236 Willis Street, Wellington.

CONTENTS

LIST OF MAPS

'*Na taku rourou, na tou rourou, ka ora ai te manuhiri.*'
'*My small flax basket and yours, together will feed the visitors.*'

At any gathering in the Maori world the orators stand to speak on the marae, but behind the scenes the workers make their pageantry possible. This is an orator's book, and many people have helped it to be heard.

Firstly, I thank the University Grants Committee for funding Rangi Motu and Ata Pedersen in their long and patient work of transcribing the tapes – without their efforts, this book could not have been written.

Gail Dallimore hunted through East Coast land court records and weekly magazines with the support of the Student Community Service Programme, and she found many of the photographs that illustrate the text.

Ulva Belsham of Riverton, John Hall-Jones from Invercargill and June Starke at the Alexander Turnbull Library answered innumerable queries about William Stirling and his descendants in Bluff; the Department of Lands and Survey sent documents relating to William Stirling's land at Stirling Point, and Lyn Williams of the Southland Museum took photographs of Stirling's grave. My brother Geoff Thorpe made enquiries at the Maori Land Court Office in Christchurch, and Ulva Belsham sent some South Island genealogies of Makere Te Whanawhana. Sharon Dell of the Alexander Turnbull Library, Sir Robert Hall at the Gisborne Art Gallery and Museum, and the staff of National Archives helped to locate East Coast documents, and Judge Nicholson of the Tai Tokerau Land Court and the staff of the Rotorua and Gisborne Maori Land Courts gave invaluable advice on the use of land court records. Anne Leahy of the Historic Places Trust loaned a copy of the site survey for Kirieke pa at Raukokore, and the staff in the Gisborne Lands and Survey office found a number of early East Coast survey maps. Haare Williams and Whai Ngata of the Maori and Pacific Islands Unit (Radio New Zealand), and the Archive of Maori and Pacific Music (University of Auckland) contributed tapes of talks by Eruera Stirling over the past 15 years, and I am very grateful to Bruce Biggs for permission to use a discussion between Eruera Stirling, Arnold Reedy and a number of other elders, taped by him in 1966. I thank all these people for their kindness – he nui nga mihi ki a koutou katoa.

I also thank the headmaster of the Raukokore School and the local community for their kind permission to reproduce material from the Raukokore School Jubilee publication (1962) in an appendix to this book; Merimeri Penfold and Ata Pedersen checked some of the Maori texts and my efforts at translation, and Roka Paora, helped by Tini Paora and Waranga Maangi carefully checked over the manuscript – any errors that remain are my responsibility, of course, and not theirs. I would be very glad if readers who detect any mistakes or misunderstandings in the text could let me know about them, so that they can be corrected.

Dave Simmons and Cliff Whiting generously supplied photographs of East Coast ancestral carvings, John Miller loaned photographs of Wairuru marae in 1973, and David Charteris supplied the photographic record of the Raglan confrontation. Wendy Harrex has been an admirable editor, and my beloved husband Jeremy took many of the contemporary photographs in the text, drew the maps, and gave me time and peace to write.

Eruera's family – Amiria, Lucy, Wahawaha, Lilian, Marama, Kepa and the others have been a constant source of kindness over the years; and Max Rimoldi, Eleanor Horrocks, Jeff Sissons, Tomas Ludvigson, Merimeri Penfold, Wharetoroa Kerr, Gail Dallimore, Judith Binney and other friends and colleagues at the University of Auckland helped me to understand the difficulties and challenges of working within a Maori tradition of knowledge.

In the end, though, as is proper, the orator stands alone on the marae and speaks. Eruera decided that the manuscript should be written, he dissolved the difficulties and blessed our enterprise from beginning to end; and this book is his gift to a new generation.

May his voice go out across the maraes of New Zealand.

ANNE SALMOND
Auckland, July 1980

Eruera Stirling speaks on the marae at Pine Taiapa's tangi, Tikitiki, 1971. *Jeremy Salmond*

I can not Stop
all articles of old Histories just at this
very Period of time, all seems to have
a way of Bringing up the Hidden
Treasures of family Lore and
Tribal Traditions, to make way
and Prepare the Path way of the
Young Leaders of today, many of the
Young Leaders, all are graduated in
the Atmosphere of the time obtained
from the University of all Laws
Education and Highlights of Leader
ship far beyond, better than the
Generations of my time,
and my mind Directing me to bring
this unwritten histories of our
grandfathers and other Great
chiefs and young Leaders of the day moving up into the High
Ladders of History . . .

. . . the time
has arrived and we must go forward
to catch up with the Needs of the People
ways and means that will improve
our own ambitions, and get closer to
the Leading nations that surround
the four winds of the world.

from *The Centennial of the Waiomatatini Maori School*
by Eruera Stirling, 1978

1
THE BOOK
OF THE ANCESTORS

CHAPTER ONE
My Great-Grandpeople

Tihere – mauri ora!
I sneeze – it is life!
Whakarongo! Whakarongo! Whakarongo!
Listen! Listen! Listen!
Ki te tangi a te manu e karanga nei
To the cry of the bird calling
'Tui, tui, tuituia!'
'Unite, unite, be one!'
Tuia i runga, tuia i raro,
Unite above, unite below
Tuia i roto, tuia i waho
Unite within, unite without
Tuia i te here tangata
Unite in the brotherhood of man
Ka rongo te po, ka rongo te po
The night hears, the night hears
Tuia i te kawai tangata i heke mai
Unite the descent lines
I Hawaiki nui, i Hawaiki roa,
From great Hawaiki, from long Hawaiki,
I Hawaiki pamamao
from Hawaiki far away
I hono ki te wairua, ki te whai ao
Joined to the spirit, to the daylight
Ki te Ao Marama
To the World of Light

a patere or chant

First of all, I remember my great-grandpeople, who brought me into this world.
On my East Coast side Poututerangi married Wharerakau and begot Maaka Te
Ehutu, Maaka Te Ehutu married Ruiha Rahuta and begot Mihi Kotukutuku, my
mother; and on the South Island side, Captain William Stirling married Te
Huikau of Ngai Tahu and begot John Stirling, John Stirling married Elizabeth
Davis and begot Duncan Stirling, my father.

My great-grandfather Captain William Stirling[1] was from the town of Stirling in
Scotland, and when he was a young boy his one idea was to join the navy as a sailor.
His ancestors before him were all sea-faring people, but the trouble was, his

mother wouldn't let him go to sea. He was the only son and she didn't want to lose him. Every time he tried to join the navy his father would agree, but his mother said, 'No, you're not going!'

According to law in those days you had to go into the army or navy at a certain age, but the people who had the money in England could put down £800 for their sons, and they'd be free from everybody. Captain William Stirling's mother paid the money and stopped him from going to sea, so in the end he just disappeared from home, changed his name to William Pankhurst (a name from the other side of their family) and joined the navy. His mother looked around for him but she couldn't find him anywhere.

As the years went by he worked up in the ranks, and when he was promoted to Second Lieutenant he changed his name back to Stirling. In that year they were arranging a big battle between the French and the English people, the Battle of Trafalgar Bay 1808,[2] and William Stirling thought, this is one time I will go and see my mother. Of course she had a big surprise when he came home and told her,

'Well, Mum, I'm an officer now and I'm going to the Battle of Trafalgar Bay!'

The British people defeated the French fleet at Trafalgar, and afterwards Stirling told his mother that he was moving away from Scotland. He worked his way around and settled in Australia, and after he'd been there for a few years, he heard of the great work of the whaling stations in New Zealand. At that time whaling was a very prosperous job, and hundreds of people were coming down to New Zealand – Americans, Norwegians, Swedish and all sorts! Stirling met a man in Australia called Captain Williams who had a team of whaling ships going down to Southland, and he decided to go to the South Island to see the whaling for himself.

My great-grandfather left Australia in 1830 and sailed for the Bluff with two ships, the *Success* and the *Frolic*.* He came to Bluff Harbour one day in the late afternoon, and he could see a lagoon there beyond the point, but it was starting to get dark and the tide was out. He told his sailors to anchor off the point, and when they woke up in the morning, the sun was shining and the tide was starting to come in like a river through the strait. The two ships went in on the morning tide, and the current carried them into a small cove, just big enough to hold them both They anchored there for the day and after a while the sailors heard voices, and a crowd of people came down the hill behind the cove to look at them, then went back again. The cove was deep, the sun was shining and everything was bright, and they could see a Maori pa on top of the hill. Captain Stirling knew something about the Maori people because some of the whalers had Maoris on their ships, so he said to the sailors,

'Whatever you do, when the Maoris come down the bank to look at us, don't interfere with them! We want to get close to these people!'

The next day, and for a few days after that, the people from the pa came down the hill each morning to look at the ships and the sailors, then went back to tell their old chief everything that they had seen. Finally one day a small group came

---

*William Stirling owned two ships in the course of his whaling career, the *Success* and the *Frolic* (J. Hall-Jones, *Bluff Harbour*, p. 28).

Captain Peter Williams, who founded the first whaling station in Southland at Cuttle Cove, Preservation Inlet in 1829. William Stirling came there to work for him in 1830. (*Western Star*, 5 October 1920) *Cyclopaedia of New Zealand*

down the hill with one man out in front, and that was the old chief himself. Stirling said to his men,

'When the Maori people come nearer, get the food ready, and when they are close to the ship, I want you all to start eating!'

The chief brought his people down and found Captain Stirling and his sailors sitting on the bank, eating corned beef and biscuits and cheese, and drinking tea. When they stopped and stared, Captain Stirling called out to the chief and handed him some food, and signed him to eat it. The chief took some meat and biscuits and tasted it, then he turned back to his people and said,

'E kai – eat it, it's good!'

One man came over and the sailors gave him bread, then another and another, until they were all there tasting the food and looking at the sailors, and they were happy. Stirling told his men,

'I want you to do this every day, until you get used to the Maori people and start to understand them.'

As time went on the people became closer and closer, and a few of the Maoris

'Lookout Point at the Bluff', sketched by an unknown sailor on the *Lucy Ann*, 1838.
William Stirling managed the Bluff whaling station from 1836, and when Edward
Shortland visited there in 1843 he wrote, 'Mr Sterling the Superintendant employs
natives with much success – Last season most of his boats were partly manned and one
entirely by natives.' (Shortland report ms, courtesy June Starke) *Old Dartmouth Historical
Society Whaling Museum*

joined in with the ship work and the whaling, and they took a liking to the work.
They were all working together, and the good friendship between the Maori and
the pakeha grew, but only in this part, not in any other area; because Stirling kept
his men in good order.

In the end the old Chief Makere Te Whanawhana thought, 'Well, Captain
Stirling is a really good man! He goes with the people, he takes food to the pa and
he shares everything with us! When some of the people go out whaling on his
ships, he gives them plenty of meat to bring back.'

Did you know that you get really good meat from the whale? We kept big stores
of whale meat in the Bay of Plenty in my young days, and we used to cut it up and
eat it just like beef – beautiful! Anyhow, Makere Te Whanawhana told Stirling to
come up to the pa, because there was a little point up there called Te Taumata o Te
Huikau where you could stand and see the whales at certain hours of the day, some
going north, some going south, and others spouting. Stirling sent a man up there
to have a look, and when the sailor came down, he said, 'Oo-h yes, you can see!'

So Makere Te Whanawhana and William Stirling posted a Maori on the point to
keep a lookout, and whenever he saw a whale, he'd give them the sign, and the
whaling boats rushed out to sea.

Not long after that the Chief said to Captain Stirling, 'You've been so good to my
people, and helped us and everything – I'm going to give you my daughter to be
your wife.'

His daughter Te Huikau was named after the man who sat on that point years ago, so that it was called 'Te Taumata o Te Huikau' (Te Huikau's summit), and after the marriage Makere Te Whanawhana gave Tiwai Point to Captain Stirling as a present. That is how Captain Stirling married Te Huikau and begot John Stirling, and John Stirling[3] married Elizabeth Davis, who begot my father Duncan Stirling and his brothers William Stirling and Richard S. Stirling, and his sisters Euphemia Stirling and Hera Stirling. These are the grandchildren of Captain William Stirling and Te Huikau of Ngai Tahu:

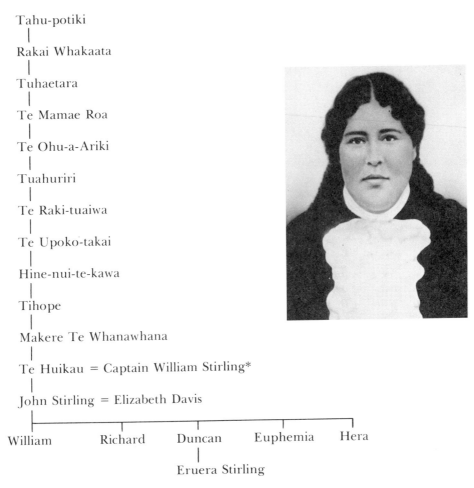

Tahu-potiki
|
Rakai Whakaata
|
Tuhaetara
|
Te Mamae Roa
|
Te Ohu-a-Ariki
|
Tuahuriri
|
Te Raki-tuaiwa
|
Te Upoko-takai
|
Hine-nui-te-kawa
|
Tihope
|
Makere Te Whanawhana
|
Te Huikau = Captain William Stirling*
|
John Stirling = Elizabeth Davis

William   Richard   Duncan   Euphemia   Hera
                                |
                        Eruera Stirling

*See Appendix C for a South Island version of this whakapapa.

Above
Elizabeth Davis married John Stirling at Ruapuke in 1858, when she was sixteen years old and he was eighteen. She was the daughter of 'Big George' Davis and Kutamamoe, an important woman of Ngati Mamoe and Ngai Tahu, 'whose word was law in her district'. (Herries Beattie ms) *Stirling family*

John Stirling lived at Riverton, 'erecting his homestead upon the portion of the Native Reserve allotted to his wife, and finally ended his days there. (He) was noted for his kindly, lovable Christian disposition.' (*Western Star*, 5 October 1920) *Stirling family*

It was about 130 years later when I got interested in the Maori Land Court, and I went down to the South Island to search all the records there. I found out my father's interests and my grandfather's interests, uncles and everything, and I put in a claim for the Stirlings in the North and the Stirlings in the South Island. I discovered that the land given by Makere Te Whanawhana was still in Captain Stirling's name, so I thought, well I'll claim it. I made an application to the court, but then my solicitor told me that an objection had been sent against my claim by the Stirlings in England, they reckoned we were not entitled to the succession from William Stirling because our great-grandmother didn't marry Stirling in the proper way. That is how we lost the case. Anyhow, we put it through the court again, and my lawyer said to me,

'Well, the Stirlings in England have no right to this land, because it came through Makere Te Whanawhana's daughter Te Huikau, and not from England! The Stirlings here are more eligible to claim this land.'

This time the court agreed that we, the Stirlings in New Zealand, had full rights to the land, and they made an order in favour of my family and the Stirlings down in Invercargill. But as time went on, we went through all the channels until I got a letter from my lawyer saying, well, the Government has wiped the claim! According to custom, property unclaimed for more than one hundred years goes back to the Crown, and that is why we lost Tiwai Point and Stirling Point. Now the Government has got New Zealand's aluminium smelter there, right at Tiwai Point. The biggest aluminium smelter in New Zealand!

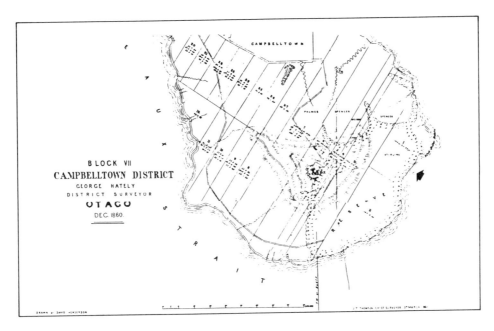

A map of 'Campbelltown' district at Bluff, showing William Stirling's land (arrowed). 'Tuhawaiki, a Native Chief, not understanding the nature of an Oath but declaring to tell the truth States – "Some years ago I sold a piece of land to William Stirling – Situated in the harbour of the Bluff (Awaroa) at Motupohue point . . . I received £40 Stg in payment for it. I had the sole right to sell the land and no one has ever disputed this right." Edward Shortland (interpreter); taken in Court 5 October 1843.' *National Archives OLC file 1023*

Stirling Point at Bluff, showing the pilot station built on the site of William Stirling's whaling station. *Alexander Turnbull Library*

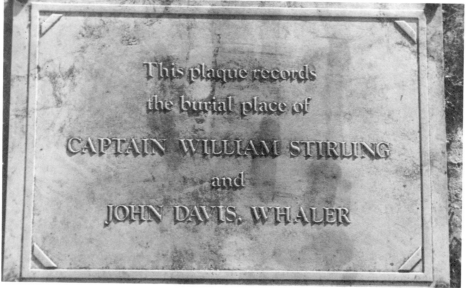

When the aluminium smelter was being constructed at Tiwai Point, a bulldozer driver uncovered an elaborate Maori burial of a European man. The burial (which included a button from a naval uniform) was excavated by Southland Museum staff over 1970–71. It was thought to be William Stirling's grave since early surveys showed his grave marked at the highest spot on Tiwai Point. The grave is now marked by a plaque. (*Southland Times*, 16 June 1971) *Southland Art Gallery and Museum*

John Stirling's three sons, William Stirling, Richard S. Stirling and Duncan Stirling, all went to the Riverton School, and Duncan, my father, was very talented. He was well advanced in his school work and when it came to the Proficiency Certificate, the two older brothers missed it – but Duncan beat both of his brothers and he passed! In those years the Proficiency Certificate was the top ticket, if you had Proficiency you could get into any government department anywhere. He applied for a job in the big shop run by Johnny Jones in Riverton, and when Mr Jones asked him, 'Have you got any qualifications?' he pulled out his two certificates, the Competency and the Proficiency.

When Mr Jones saw those tickets he said,

'Well, Duncan, I'm not going to use you for selling goods; you'd better come and work with the girls in the office and do all the figuring work for us.'

He made him the senior in the office, because none of the girls had those qualifications, and Duncan was quite happy there for a while, but one day he saw an advertisement in the paper, placed by the Williams Construction Company in Dunedin. They wanted carpenters, bricklayers, interior decorators and plumbers, and when he saw the advertisement Duncan said to his mother,

'I'm going to study for that job! I'm leaving home.'

'No, you're not going! You've got to stay here.'

'Well Mum, I'm determined. I *am* going to Dunedin to study for that job!'

His mother started to cry and things like that, so early one morning, when everyone was still sleeping, Duncan left the house and walked to Invercargill, and caught the bus to Dunedin.

When he arrived in Dunedin he went to the Williams Construction Company, and asked to see the manager. They asked him,

'What do you want?'

'I want to be a builder and a carpenter, all that kind of work.'

'Well, do you have anything to show us? We'd like to see your credentials.'

He pulled out his two certificates, the Competency and the Proficiency, and when the manager saw those tickets he gave him a job in the office. The people at Williams Construction Company soon found out that Duncan was very good with figures; he could estimate anything to do with houses in his own mind, without putting it down on paper. The manager wanted to keep him on in the office, but Duncan said,

'No – I want to be a builder!'

The manager thought about it for a while, and then he told him,

'Look here, Stirling, you can still be a builder. I tell you what we'll do . . . Here is an architect's plan – you estimate all the quantities and how to cut the timber for this house, and when we're ready to build it we'll let you know.'

'All right.'

So Duncan figured out the quantities of bricks, timber, plumbing and everything for that house, and when they started to build it the supervisor called him to come and help. After a while he got used to the work, and in the end he built a house by himself, right from setting out the plan to the plumbing, bricklaying, carpentry and interior decorating. Then the manager of the construction company said to him, 'Well Stirling – now you are a fully qualified builder.'

Duncan Stirling. *Stirling family*

Duncan did very well in Dunedin, and everybody knew him around there. When I went down to the South Island, all the old people knew him. He was a very musical man, he could play the piano and other instruments, he was a good dancer and good at everything! They reckoned that Duncan Stirling was one of the finest men that ever travelled, and the womenfolk were chasing him everywhere. When my son Waha got married in the South Island, his wife's grandmother stood up and said,

'Well, I'm very pleased that my mokopuna is marrying the grandson of Duncan Stirling. Duncan and I were going together for a long time and we were supposed to get married, but he was such a fine-looking man that most of the women around here were also after him. Some of those women interfered and in the finish we couldn't get married, but now that Mina and Waha are married I'm very proud. Our grandchildren have joined us together!'

Duncan got into a lot of entanglements in the South Island, and one day he saw an advertisement in the paper placed by a leading farmer on the East Coast, Thomas Sydney Williams. He wanted a builder to help him start the Kuhirerere

Station, so Duncan got on the sailing ship and went to Gisborne. He stayed at the pub in Gisborne for a few days and while he was there he read in the paper that Mr Sherratt wanted a woolshed shifted on his property near Gisborne† so he thought, 'Well, I'll give it a go!' He got his tender ready and went to see Mr Sherratt, and when Mr Sherratt saw the papers with all his qualifications, he cut off the other tenderers straight away. Duncan got the contract, and one day when he was getting everything prepared he saw Frank McDonald, a 'bullocky' who used to cart all the logs from the bush into the mills in Gisborne. He pulled up Frank McDonald and said to him,

'I wonder if you can do something for me?'

'What's that?'

'I'd like a hundred or so posts of manuka, to use for sneaks.'

'All right,' said Frank McDonald, 'I'll make a special trip into the bush to get them.'

Manuka was the best timber for sneaks, because there is a lot of slime under the bark, and Duncan's plan was to lift the woolshed onto a sledge and roll it along on these manuka sneaks to its new position. He made the sledge with its skids, then he hired some Maori people from Tolaga Bay to help him lift the woolshed with big jacks and lower it onto the sledge. Frank McDonald came along with his team of bullocks, about nine or ten of them; they laid the manuka sneaks in front, and as soon as the bullocks pulled the sledge onto the sneaks the slimy stuff in the manuka made it go just like that! Mr Sherratt was very pleased with the job and he paid Duncan a good price for the contract.

After that Duncan went down to the East Coast and worked for Thomas Sydney Williams, first at Kuhirerere Station and then at Pakihiroa Station building woolsheds. The people from Tolaga Bay who had helped him shift Mr Sherratt's woolshed went home and told their relations that Stirling was a pretty good carpenter, so the Tolaga Bay people said, 'Oh, we'd better bring him here!'

He built some private homes in Tolaga Bay, good big houses with three or four bedrooms, one for the Rangiuias and one for the Hindmarsh family; and even

†'Sherratt' was probably Richard Sherratt who came to Gisborne to manage the Wainui run in 1881 (*Poverty Bay Herald*, 14.12.38), or his brother William, who came to Gisborne as a station manager at about the same time (*Gisborne Herald*, 16.11.43).

Shifting a house by bullock team. *Auckland Weekly News, 14 March 1907*

when he was in Tolaga the womenfolk were chasing him all the time. I heard the old ladies from around there talking about it,

'When Duncan Stirling was a young man, he was so fine-looking– well! I'd be for him tonight, and tomorrow he'd be somebody else's . . .'

He stayed in Tolaga for a while and then the people asked him to build them a church, so he ordered the timber from Auckland and the schooner landed it at Tolaga, and Duncan built that church; then he built one at Tokomaru Bay, Tuatini; one at Mangahanea; one at Te Horo near Waiomatatini; the old church at Tikitiki; one at Te Araroa, but that's been renewed; Torere, and the church at Hicks Bay that went down in a storm a few years ago. He also built the old Kemp homestead, still standing in Ruatorea today, and the Ngai Tai meeting-house 'Te Roroku' that stood at Torere. He ordered all his timber from the Kauri Timber Company in Auckland, and Captain Skinner brought it down on the *Kaeo*, the schooner that used to run from Auckland right down to Gisborne, dropping off flour and sugar for all the shops, and taking back kumaras, wheat, and maize from the Maori people.

While Duncan was building the church at Te Horo for the Kaua family, some of the people there said,

'Oh, Duncan Stirling is a very fine man, he's a good boss, he treats everyone well. And he never drinks!'

Then the old man Kaua said,

'Well, I think this is going to be the husband for our cousin Mihi Kotukutuku.'

That is how the match marriage began between Duncan Stirling, the descendant of Captain William Stirling and Te Huikau from the South Island, and my mother Mihi Kotukutuku, descended from those great East Coast chiefs, Paikea, Porourangi, and Apanui.

Uia mai koia
Ask me
Whakahuatia ake
To name
Ko wai te whare nei e?
This house?
Ko Te Kani!
It is Te Kani!
Ko wai te tekoteko kai runga?
Who is the carved figure up there?
Ko Paikea! Ko Paikea!
It is Paikea! Paikea!
Whakakau Paikea
Paikea swam
Whakakau te tipua
The sea god swam
Whakakau te taniwha e
The taniwha swam

Hicks Bay church, built by Duncan Stirling. *Gisborne Museum, Williams collection*

Ka u Paikea
And Paikea landed
Ki Ahuahu – pakia!
At Ahuahu
Kei te whitia koe
You changed
Ko Kahutia-te-rangi!
Into Kahutia-te-rangi,‡
E ai to ure
And copulated
Ki te tamahine
With the daughter
A Te Whironui!
Of Te Whironui!
Nana i noho
Who sat
I te kei o te waka
In the stern of the canoe
Aue! Aue!
Alas! Alas!
He koruru koe, koro e!
You are a carved face
on a house, old man!

a chant for Paikea (Ngati Porou)

The history of our family on the East Coast side goes right back to that far-off land, Hawaiki. The great East Coast ancestor Paikea[4] was a high chief in Hawaiki, and when he came to New Zealand he brought with him all the histories from the Whare Wananga of Hawaiki-nui, those Houses of Learning called Te Whakaeroero, Te Rawheoro, Rangitane, and Tapere-nui-a-Whatonga.

Paikea travelled to New Zealand on the back of a whale, and when they landed on the East Coast in the early hours of the morning, the star Poututerangi was just rising above Hikurangi mountain. Paikea looked around at the mountains and the sea, and the landscape reminded him of his birthplace back in Hawaiki, so he named his new home Whangara-mai-Tawhiti, Whangara from the far-off-land, and he gave the names of other places in Hawaiki to the mountains and rivers and the headlands – Tawhiti Point, the Waiapu River running below Hikurangi mountain, and Tihirau-mai-Tawhiti, the mountain at Cape Runaway. Paikea settled in his new land and married Huturangi the daughter of Te Whironui and begot Pouheni; Pouheni married Uekaiehu and begot Tarawhakatu, and Paikea's sons and grandsons lived on the lands around his pa Ranginui, cultivating their

‡'. . . the name of Paikea when he lived at Hawaiki was Kahutiaterangi; and the reason of his being called a new name – that is Paikea – was on account of his coming on the back of a sea monster to these Islands' (Nepia Pohuhu, *AJHR* 1880 Vol. II).

Paikea rides his whale – tekoteko at the Whitireia meeting-house, Whangara. *Cliff Whiting*

kumara and taro gardens in peace and holding fast to the memories of their ancestors.

Paikea was the great ancestor of the East Coast tribes and most of our genealogies go back to him, but some ancient descent lines of our tribe Te Whanau-a-Apanui also come down from Motatau-mai-Tawhiti, an ancestor who came to Cape Runaway on his canoe Tauira not long after the Great Migration.§ Only a few people know about that, and one time when Apirana Ngata called a meeting at Poho-o-Rawiri meeting-house in Gisborne, I went there with a group of elders from our tribe. A man from Te Aitanga-a-Hauiti stood up on the marae and greeted us,

'Welcome, Te Whanau-a-Apanui, te iwi e kore waka – the tribe with no canoe!'

The old people in our party didn't like to hear that kind of talk, and Tane Tukaki of Te Kaha turned around to me and said,

'Oh, that fellow makes me feel ashamed!'

§'The Ngariki people in the Tauira canoe under their ancestor Motatau-mai-Tawhiti . . . are the ancestors of Te Whanau-a-Apanui and their blood will be found in the foundations of Ngai Tai, Te Whakatohea and coastal tribes as far west as Waihi near Maketu.' (A. T. Ngata, *Rauru-nui-a-Toi lectures*, Lecture 2, p.4).

Paikea – poutokomanawa (centre-pole) from a former meeting-house at Tolaga Bay, now held in the American Museum of Natural History. *David Simmons*

I told him, 'Never mind, I know how to answer him back . . .'

When the time came for our speakers to return the home-side greetings, I stood on the marae at Poho-o-Rawiri and greeted their chief Te Kani Te Ua, and then I turned to that man and said,

'Te Aitanga-a-Hauiti! You say that we of Te Whanau-a-Apanui have no canoe! But I have my canoe – Tauira, that carried Motatau-mai-Tawhiti to these islands. We brought the kumara for you, the chiefs! You should not have spoken to me, for where is your canoe? Na te tohora ra koe i tiko ki uta – you were shat ashore by a whale!'

I was talking about Paikea, of course. Well, the next minute old Te Kani Te Ua was up on the marae, stamping his feet and waving his carved stick around, and he shouted at that fellow from Te Aitanga-a-Hauiti,

'Pokokohua – taurekareka! Meathead – slave! Fancy telling our relations of Te Whanau-a-Apanui that they have no canoe! You have killed us both – now we are called 'tutae' – whale dung – on our own marae!'

Then the old man turned to me and said, 'My grandson, Eruera – greetings. You spoke with the voice of the old people and you spoke the truth. It was that mad fool over there who threw his words around . . .'

Te Kani Te Ua, chiefly elder of Gisborne. *Gisborne Herald*

The man from Te Aitanga-a-Hauiti had to stand up and leave the marae, and he was really disgraced. It's no good making that kind of remark on the marae unless you know the background of your tribal history.

From Paikea right down to the present day, the descendants of the high chiefs from Hawaiki have remembered their whakapapa and the stories of their ancestors, and in the Maori world you have to know your tribal history and your whakapapa, otherwise you're nothing! You can't say anything, you can't do anything, you can't move in the right way and you're nobody. Only when you know your whakapapa can the mana of your ancestors shine on you. The most important part of any whakapapa is the tahuhu, the main line of descent through the senior men, and it is the tahuhu that moves the tribes. The man who can claim seniority over all the other chiefs is the strong person in the area – people will help him and do what he says, because he is the recognised senior and inherits the mana and supreme power of his ancestors. The same thing happens in the pakeha world, you can see that the line of kings is still going on in England, from Queen Victoria down to Queen Elizabeth. They believe in the whakapapa, just like the Maori people; they started their line of kings in the year 802 with King Egbert, and Maoris started theirs in 1350, when the canoes landed in New Zealand. They're doing it in England and we're doing it here too – without that whakapapa, you'll go nowhere!

I have collected the genealogy of the kings and queens of England and written it in my whakapapa book so I will know the chiefly background of both of my sides, the Maori and the pakeha. If you gather these treasures of history and bring them together in one place, you can see the seeds from which you have sprung, and you will stand tall wherever you may travel. That's what my father always told me when I was a young man, 'Don't forget that you are also a Scotsman!'

That was one thing about my father, he liked me to be proud of both my sides, the pakeha and the Maori, and one day when he heard me learning my Maori whakapapa he said,

'Well son, I think you'd better learn your Scottish background too!'

He sat down beside me and taught me a Scottish poem, and I still remember some of the verses:

> A chieftain to the Highlands bound
> Cries, 'Boatman, do not tarry!
> For I'll give thee a silver pound
> to row us o'er the ferry!'
>
> 'And who be ye would cross Lochgyle
> This dark and stormy water?'
> 'Oh, I'm the chief of Ulva's Isle
> And this, Lord Ullin's daughter!'
>
> And fast before her father's men
> Three days we fled together
> And should he find us in the glen
> Our blood shall stain the heather . . .||

||See T. Campbell in F. T. Palgrave, *The Golden Treasury*, 1946.

The whakapapa of the Kings and Queens of England, written by Eruera Stirling in his whakapapa book.

I sometimes use that poem as a patere on the marae, and it has stood me in good stead ever since.

When you look at the whakapapa of the kings of England it sometimes comes down to a woman, and the same thing happens on the East Coast. Quite a few of the meeting-houses and sub-tribes are named after senior women, and sometimes the main line of descent lands on a woman – Materoa Reedy, Rutu Tawhiorangi and Heni Houkamau were all women who came on the senior line in my young days. It can cause a lot of trouble, though, because the people don't like womenfolk to take over the area. If you look at the pakeha world and the Maori world, you will see the same things coming out.

The taumau marriage is also carried on by the kings and queens of England and if you're a prince or a princess you don't marry just anybody, a wife or a husband is found for you from the senior line of descent. The Maori people selected their wives like that, to carry on the tribal histories and bring the descent line together; the old people would say, 'Well this chap can marry that woman, because he's so-and-so and she's so-and-so' and often that was the first thing the young people knew about it. All the same, most taumau marriages were just as happy as anything, and very few of them were broken.

Porourangi meeting-house at Waiomatatini. *Cliff Whiting*

The main descent line from Hawaiki carried on down to Paikea's grandson Tarawhakatu; he lived in Whangara and had a son called Nanaia, who married Niwaniwa and begot Porourangi, the founder of Ngati Porou, and his younger brother Tahu-potiki, the founder of Ngai Tahu and my ancestor on the South Island side.

Porourangi and his younger brother Tahu-potiki were born at Whangara, where their people had lived since Paikea's migration to New Zealand. When they grew to manhood the tribe started to build a big new marae at Whangara, and they appointed Porourangi their high chief with the titles Te Ariki-matara-a-whare and Te Tuhi-mareikura-a-oho,¶ and gave him Hamo-te-rangi, a high born woman, to be his wife. Hamo-te-rangi had three children with Porourangi: Hau-te-rangi the eldest son, Rongomaianiwaniwa a daughter, and Ueroa the youngest son, and all the tribes and sub-tribes of the East Coast trace back to these three children.[5]

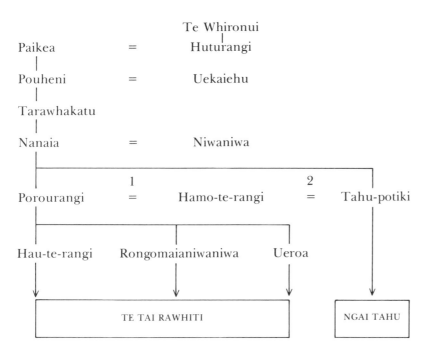

They unite the descent lines of all the main districts of Te Tai Rawhiti, right from Nga Kuri-a-Wharei hills behind Katikati to Tihirau mountain at Cape Runaway, from Tihirau to Tawhiti mountain, from Tawhiti to Kaiti in Gisborne, and from Kaiti to that proverbial hill in Heretaunga called 'Te taumata-whakatangi-hanga-koauau-a-Tamatea-pokaiwhenua-ki-tana-tama' ('the summit where Tamatea-pokaiwhenua played his flute to his child').

¶'Porourangi (had the) titles Te tuhi mareikura o Rauru, a full-blooded man, (and) Te Ariki-matatara-a-whare, a name which you will find today in Rarotonga as that of the high priest under Makea.' (A. T. Ngata, *Rauru-nui-a-Toi lectures*, Lecture 2, p.6).

Porourangi and his younger brother Tahu-potiki lived happily together at Whangara and carried out the teachings of their elders, and the people were very pleased with them. Tahu-potiki was a fine-looking man and very hardworking; whenever there was work to do around the pa he was always there, and he was a leading man in all the tribal activities. Only one thing puzzled the old people about Tahu-potiki, he didn't seem to be interested in getting married. No matter what women came to him he took no notice, he just kept on working. The elders wondered, 'Why is he like that?'

In the finish, they got really worried about it, so one night the old people asked the high priest to come to the pa and tell them something about Tahu-potiki's future life. They said to the priest,

'We want to ask you, why is Tahu-potiki still leading a single life? There are plenty of fine-looking women in the tribe, but he refuses to get married.'

The tohunga said to them,

'Very well.'

He turned aside and made offerings, and chanted prayers to Io-matua-te-kore, and when he came back to them he sat down and told them the secret life of Tahu-potiki.

'This man will not marry because he is in love with his brother's wife! There is no trouble between them but he thinks about her all the time and that is why he cannot look at any other woman. He will have to leave the district; tell him to seek a place called Rapaki, and when he sees red fires gleaming on the mountains of Tamatea-pokai-whenua, there he will find his new home.'

When the elders heard the tohunga's words they called a meeting the next morning, and asked Tahu-potiki to come to the marae. He came and sat down, and the old people said to him,

'Well, e tama Tahu-potiki, we have met and decided that you must leave the district. The high priest has told us that you are in love with Hamo-te-rangi, your elder brother's wife, and although you have not caused any trouble it cannot go on. We are preparing a group of men to travel with you tomorrow – go to the mountains of Rapaki in the South Island, and when you see the burning rocks of Tamatea-pokai-whenua, you will find land there for yourself and your people. You must leave in the early hours of the morning; do not come back here to

Above
Wall panels in Hine Tapora meeting-house at Mangahanea, showing the genealogy.
Paikea = Huturangi; Pouheni = Uekaiehu; Tarawhatu = Hau-a-Tikiteora;
Nanaia = Niwaniwa; Porourangi = Hamo-te-rangi. *Hirini Mead*

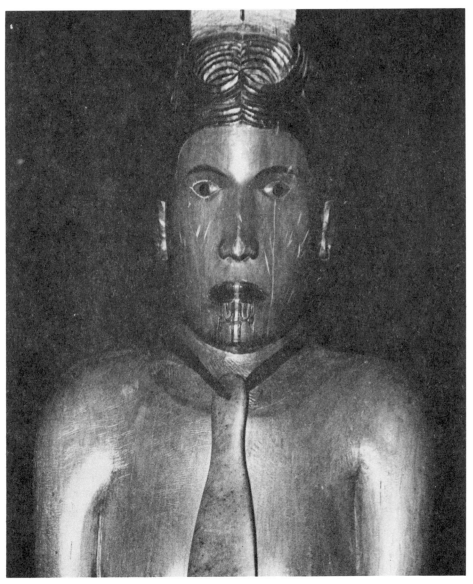

Hamo-te-rangi, the wife of Porourangi – poutokomanawa in Porourangi meeting-house, Waiomatatini. *Cliff Whiting*

interfere with your tuakana,* Porourangi!'

Tahu-potiki listened to them, and said nothing. The next morning he moved out with a selected group of fighting-men, and before they had gone very far they saw a war party standing in their pathway, ready for battle! In those days you couldn't just walk into the territory of another tribe, you had to ask them for special permission or they would think you had come to cause trouble, and kill you. So Tahu-potiki had to start fighting and he defeated those people and moved on to Gisborne, fighting all the way. From Kaiti Pa he travelled to Mahia and fought his way to Heretaunga, Wairarapa and the Rimutaka mountains, and in every place, he selected warriors to join his party. By the time he reached Nga Pito-one Pa at Wellington, he had a large army of fighting-men, and they defeated Te Atiawa and captured the pa. Tahu-potiki and his men stayed at Pito-one for a while, then he remembered the words of the high priest at Whangara,

'Haere e Tahu, e tae koe ki runga o Rapaki, ka kite koe i nga pohatu whakarakaraka a Tamatea-pokai-whenua, i runga i a Kaikoura, koiana te kainga mohou . . . go Tahu, and when you come to Rapaki, you will see the glaring rocks of Tamatea-pokai-whenua burning above Kaikoura; there you will find your home.'

He sent his people into the bush to fell trees for rafts, and when the logs were lashed together and the mokihi rafts were finished, Tahu-potiki's party crossed to Kapiti Island and fought the people there, and captured all their canoes. After that they crossed Te Moana-a-Raukawa (Cook Strait) to Rapaki in the South Island. As they approached Rapaki mountain Tahu-potiki looked up and saw red fire flickering on the rocks of Tamatea-pokai-whenua, and he said to his people,

'We have come to Te Turanga-a-Maui, Maui's standing-place in the South Island, and up there on the mountain you can see the sign that this land will be our new home.'

The canoes landed at Rapaki and stayed for a while, then they travelled on until they came to Waitahanui beach near Christchurch. Tahu-potiki and his people landed on the plains of Waitaha and fought the Moriori tribes and drove them beyond Aorangi mountain, killing most of them in the bush. Now Tahu-potiki's people settled on the land and made it their home. Time passed, and after a while word came to the South Island that Tahu-potiki's older brother Porourangi had died. Tahu told his people to prepare everything, and they travelled by canoe to the tangi. When the people at Whangara saw a strange canoe approaching the beach they looked out and hah! it was Tahu-potiki. The elders gave him a big welcome, and he stayed at the marae for the tangi. When everything was over and it was time for him to go home, he said to the people of Whangara,

'I have come to fetch my older brother's wife.'

The tribe agreed, and Tahu-potiki took Hamo-te-rangi with him back to Kaiapoi, and together they founded Te Whanau-a-Tahu-potiki, now the tribe of Ngai Tahu in the South Island.

---

* Senior in descent, elder brother.

† Te Ari Pitama was one of the first Maori radio announcers; he was from Tuahiwi, of chiefly Ngai Tahu descent.

When I went down to the tangi of Te Ari Pitama† in the South Island, I found out that the people down there didn't know the story of Tahu-potiki's migration from Whangara – they didn't know where Tahu-potiki was born. I stood on the marae and told them this story, and traced my father's descent from Tahu-potiki and Ngati Rapa and Ngati Mamoe, because I am a taharua with descent lines from both Porourangi the senior on the East Coast side, and also from his younger brother Tahu-potiki on the South Island side.

> (Kaea – Leader)
> Tena i whiua!
> *Begin with a swing!*
> Taku pohiri e rere atu ra
> *My call has gone out*
> Ki te hiku o te ika
> *To the tail of the fish*
> Te puku o te whenua
> *To the belly of the land*
> Te pane o te motu
> *To the head of the island*
> Ki te whakawhitianga i Raukawa
> *By the crossing at Raukawa*
> Ki te Waipounamu, e . . .
> *To the land of greenstone waters!*
>
>
> (Katoa – All)
> E i aha tera e!
> *The call has gone out*
> Haramai koe i te pohiritanga
> *So come at the welcome*
> A taku manu!
> *Given by my bird!*
> Haramai koe i te pohiritanga
> *Come at the welcome,*
> A taku manu!
> *Given by my bird!*
> He tiwaiwaka hau na Maui!
> *I am a fantail of Maui*
> Tiori rau e he ha'
> *Chirping restlessly, here and there*
> He tiwaiwaka 'hau na Maui',
> *I am a fantail of Maui*
> Tiori rau e he ha!
> *Singing, flitting here and there!*
> Ko tou aro i tahuri mai
> *Turn yourself to me*

Ko toku aro i tahuri atu!
I turn myself to you
Takina ko au! Takina ko au!
You have challenged me!
Ko tou aro i tahuri mai,
Turn yourself to me
Ko toku aro i tahuri atu!
I turn myself to you
Takina ko au! Takina ko au!
You have challenged me!
Porou koa!
It is Porou [Porourangi]!
Ko Hamo te wahine koa!
Hamo is his wife [Hamo-te-rangi]!
Ko Tahu koa!
It is Tahu [Tahu-potiki]
Ko Hamo te wahine koa!
Hamo is his wife!
Nana i tohatoha ki Niu Tireni ka hipoki!
Their children have scattered and covered New Zealand!
Haere mai, haere mai!
Welcome! Welcome!
Haere mai, haere mai!
Welcome! Welcome!
Taku hui! Hei!
To my hui – hei!

a women's haka (Ngati Porou)[6]

Back in Whangara Porourangi's eldest son Hau married Takotowaimua and begot Kehutikoparae, then he married his second wife Tamateatoia and begot Rakaipo; Rakaipo begot Manutangirua, and Manutangirua married Kehutikoparae, Hau's eldest daughter and begot Hingangaroa, the great carver who founded Te Rawheoro School of Learning at Uawa, Tolaga Bay.[7]

When Hingangaroa married Iranui they had three sons, Taua, Mahaki and Hauiti, and these three sons are very important in the history of the East Coast. Taua's eldest son was called Apanui-Waipapa, and all the chiefly descent lines of Te Whanau-a-Apanui and Ngati Porou tribes come down from him and his wife Hine Mahuru; Mahaki, the second son, was the ancestor of Te Aitanga-a-Mahaki people around Gisborne; and Hauiti's descendants became Te Aitanga-a-Hauiti, the tribal people at Tolaga Bay.[8]

Hauiti, the potiki or youngest son was very jealous of his older brothers, and he tried to take over the senior line by driving them out of the district and killing all their children, so that his own children could come out on top. He fought against Taua and Mahaki and they fled to the mountains, and Taua's son Apanui-Waipapa shut himself up in his pa at Whangara with his eight children, Te

Tukutuku panels for Porourangi meeting-house, showing Taua (second from right, top), Hauiti, and other important ancestors. *Auckland Institute and Museum*

Apanui-Waipapa and his wife Hine Mahuru – poupou in Tukaki meeting-house. *Cliff Whiting*

Ao-puhara the eldest, Te Ao-te-ngahoro, Te Ao-takaia, Taikorekore, Pararaki, Mokaitangatakore, Rongomaihuatahi his daughter and his youngest son Matapiko.

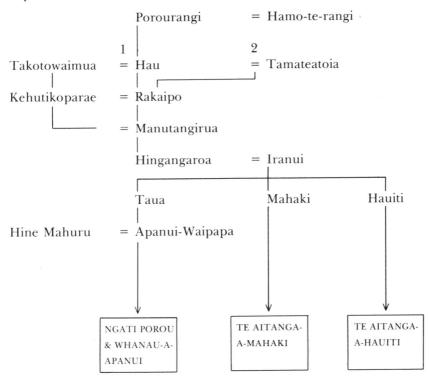

Hauiti collected his warriors together and one day when Apanui's children were out gathering food, Hauiti laid an ambush for Apanui and killed him. When the children came back to the pa the people told them that their father had been murdered, and Hauiti's men shut off the entrance to the pa and trapped them inside.

One of the warriors in Hauiti's party was related to Apanui and he felt sorry for those children, so he took a blade of flax and knotted a message onto it, and crept up to the pa and tossed the flax inside. When Te Ao-takaia saw the flax land on the ground he picked it up, and he realized that the knots in it made a message, saying, 'Escape from the pa tonight or you will all be killed. Wait on the right side of the pa, not on the left, or you will die.'

Te Ao-takaia gathered his brothers and their sister and they waited on the right side of the pa. Soon Hauiti's warriors came moving up on the left side of the pa, and as they approached Te Ao-takaia led his brothers and sister over the palisades on the right-hand side and they all managed to escape. If their relation had not sent them a warning all of Apanui-Waipapa's descendants would have been wiped out, and there would be no Te Whanau-a-Apanui tribe today![9]

Apanui's children fled from Whangara to Maraenui in the Bay of Plenty, and then they sent word to Turirangi of Te Arawa to come and help them fight Hauiti.

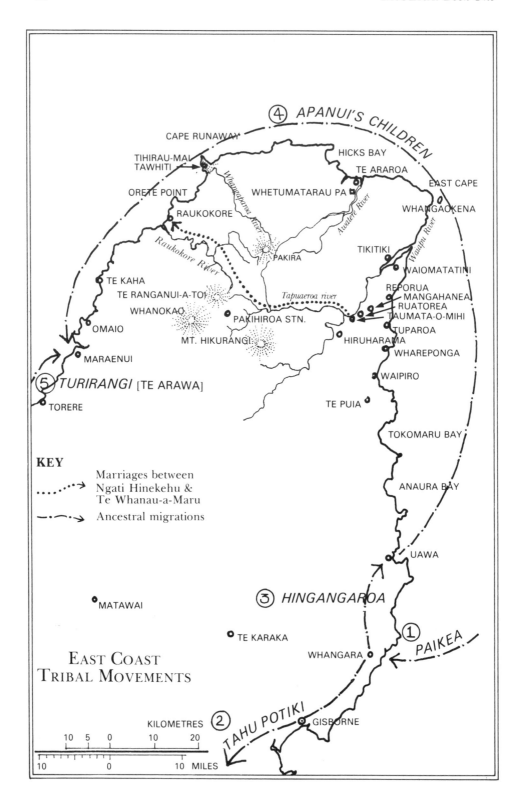

KEY

········> Marriages between
Ngati Hinekehu &
Te Whanau-a-Maru

—·—·—> Ancestral migrations

EAST COAST
TRIBAL MOVEMENTS

KILOMETRES

10 5 0   10   20

10   0   10 MILES

Rongomaihuatahi meeting-house at Omaio. *David Simmons*

Turirangi was related to them in the ancient descent lines from Muturangi[10] so he came with a party of his warriors to Maraenui, and when Hauiti's canoes came chasing the children of Apanui, Turirangi fought Hauiti on the Maraenui beach and killed him.

Te Ao-takaia and his brothers were so grateful to Turirangi that they gave him their sister Rongomaihuatahi to be his wife, and Turirangi settled down in the Whanau-a-Apanui district and lived there for the rest of his days. Turirangi was descended from the eldest son of Tama-te-kapua, the captain of the Te Arawa canoe, and the rest of Te Arawa come down from Tama-te-kapua's second son, Kahumatamomoe:

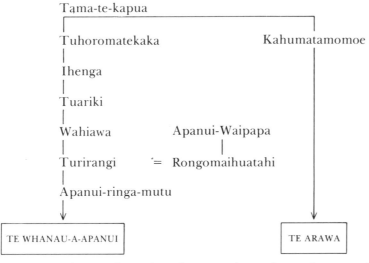

In these descent lines the Whanau-a-Apanui people are senior to the tribal people of Te Arawa.

Tama-te-kapua meeting-house at Ohinemutu, Rotorua. *Alexander Turnbull Library*

In 1917 when the youngest son of Tiweka Anaru died overseas, a big party of Te Whanau-a-Apanui people went to the tangi at Ohinemutu in Rotorua. Tiweka Anaru was the Registrar of the Native Land Court in Rotorua at that time, but he came from Raukokore in the Whanau-a-Apanui district, so all the main chiefs of Te Whanau-a-Apanui travelled to the tangi.

When they arrived at the marae a speaker from Te Arawa stood to welcome them, and then the elders of Te Whanau-a-Apanui didn't know what to do! My mother was the most senior one amongst them, and it was really for her to speak. Koopu of Maraenui and the other chiefs looked at each other, and the next thing my mother stood up on the marae in front of Tama-te-kapua meeting-house.

As soon as she stood, the old chief of Te Arawa, Mita Taupopoki, called out,

'E tau! E tau, e tau, *e tau*! Sit down, sit down! Get your feet off my marae! It is not right for my marae, my tribal etiquette to be trampled by a woman! E tau ki raro! Sit down!'

It was not customary for women to speak on the marae in Te Arawa. Well, my mother stood there and waited for Mita Taupopoki to finish, and when he had stopped speaking she said,

'E Mita! You cannot speak to me! I am standing on *my* marae, in front of *my* ancestor Tama-te-kapua – I am a descendant of his eldest son Tuhoromatekaka, and I am a descendant of Apanui! It is not right for you to speak to me – *you* sit down! You come from the junior line, from Tama-te-kapua's younger son

Kahumatamomoe – you, and all your people of Te Arawa! And I think I heard
you saying something about women – listen, child, how do you think you were
born into this world?'

My mother turned round and bent over, and she threw up her skirts and said,
'Anei! Here is the place you came from, here between my thighs! Your grey hairs
come from a woman's belly, out into the world – so don't you speak to me!'

When my mother finished her whaikorero all the speeches were shut off.
Wiremu Kingi the chief of Ngai Tai stood on the marae and said, 'Well, Te Arawa,
this woman speaks according to her kawa, on her ancestral marae – who amongst
us can answer her? Who?'

No one said a word.

Nearly forty years later, in 1956, when my mother died at home in Raukokore
Te Arawa heard about it and they gathered to come to the tangi. The people came
to Wairuru marae from far and near, Ngati Porou, Ngai Tai, Ngai-te-Rangi, Ngati
Awa and Te Whanau-a-Apanui, and the tangi lasted for days. Finally Ngati Porou
asked that my mother should be buried because they had to return home, but I
said to them, 'No – wait a while longer. Her people of Te Arawa are still on the
road.'

A full busload of elders came from Rotorua, and when they stopped at Opotiki
for a rest one of the old chaps invited Kepa Ehau to come and have a drink at the
pub. Kepa Ehau was fond of his beer, but this time he said,

'No! For this one tangi I am going to keep right away from liquor. I want to go in
a chiefly way on to the marae, and smash my words upon that woman's head!'

(Left) Mihi Kotukutuku. *Stirling family.* *(Right)* Mita Taupopoki, Te Arawa chieftain.
Alexander Turnbull Library

When Te Arawa arrived at Wairuru marae we were waiting for them, and the elders of Te Whanau-a-Apanui and Ngati Porou gave their speeches of welcome. The next thing we saw Kepa Ehau leap up on to the marae with his tokotoko flashing and his feet stamping, and he yelled out at my mother,

'Pokokohua a Mihi Kotukutuku, purari paka! You bloody bugger, Mihi Kotukutuku – slave! Good job you died! The woman who trampled upon the spirit of Te Arawa! Right from the times of our ancestors down to today, no woman has stood on a Te Arawa marae – only *you!* Now there'll be no Mihi Kotukutuku to stand upon our heads – you were the first and the last! Kai toa koe kia hemo noa atu! Good job you died!'

The tears were streaming down Kepa Ehau's face as he spoke like that to my mother, and when he had finished my younger brother Mark said to me,

'Hika, Eruera! Aren't you going to answer him back? That fulla has got a cheek to talk like that about Mum!'

Mark wanted to go over and belt Kepa Ehau for saying those things about our mother, but I told him,

'No, Mark. Let the words of a chief lie upon the marae. Kepa Ehau has honoured our mother today and made her a chief – kua rangatira a ia. Sit down – you don't understand . . .'

The people of Te Arawa wept a long time for my mother, and when their tangi was finished I called out to them,

'Te Arawa, you have come, and your long hurt is over. Now let your relation Mihi Kotukutuku down into the belly of the earth . . .'

That finished it.

Back in the old days, after our ancestor Turirangi of Te Arawa had killed Hauiti at Maraenui and married Rongomaihuatahi, the eight children of Apanui-Waipapa and Hine Mahuru settled down on the land between Maraenui and Cape Runaway, and called for their mother to join them. Hine Mahuru came to the Bay of Plenty and settled at Kirieke pa in Raukokore, and she laid claim to the mana of all the lands below Whanokao mountain in the Raukumara ranges, including Whangaparaoa, Tihirau, Ranganui-a-Toi and Rangamuatai. Her name was given to the fishing grounds and mussel beds where the Raukokore river comes out into the sea, 'Te Kopua-a-Hine Mahuru', the deep waters of Hine Mahuru. She was a woman who was a leader of her people and she had the power to lay claim to all things and to do all things, and her power was passed down to her descendants.

Our meeting-house at Wairuru marae in Raukokore is called 'Hine Mahuru', Kirieke pa stands on the hills behind it, and Hine Mahuru is our ancestress and our resting-place.

Apanui-ringa-mutu was the eldest son of Turirangi and Rongomaihuatahi, and one time when he was a young man his relations invited him to visit them at Rotorua. Apanui-ringa-mutu left his home in the Bay of Plenty and travelled to Rotorua, and when he arrived there he passed by the pa of a Te Arawa man called Huri-tu-moana. Huri-tu-moana sent down a messenger to invite Apanui and his party into the pa, and as they climbed up the hill Apanui could smell the hangi fires

(*Left*) Hine Mahuru meeting-house, Wairuru Marae, Raukokore. Amiria Stirling is sitting in front of the door in the top photo. *John Miller, 1973*.
(*Below*) 'Te Kopua-a-Hine Mahuru' – the deep waters of Hine Mahuru. *John Miller, 1973*

burning inside. He thought they were cooking human flesh in his honour, for in those days they would kill a chief to feed another chief, that was the custom. Apanui's pet parrot flew ahead of them to take a look at the pa, though, and when he flew back he perched on the gateway of the pa and sang out to them:

> Uia te manuhuri me ko wai
> *Ask the visitor his name*
> Te Kuti, Te Wera, Te Haua!
> *He descends from Te Kuti, Te Wera, Te Haua!*
> Ko Apanui!
> *It is Apanui!*
> Moi, moi, haramai!
> *Moi, moi, welcome!*
> Kaore he kai o te kainga nei
> *There is no food in this village*
> Tou apiapi, tou apiapi
> *The marae is crowded, crowded*
> Kehu, kehu
> *The people are getting ready*
> Haramai te koki koka
> *Welcome to you*
> Ko Huri-tu-moana
> *Huri-tu-moana*
> Te o! te o!
> *Shall be the food, the food!*

Well, as soon as Apanui heard his parrot chanting he knew that the hangi fires had been lit to cook him and his people, because there was no other meat in the pa, and he warned his warriors, 'E! Those hangi fires are burning for me! We must go carefully into this pa, hiding our weapons under our cloaks, and when we get inside I want you all to sit on the right side of the marae . . .'

Soon the local women began calling and Apanui's party moved into the pa and sat on the right side of the marae. The visitors exchanged speeches with the local people and when they were invited to come and eat, Apanui saw Huri-tu-moana's hand reaching inside his cloak. Straight away Apanui-ringa-mutu jumped to his feet and cried,

'E, Huri-tu-moana! You have prepared the earth ovens for me, but I will not be eaten!'

He took his mere and killed Huri-tu-moana, and his warriors attacked the local people, and Huri-tu-moana and his people were cooked in their own hangi pits and eaten by Te Whanau-a-Apanui.

When Apanui-ringa-mutu married Kahukuramihiata, a descendant of Ruapani, he begot Tukaki, and Tukaki is the name of the carved house standing at Te Kaha today. Tukaki married Te Rangiwhakapunea and begot nine children, and their youngest son Tamahae grew up to become the most famous warrior in all the history of Te Whanau-a-Apanui.

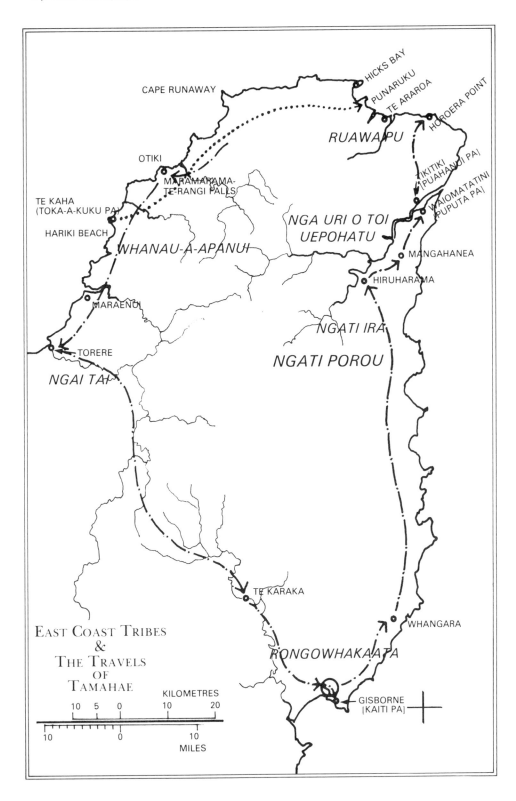

HICKS BAY

PUNARUKU

TE ARAROA

HOROERA POINT

CAPE RUNAWAY

RUAWAIPU

OTIKI

IKITIKI
(PUAHANDI PA)

MARAMARAMA-
TE-RANGI FALLS

WAIOMATATINI
(PUPUTA PA)

TE KAHA
(TOKA-A-KUKU PA)

*NGA URI O TOI
UEPOHATU*

HARIKI BEACH

WHANAU-A-APANUI

MANGAHANEA

HIRUHARAMA

MARAENUI

NGATI IRA

TORERE

NGATI POROU

NGAI TAI

TE KARAKA

WHANGARA

EAST COAST TRIBES
&
THE TRAVELS
OF
TAMAHAE

RONGOWHAKAATA

KILOMETRES

10   5   0   10   20

10   0   10
MILES

GISBORNE
(KAITI PA)

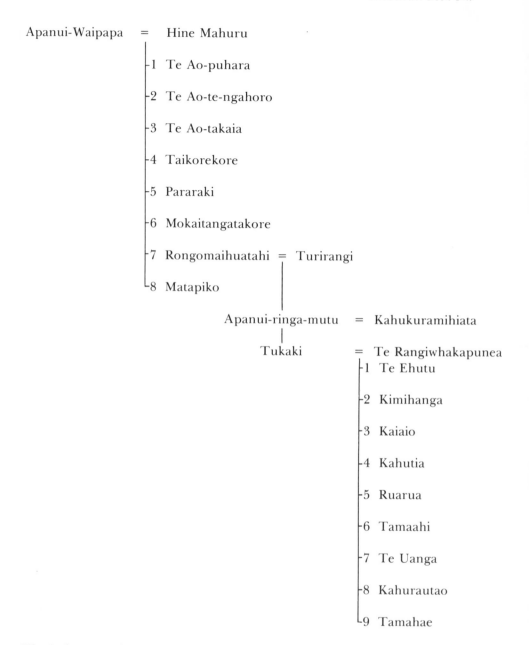

Apanui-Waipapa = Hine Mahuru

1 Te Ao-puhara

2 Te Ao-te-ngahoro

3 Te Ao-takaia

4 Taikorekore

5 Pararaki

6 Mokaitangatakore

7 Rongomaihuatahi = Turirangi

8 Matapiko

Apanui-ringa-mutu = Kahukuramihiata

Tukaki = Te Rangiwhakapunea

1 Te Ehutu

2 Kimihanga

3 Kaiaio

4 Kahutia

5 Ruarua

6 Tamaahi

7 Te Uanga

8 Kahurautao

9 Tamahae

The jealousy against the senior line was passed on down the generations, and from the time of Apanui-Waipapa's murder right down to the days of Tamahae, Ngati Porou and Te Whanau-a-Apanui were fighting against each other all the time.

One time when Tamahae's grandmother went on a visit to Gisborne the Rongowhakaata people killed her, so Tamahae grew up with one idea in his mind – to avenge the death of his grandmother.[11] He studied the art of fighting with all

Tamahae, the great Whanau-a-Apanui warrior – tekoteko on Tukaki meeting-house at Te Kaha. *Cliff Whiting*

the experts of his district, and one day his grandfather Apanui-ringa-mutu said to him, 'Good, Tamahae, learn everything you can, but your first battle is going to be against your own people. If you can kill Korokoro, then you can go outside to fight.'

Te Whanau-a-Apanui was divided into two groups in those days because the people from Cape Runaway to Te Kaha were quarrelling with the people from Waiorore to Maraenui, and Korokoro was the leader of the Waiorore and Maraenui people. Tamahae went from Te Kaha to Cape Runaway, gathering warriors and preparing them for battle, and when he brought them back to Te Kaha they came to Hariki beach (between Te Kaha and Waiorore) and saw their enemies coming down the hills. The two sides met on Hariki beach and started to fight, and the next minute Tamahae caught sight of Korokoro and called out,

'Maku a Korokoro! Korokoro's mine!'

As soon as Korokoro heard that he came towards Tamahae with his taiaha whirling through the air, and Tamahae shouted,

'Korokoro – welcome! E kore rawa nei tou upoko e meinga e au hai mounu taruke, hai rurutanga ma nga koura o Paringaere! – I would *never* use your head to bait my crayfish pots, to be torn at by the crayfish of Paringaere!' (Paringaere is a fishing ground off Te Kaha.)

Korokoro and Tamahae fought on Hariki beach and Korokoro was killed, and then Tamahae cut off his head, put it into a crayfish pot and fed it to the crayfish at Paringaere! The people of Waiorore and Maraenui were defeated and Tamahae became the leader of all Te Whanau-a-Apanui.

His first fighting expedition was to Hauturu‡ in Thames, and while he was away his older brothers travelled up the Raukokore river to the Tapuwaeroa Valley, where the local people attacked and killed them. It was the same thing coming out again – jealousy against the 'tatai rangatira', the senior line of descent. When Tamahae came back to Te Kaha the people told him that his older brothers had been killed by Ngati Porou, so he gathered a big party of Te Whanau-a-Apanui warriors and took them over the hills to Torere, and along a mountain track from Torere to Te Karaka near Gisborne, seeking revenge for the deaths of his grandmother and his older brothers. On the way he stopped at Otiki at a place by the waterfall called Maramarama-te-rangi, where a tutu bush was standing. Tamahae attacked the bush with his taiaha and smashed it all to pieces, calling out,

'E Kuriteko! Naku ano te taiaha kotahi atu, taku taiaha ra hoki i whakaheia i runga o Maramarama-te-rangi! – Hey Kuriteko! Mine is the first taiaha, my taiaha wielded up on Maramarama-te-rangi!'

Kuriteko was the chief of the Rongowhakaata people who had killed Tamahae's grandmother, Kahukuramihiata, and that's why Tamahae called out his name.

When Tamahae and his men came out from the hills at Te Karaka they killed all the people there, and from Te Karaka they went on to the big pa at Kaiti in Gisborne, where Kuriteko and his warriors were waiting. As Tamahae's party began to climb the hill one of his men called out, 'Hey Tamahae – I'll lead now!'

Tamahae answered, 'No – go back, and watch the plumes standing here upon my head. I want you to tell me which one shakes and quivers in the wind . . .'

When they climbed higher Kuriteko and all his warriors appeared upon the ramparts – hu-uu! The next minute the man at the back called out, 'Tamahae! The left plume on your head is quivering!'

‡'Hauturu' is Little Barrier Island.

That was a sign to Tamahae that Kuriteko was a right-handed warrior and weak on his left side; but Tamahae had been taught by his grandfather Apanui to fight with his taiaha on both his right and left-hand sides.

As Tamahae came to the top of the hill Kuriteko came out of the pa to meet him, and the two great warriors began their battle, watched by all the rest. Kuriteko struck at Tamahae with his patu and Tamahae parried to the left, and Kuriteko struck out again and Tamahae parried, then Tamahae shifted his taiaha to his left side and lunged at Kuriteko, and hit him on the forehead. As Kuriteko fell to the ground Tamahae called out,

'E he noa ra aia, taku taiaha ki te marahea! – I'd be wrong to waste my taiaha on a man of no importance!'

Kuriteko looked up at him and said,

'E Tamahae, he marahea hoki au? E ko au ra tenei ko Kuriteko. – Am I indeed so insignificant? For I am Kuriteko!'

Then Tamahae lifted his taiaha and cried,

'A, taku taiaha i whakaheia ra hoki ki runga o Maramarama-te-rangi. – Oh, my taiaha, wielded upon Maramarama-te-rangi!'

He plunged his taiaha downwards and killed Kuriteko, and his warriors attacked the people of Rongowhakaata and wiped them out. That was Tamahae's revenge for the killing of his grandmother Kahukuramihiata at Gisborne.

Now Tamahae turned for home and travelled along the East Coast, seeking revenge for the deaths of his older brothers. He killed a lot of people at Whangara and when he came to Hiruharama he killed Te Kokere, a great chief of Ngati Porou. Kokere's people had all fled into the bush, and when Tamahae came to the pa at Hiruharama Kokere called out,

'E Tamahae – I am the only one here!'

Tamahae replied, 'Where is this solitary man?'

Kokere knew that Tamahae had come to kill him as payment for his older brothers, so he answered,

'E Tamahae, e patu koe i a au, waiho aku toto kia heke ki roto ki nga wai ratarata o Makarika me Tatara e maru ana – i a au te tangata, i a au te whenua, i a au nga mea katoa. I tenei ra, ko au anake. – When you kill me, Tamahae, let my blood flow into the clear waters of Makarika, and Tatara shading them. I had men, I had the land, I had all things – but today I'm on my own.'

Tamahae struck Kokere down, and killed him.

When Tamahae went on to Mangahanea, all the pas along the way had been abandoned. He came to Mangahanea pa and found the old chieftainess Hine Tapora sitting there alone because she had refused to run away with her people, and Tamahae killed her there, the upoko ariki, the head of all the chiefly lines of Ngati Porou.

After that Tamahae went to Puputa pa at Waiomatatini, where Makahuri was waiting for him. When Tamahae saw Makahuri up in the heights of the pa he called, 'Come down!'

Makahuri stood on the ramparts and turned his bare backside to Tamahae and gave a resounding fart – that was his answer!

Tamahae cried out, 'E, akiaki ana ra aia te whero o te tama a Te Atahaia!

Rongona ana te harurutanga i runga o Kauwharetoa i runga o Puke-a-maru, te pihau nei! Listen to the exploding backside of Te Atahaia's son! You can hear his fart thundering from Kauwharetoa to Puke-a-maru!'

Makahuri stayed up in his pa though, and he didn't come down to fight.

From Puputa Tamahae went on to Puahanui near Tikitiki and Putaanga was up in the Puahanui pa. Tamahae called out to him, 'Come down!'

'No!'

So Tamahae said, 'E, te kino tangata e wero iho nei.– What an ugly-looking fellow to challenge me!'

Putaanga answered,

'E, he kino tangata ra no ro Tau-o-te-wai, no roto i te mara kotipu a Tumoanakotore.– An ugly man indeed, descended from Tau-o-te-wai and the nursery gardens of Tumoanakotore!'

Tamahae was descended from those ancestors on the senior line, while Putaanga came down from Tumoanakotore's second son Tamataua, so he called out to his relation,

'A, taua taua – we are one!'

Tamahae left Puahanui and went on his way in peace. He and his men went over the hills to Te Araroa in the early hours of the morning and on the way somebody warned them that Te Whanau-a-Tuwhakairiora, Te Whanau-a-Rerekohu and Te Whanau-a-Hukarere were all gathered in the pa at Horoera. Tamahae said to his warriors,

'We will approach the Horoera pa at daybreak along the beach, and as we go I want about forty of you to walk together in a group, but the rest can wriggle along the sand like seals, keeping out of sight . . .'

As the sun rose that morning Tamahae's party came along the Horoera beach, some walking upright but most of them crawling on their bellies like seals. The Ngati Porou people looked out from their pa and saw a small group of Whanau-a-Apanui warriors approaching, and they said to each other,

'Ha! Tamahae's got hardly anybody left!'

They broke out of the pa waving their weapons, and when Tamahae's men saw them coming they turned and ran back down to the beach. The Ngati Porou warriors chased after them, and as they came on to the beach Tamahae called out to the rest of his party,

'E tu! Stand up!'

The next minute all of the Whanau-a-Apanui warriors were on their feet, and the people of Horoera looked at them and said,

'Oh, there are a lot of them all right!'

They fled back to their pa.

In the meantime a cousin of Tamahae's who was married to a Ngati Porou woman had gathered a group of warriors and brought them to Horoera, and when he saw the Horoera warriors running back to the pa he said to his party, 'Let's go and help my cousin!'

They charged out and attacked the Horoera people in front of the pa and drove them back down the hill. Tamahae attacked them from the beach, and on that day all the fighting-men of Te Whanau-a-Tuwhakairiora, Te Whanau-a-Rerekohu

Te Maniaroa beach at Te Araroa. *Auckland Institute and Museum*

and Te Whanau-a-Hukarere were killed on the sands of Horoera. A tapu was placed on the beach and it was reserved, and you can still see the bones heaped up there today, washed clean by the rain. This was Tamahae's last battle before his return to Te Whanau-a-Apanui.

Not long after Tamahae's return a big war party came from Ngati Porou to the Bay of Plenty looking for revenge, and it was led by 'Nga Kuri Paka a Uetuhiao' (the brown dogs of Uetuhiao), the three sons of that ancestress.

When Te Whanau-a-Apanui heard that Kuku, Rongotangatake and Korohau were bringing their taua to Te Kaha, Tamahae said to his grandfather Apanui-ringa-mutu,

'Look here! I will lead our people into battle at Punaruku – you stay at home.'

Apanui replied,

'No! I am coming, and *I* will hold the last taiaha at the battle of Punaruku.'

Apanui and Tamahae took the fighting-men of Te Whanau-a-Apanui to Punaruku, this side of Te Araroa, and when they got to the beach 'Te Maniaroa' they saw Ngati Porou coming – the beach was black with people! Apanui led his people on to Te Maniaroa beach and Tamahae came behind him, and that day all the chiefs of Ngati Porou were killed by Te Whanau-a-Apanui and there were no survivors.

The last great battle between Ngati Porou and Te Whanau-a-Apanui took place when Kaka Tarau, the ancestor of Reweti Kohere, brought a taua to Toka-a-Kuku pa at Te Kaha looking for revenge, and Tamahae killed Kaka Tarau and most of his warriors from Ngati Porou.[12]

E kui ma e! He oti tou te manako
Old women! All I think about
Ko koe nei te tane ki roto te ngakau, e
Is this man within my heart
He aha te inaina, e kohi ai te mahara
With the sun on my body I gather thoughts
He aha te ao pango
Under black clouds
E kapo ai te aroha e
Love flashes
Aroha rawa au ki Hikurangi ra ia
I look with longing at Hikurangi
Te maunga ka hira, ka kite mai te whenua
The high mountain, that all the land can see
Ka tiro mai Otiki, e
Even from Otiki.
Takoto ai te marino, horahia i waho ra
The sea lies calm out there
Kaupapa haerenga nou e Tiakitai, e.
The sea where you travelled, Tiakitai.
E whanatu ana koe ki aku kaingakau
Going to my loved ones –
Ina ia te wa i tau ai ki raro
Now my mind alights and rests
Ka pau te tute atu e te ope whakataka
The war party has been commandeered
Nau ra e Pape e
By you, Pape
Hinga mai to ika me ko Tu-ki-te-rangi
If your fish falls to the war god,
Whenua noa i mahue
The land will be desolate.

a love song for Te Manana Kauaterangi
by Turuhira Hine-i-whakinaterangi (Ngati Porou)§

After the battle at Toka-a-Kuku pa, Tamahae thought it was time to make peace between the two tribes, so he travelled to Puputa, Makahuri's pa at Waiomatatini, and said to Makahuri,[13]
'E Makahuri, I have come to make a covenant between our two tribes, Ngati Porou and Te Whanau-a-Apanui – there has been enough fighting between us.

§From A. T. Ngata, *Nga Moteatea* Part I, No. 23, pp. 86–7; a song written by Turuhira for her husband Kauaterangi when he went with Ngati Porou under Kaka Tarau (also called Pape) to attack Te Toka-a-Kuku pa at Te Kaha.

Now let it stop! Give me two young chiefly women and I will marry them to my grandsons.'

Makahuri agreed to the covenant and his grand-daughters, Te Muiora and Te Kohiku, were chosen, and Tamahae took them back to the Bay of Plenty and married them to his grandsons. Upon his return he built a pa in Waihau Bay (near Pera Stewart's place), and called it 'Te Rangi-pa-tu-riri', and Ngati Porou agreed not to go past that spot into the territory of Te Whanau-a-Apanui.

That is the story of Tamahae's revenge – he killed Kuriteko of Rongowhakaata for the death of his grandmother Kahukuramihiata, and he killed Kokere and Hine Tapora of Ngati Porou for the deaths of his older brothers; he defeated two Ngati Porou war parties that came to Te Whanau-a-Apanui, then he made a lasting peace between the two tribes and bound them together by marriage.

I am a descendant of Tamahae but my mother's line goes back to the senior descent line from Te Ao-puhara, the eldest son of Apanui-Waipapa and Hine Mahuru. Apanui-Waipapa married Hine Mahuru and begot Te Ao-puhara, Te Ao-te-ngahoro, Te Ao-takaia, Taikorekore, Pararaki and three other children; Te Ao-puhara married and begot Ruatahi; Ruatahi married her uncle Te Ao-te-ngahoro and begot Hinerangi; Hinerangi married her uncle Te Ao-takaia and begot Apahoua; Taikorekore married Te Kawekuratawhiti and begot Hinetera; Hinetera married her uncle Pararaki and begot Maruhaeremuri; and Maruhaeremuri married her cousin Apahoua and became the ancestress of the Whanau-a-Maru people at Raukokore. On the next page are the descent lines from Apanui-Waipapa and Hine Mahuru, right down to my great-grandfather Poututerangi, my mother Mihi Kotukutuku, and myself.

All through the years after Tamahae's covenant the two tribes Ngati Porou and Te Whanau-a-Apanui kept up strong ties with each other, and one of the closest relationships was between Ngati Hinekehu[14] of the Tapuwaeroa Valley and Taumata-o-mihi, and our own sub-tribe Te Whanau-a-Maru of Raukokore.

Tihere mauri ora!
Tihere mauri ora!
Ko te whakaariki, ko te whakaariki
An invading army is coming,
Tukua mai kia piri, tukua mai kia tata
Come closer, draw near
Ki te paepae o taku tipuna
To the threshold of my ancestral house
Ko Rauru-a-Toi, e tu nei
Rauru-a-Toi, standing here!
He atua, he tangata hou!
A god, a new man!

a patere or chant by Eruera Stirling

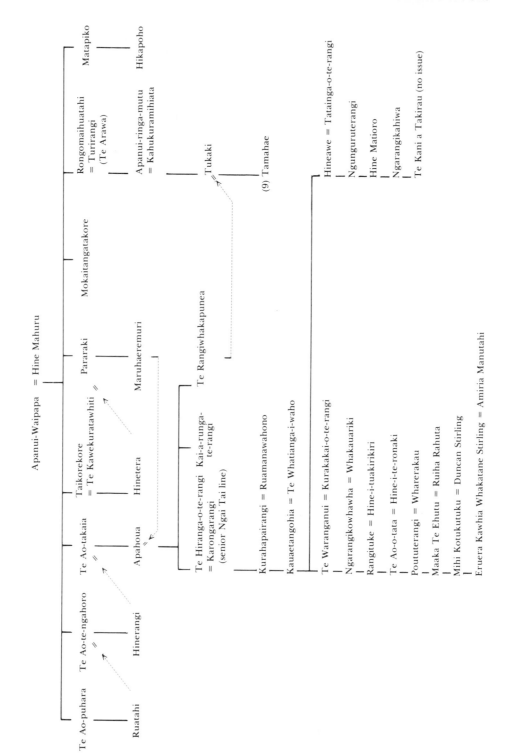

Eruera Stirling's descent line from Toi, written in his whakapapa book.

The Ngati Hinekehu people go right back on the very old descent lines from Toi,[15] the first man to come to New Zealand – he was a traveller who went back and forth, visiting all the islands, and his descendants from Rauru-nui-a-Toi down to Uepohatu settled in the Tapuwaeroa Valley next to the lands of Te Whanau-a-Maru, and claimed the territory from Hikurangi Mountain to Tuparoa on the East Coast. The great pas of Tapuwaeroa were Wharawhara, Takuahikereru, Te Kumi-ki-tua, Tauwharenikau and Te Ranganui-a-Toi, which stood near Whanokao mountain and marked the boundary between the lands of Te Whanau-a-Apanui and Ngati Porou. From Te Ranganui-a-Toi the Manga Raukokore stream runs to join the Raukokore river at Kawa-a-kura on Whanau-a-Maru land. The boundary between the lands of Ngati Hinekehu and Te Whanau-a-Maru starts at the western end of Whanokao mountain and runs along the Ranganui-a-Toi ridge in the Raukumara ranges to Te Pakira, then along to Potikirua mountain where it turns towards the sea, straight towards Tihirau mountain, to Ratanui and the mouth of the Whangaparaoa-mai-Tawhiti river. These are the boundaries told to me by my grandfather Maaka Te Ehutu.

The first marriage between Ngati Hinekehu and Te Whanau-a-Apanui took place in ancestral times when Tamataonui, Hinekehu's son in the aristocratic descent line from Porourangi, married Te Ikiwa-o-rehua of Te Whanau-a-Apanui;

        Porourangi
          |
(1)[ll] Hau
          |
(1) Rakaipo
          |
(1) Rakaiwetenga
          |
(1) Tapuatehaurangi
          |
(1) Tawakeurunga
          |
(1) Hinekehu
          |
(1) Tamataonui = Te Ikiwa-o-rehua of Te Whanau-a-Apanui

and this began a long tradition of intermarriages between the two groups. When it came to the generation of my great-great-grandfather Te Ao-o-tata, he was married to Hine-i-te-ronaki, a descendant of the Ngati Hinekehu chief Mahu-tai-te-rangi[16], and they had a son called Poututerangi. Poututerangi grew up and when he was old enough the Ngati Hinekehu people met at Tuparoa and decided to marry him to Wharerakau, another high-born woman of the Mahu-tai-te-rangi line; they carried her up the Tapuwaeroa Valley and over the hills to Raukokore, and there was a great celebration on the Wairuru marae when Poututerangi married Wharerakau.

[ll](1) = eldest child.

Amiria Stirling sitting on the pae of Rauru-a-Toi meeting-house, Ngati Hinekehu, at Taumata-o-mihi. *Jeremy Salmond, 1976*

These marriages between the two tribes were one way to settle fights over land boundaries, and over the years Ngati Hinekehu and Te Whanau-a-Maru helped each other quite a lot. In the time of my great-grandfather Poututerangi, the Whanau-a-Te Ehutu people of Te Kaha tried to take the Kawa-a-kura plantations off our people at Raukokore. The leaders of Te Whanau-a-Te Ehutu sent a patrol through the hills and built a hut on the Kawa-a-kura flats, and when the Whanau-a-Maru people went up to Kawa-a-kura looking for fern-root and eels, they found this new hut standing on the land. A man came up to them with quite a number of others and told them,

'This land belongs to my ancestor Ruarua – here is a feather from Ruarua's pet parrot, found on the Kawa-a-kura plantations! Get off!'

One of the men from Whanau-a-Maru, Arapeta Pohoi, rushed back to Raukokore and told them about this, so they had a meeting on the marae and the local chiefs sent Arapeta Pohoi to Te Kumi-ki-tua pa at Tapuwaeroa with a message to ask the Ngati Hinekehu chief Tama-i-ua-te-rangi for help. As soon as Tama-i-ua-te-rangi got the message he sent a big force of men to punish the invaders, and he threw Te Whanau-a-Te Ehutu right off the land and sent them back to Te Kaha. It was the tradition of marriage between our people and Ngati Porou that saved Whanau-a-Maru from the claims of outside tribes.

In those years, too, Hongi Hika was running around all over the country, shooting up people with his muskets; he came down from Nga Puhi to Tauranga and Te Arawa, and he conquered all those tribes because he had guns, but most of the other Maoris didn't have any. After a while he came on to the Bay of Plenty into the territory of Te Whanau-a-Apanui, and when he came to Toka-a-Kuku pa at Te Kaha he went right past it, and travelled on to Raukokore. He couldn't go ashore at Raukokore either, because the pa was right by the sea and and there was no way up, so he continued on to Whangaparaoa. Two brothers from Raukokore called Te Kainui and Te Ihu-i-te-kore heard that Hongi Hika was on the coast, and when they found out he was heading for Whangaparaoa Te Kainui said to his younger brother,

'Let's go there!'

At Whangaparaoa there is a landing-place, down the hill near Dick Waititi's marae by a rata tree, and Te Kainui and Te Ihu-i-te-kore headed straight for that place. They hid in some bushes at the top of the hill, and before long they heard voices out at sea, and Hongi Hika's canoes came around the point. One of the canoes paddled into the landing-place and dropped off a warrior called Ngaure, the top man on the canoe – he was coming to have a look around. When Te Kainui caught sight of this chap he said to his brother, 'O-o-o! Big man coming!'

Ngaure started to climb the hill and Te Kainui said,

'Hey brother, you get in behind me here, and if I can't kill this chap, you finish him off.'

When Ngaure reached the flats near the top, Te Kainui went on with a swing and attacked him with his taiaha. Ngaure was a famous warrior but Te Kainui was pretty good too, and he gave his enemy one tap on the head and knocked him flat. He stood over him with his taiaha raised, then he lowered it and said,

'Go back!'

Ngaure stumbled back to the canoes, and when Hongi Hika saw that his man was wounded he called out to his people,

'We're not landing here – this is a bad sign!'

When the canoes left Whangaparaoa and went on to Te Araroa, the people there had heard that Hongi Hika was coming and they were all crowded in to the Whetumatarau Pa. When Hongi Hika saw that pa standing on steep cliffs, full of people and with no access to the top, he knew it would be a big job to beat them. He decided to stay there for a while and starve them out, so he posted his men to stop the people coming down to collect kumaras and sea food. While they were there, Pomare, one of the Nga Puhi chiefs noticed a beautiful woman called Te Rangiipaia up in the pa, and one night he called out to her husband,

'Friend – sleep in the pa with our woman tonight, tomorrow she will be mine!'

The next morning Hongi Hika's fleet sailed on a calm sea around Matakaoa Point and landed there. The people in Whetumatarau Pa thought that Hongi Hika had left the district, but that night when everybody was asleep, the Nga Puhi warriors came back by an inland track, broke into the pa and killed all the people, and Pomare captured Te Rangiipaia and took her as his wife.[17] A chief called Te Whetu Kamokamo came to try and rescue Ngati Porou from Hongi Hika, but Hongi's men caught him and killed him in the Awatere River.

Whetumatarau Bluff at Te Araroa. *Gisborne Museum and Arts Centre*

E kainga iho ana e au nga kai ki roto ra
I eat
Tutoko tonu ake e aku tini mahara
And my thoughts overcome me
He mea koroukore i te wa e ora ai, e
When you lived, I ignored you
Taria me he mate, ka hao au te mahara e
Now you are dead, memories enslave me.

Kai wawewawe atu e te mate i ahau e
Take me quickly, death
Kia wawe te wairua te tae ki Taupo
Let my spirit hurry to Taupo
Kei noho i te ao kairangi atu ai e
Or it will stay in the world
Ki te ao o te tonga e koheri mai ra
wandering below southern clouds, scattered
Na runga ana mai te hiwi ki Tikirau
Over the peak of Tikirau –
Kei tua koutou ota ora i ahau . . .
Beyond it, you are eating me alive

a song of yearning
by Te Rangiipaia (Ngati Porou)¶

After that Hongi moved on to Kokai Pa at Whareponga, and there the people screamed out insults at him.

'Enei whamamaku ki ena, pokokohua! Your pop-guns against ours, you bastard!'

They thought that Hongi's men were armed with the old style of pop-guns made from patete wood, which fired out pellets of dried kumara.

Hongi answered them, 'Tena, whakarewa to papatu, e mara! – All right then you lot, show us your backsides!'

The people of the pa stood on the ramparts and turned round, exposing their backsides to Hongi Hika in the worst of all Maori insults. Hongi's marksmen took aim and fired, and the people of Ngati Porou toppled over the cliff, shot by Hongi's muskets. Hongi was so wild with them that he killed them all except two women, Mokikiwa and her younger sister, whom he took back to Nga Puhi and married to prominent chiefs. Mokikiwa married Hare Hongi, and many of the important people of Nga Puhi are descended from her. That is the history of Hongi Hika's raid on the East Coast – he wasn't much of a fighter, but he had plenty of guns.

After my great-grandfather Poututerangi married Wharerakau from Ngati Hinekehu, they had a son called Maaka Te Ehutu and a second son called Pekama Ngatai. They lived in the hills on the Tapuwaeroa block between the lands of Te Whanau-a-Apanui and Ngati Porou, and Poututerangi kept the fires burning in the pas of his ancestors, Wharawhara, Takuahikereru and Te Rangiweherua, growing food for all his people and travelling back and forwards over the Tapuwaeroa Valley. The Whanau-a-Apanui came to visit him at Tapuwaeroa, bringing food from the coast with them, and that was the work of that old man – he gave food to everybody who came on the land. When the first Maori Land Court sittings were held in the district, Poututerangi was the senior man in the back country and all the people could see that his claims to the land around Tapuwaeroa were very strong, because he was a taharua, descended from both Whanau-a-Apanui and Ngati Porou, and he was living in the area; so Ngati Porou started to get jealous. My great-grandfather was a descendant in the senior line from Tamahae, and that was another reason for Ngati Porou to hold a grudge against him.

Well, one time when Poututerangi was living up in the backblocks at Tapuwaeroa, some of the Ngati Porou people at Reporua invited him to visit them at Te Houanga pa on the coast and feast on the beautiful seafoods of the area, crayfish, parengo and hapuku. He came down from the hills with his wife and his

¶ From A. T. Ngata, *Nga Moteatea* Vol. 1, No. 22, pp. 82-3: 'When Ngati Porou were defeated by Nga Puhi at Te Whetumatarau, Te Rangiipaia became the prize of Pomare, leader of the Nga Puhi war party. It was he who, during the siege of Te Whetumatarau Pa, called out to Ngarangitokomauri: "Sleep, o friend, with our woman this night." After her capture by Nga Puhi, Pomare wed Te Rangiipaia and took her to the north. After a while Pomare came back to make peace with Ngati Porou. Returning from that mission he met his death at Waikato, and Te Rangiipaia became the wife of Te Kariri of Ngati Haua. They lived at Maungatautari and it was from there that Te Rangiipaia sang her song of yearning for her own people.'

two sons Maaka Te Ehutu and Pekama Ngatai and spent the night at the marae, and the next morning somebody said to him, 'Come on, we're going down to the beach to see the canoes coming in!'

It was a beautiful day, the sun was shining, and as Poututerangi stepped on to the beach at Reporua a man hiding in the bushes shot him dead. No one at the marae saw who did it.

When Te Awarau of Te Whanau-a-Iritekura heard that Poututerangi had been murdered at Reporua, he came with all his people and took the body to lie at Waikawa, then they carried my great-grandfather up to the Tapuwaeroa Valley and over the hills to Raukokore. They buried him in a cave in the hills at the back of Raukokore, a special cave at the old pa called Mahirau where the bones of his ancestor Tamahae were hidden. I went there once, it was a beautiful cave and I saw the bones of my ancestors laying around washed clean by the rain, but I wasn't frightened – I knew I was entering into my own people.

When Apirana Ngata talked to me about the murder of Poututerangi, he said, 'It all led back to old grievances, Eruera, your great-grandfather didn't do anything wrong. The Ngati Porou people remembered those battles with Tamahae and that is why they killed the top man on the Tamahae line – hei ito mo nga mate o nga rangatira katoa o Ngati Porou – to pay for the deaths of all the chiefs of Ngati Porou!'

After the tangi my great-grandmother Wharerakau composed a lament for her husband and years later Ngata wrote it down in his book *Nga Moteatea*. My mother used to sing Wharerakau's chant† on the marae at home, but my voice could never get round the tune of that lament:

> E haere noa ana, e karanga noa ana, e u e
> *I wander about, calling out*
> Kia whakaoho koe i te ahiahi nei
> *Trying to wake you this evening*
> Ko te whanau koe a Matukutangotango, e u e
> *You are from Matukutangotango's family*
> Mate atu, ara mai kai runga te marama
> *That die away, then rise up to the moon*

> E hua i te tamaki, e whakatipua nei e u e
> *I thought I glimpsed a terrifying omen*
> Ko te hoa kairiri kei te haohao mai
> *Of an enemy plotting evil*
> Tenei tata tonu kei te huka o te kaka, e u e
> *Like the scarecrow fringes of a cloak*
> Kiia ai pakura, e ora i te whakaware . . .
> *Warning the swamp hen of danger . . .*

†From A. T. Ngata, *Nga Moteatea* Part I, pp.52-3: 'Poututerangi was a great chief; his father Te Aotata was one of the Whanau-a-Apanui, claiming descent from the aristocratic and warrior lines; his mother Hine-i-te-ronaki, was of Ngati Porou, a descendant of Mahutaiterangi, a leading Ngati Porou ancestor. Poututerangi's wife Wharerakau, who composed this lament, was also descended from Mahutaiterangi.'

... E kore ra e houa i te po wananga, e u e
... this will not be settled when the white clematis blooms
I te pitau tutu, i te kowhai angaora
When the tutu send up shoots or the kowhai flowers
Taria e ahu mai ki to waitohunga, e u e,
Wait, show yourself to your chosen wife
Ki to whakapapanga, i waiho i muri nei, e
And to the descendants you have left behind.

from a lament for Poututerangi
by Wharerakau (Ngati Porou)

Even though Poututerangi was killed at Reporua his title to the land remained, and when the Tapuwaeroa case came to court an old kaumatua called Wi Tahata gave evidence that Poututerangi had occupation rights in the area, and those rights were passed on to his eldest son Maaka Te Ehutu.‡

My grandfather Maaka Te Ehutu lived at Raukokore, and I remember him as an old man with a white beard who always wore a hard knocker on his head, even when he went to bed at night. One time my elder brother Taikorekore asked him,

'Why do you go to bed with your hat on, grandfather?'

'Cause I don't want the turehu§ to come and tiko on my head!'

He was frightened that the fairy people might come and do their business on him, eh. He would only tell Tai about it though, not me, because customarily in those days the old people only liked the senior grandchild and they'd do anything for him, but if my younger brother or I went near the old man he'd reach out with his long fingernail, shaped something like a claw or a hook, and *bang* us on the head like that! It was the same if we brought him his kai, he'd throw it out of the window and slam the door; he only wanted Taikorekore, the senior grandson. My grandfather observed all the tapu rules and he was very fussy about his kai, he would never touch food once the sun had set at night. As soon as the sun went down he'd go to bed and close the door, and if Mum was late with his kai he'd throw it out of the window, so she had to prepare his food watching the sun all the time. He told us that the turehu people start moving around after sunset, and he did not want a turehu eating beside him, picking at his kai.

My grandfather used to say that he was one of the last in the district who had eaten human flesh; my brother asked him,

'Ugh, kua kai tangata koe? Have you eaten the flesh of a man?'

'Oh yes, that's part of it, kua kai tangata au all right!'

In those days if a chief was killed in battle they'd cook his body and give the flesh

---

‡In the hearing of Tapuwaeroa No. 1 case at Waiomatatini in 1886, Wi Tahata of Te Whanau-a-Rua sub-tribe of the Uepohatu people said: 'Poututerangi strengthened the (Iringaanui) fortification as a pa of occupation by his people Te Whanauaapanui – the land was cultivated on every side of the pa and the whole of the people came to this pa to reside; they came from their own country through fear of Nga Puhi under the protection of Poututerangi who was a descendant of Uepuketa. He was related to Whanauaapanui and Whanauaruataupare, he was the father of Maaka Te Ehutu.' (*Waiapu Minute Book* No. 10, p.221).
§Fairies.

to other high born people, to pay him back for the harm he had done to their tribe. They'd kill a chief for another chief to eat, but not just the ordinary people.

One time when my grandfather was very young his tribe attacked another pa in the district, because they were still fighting each other in those days out of jealousy. The pa fell and the chief was killed, and Te Whanau-a-Maru cooked his body and cut it up; but when they heard that the relations of those people were coming to get revenge, they had to get away quickly. One of the old people put Maaka on his back and as he ran away from the pa, every now and then he'd pass him a little bit of meat to eat. My grandfather said it had a special taste, very sweet, and it was the flesh of that chief. That's why he told us, 'Oh yes, kua kai tangata au! I have eaten a man!'

Maaka Te Ehutu leans against the carved post with Paikea at its top, outside the Orete Point Native Telephone Station; Duncan Stirling holds the horse at left. *Gisborne Herald*

The trail inland along the Raukokore River, near the present bridge. *Alexander Turnbull Library*

When Maaka Te Ehutu grew to manhood, Te Whanau-a-Maru of Raukokore and Ngati Hinekehu decided to keep up the tradition of taumau marriages between the two tribes, and the Tuparoa people brought Ruiha Rahuta, a descendant of Mahutai-te-rangi over the hills to Raukokore. Ruiha and her people travelled from the Tapuwaeroa Valley down the Te Pakira ranges to Kawa-a-kura at the back of Whanokao mountain, and along the Raukokore River to the marae where all the people were assembled. The Ngati Porou chiefs who came with the party were Tama-i-ua-te-rangi, Te Keepa Takatakaorangi, Te Maru-ki-tipua, Marakai Kaihamu, Erupaata, Hotene Porourangi and Kahuroa; and on the Whanau-a-Apanui side the chiefs were Poututerangi my great-grandfather, Te Aopururangi, Te Ahiwaru, Haimona Waititi, Te Hata Moutara, Arapeta Pohoi and Te Hirata. It was one of the biggest taumau matches of those times, and after that my grandfather and my grandmother settled down together at Wairuru.

In later years Maaka Te Ehutu became very prominent in the district; he could trace his descent down all the senior lines of the East Coast and even in Te Arawa and Tuhoe, but he was always very humble. When he went to a tangi in Te Whanau-a-Apanui, Tuhoe or anywhere else, the people would reserve the special bed beneath the window of the meeting-house for him with the best of everything, but my grandfather never slept there. If the people pointed to that place and said to him, 'There's your bed, koro,' he'd say, 'No, here's my bed!' He'd walk right to the back of the house to sleep. When Maaka Te Ehutu stood up to speak though, the people listened and it went his way, because he was firm and they liked that.

In his day Maaka had a whaling station at Moutara with a whaling boat named *Horowai* after his daughter Keita Horowai, he set up a flour mill at Orete with the help of his relations from Ngati Hinekehu, he helped the people get maize and machinery from John Burns in Auckland (the locals called him 'Tione Paana') to start them off in maize-cropping, and he was one of the chiefs who went away to the Taranaki wars, along with Major Ropata Wahawaha, Mokena Kohere,

(*Left*) Major Ropata Wahawaha. *Gisborne Museum and Arts Centre*   (*Centre*) Ropata Wahawaha's flag. *Gisborne Museum and Arts Centre*   (*Right*) Mokena Kohere. *James McDonald*

Houkamau, and Wiremu Kingi from Torere.

While the Ngati Porou and Whanau-a-Apanui people were in Taranaki, they had the order to shoot; if they saw a group of Maoris coming through the bush they were told to shoot them, because the General said that those people were coming to fight against the Government! Maaka Te Ehutu didn't like that part and when he saw a party passing through the bush he'd just turn away, and Ropata Wahawaha told his soldiers not to shoot because he respected the wishes of the senior line of Whanau-a-Apanui and Ngati Porou.

Another time while they were away in Taranaki Major Ropata Wahawaha captured some of the locals who were fighting against the Government, and tied them up to be taken to gaol. My grandfather noticed one or two young boys in the crowd who looked like high-born people, and he felt very sorry for them, so he went over to them and said,

'Oh well, tonight when we go to sleep, you'd better get away!'

In the middle of the night he let them go and when the soldiers woke up in the morning, those chaps had vanished!¹¹¹ Not long after that the Taranaki wars of 1863 finished up and the East Coast people went back to Gisborne; the Government schooner was sent to take them home. I have written the story of Maaka Te Ehutu's return to Raukokore in one of my books.

A letter from Maaka Te Ehutu in Patea, 27 April 1870, requesting that Te Whanau-a-Apanui be allowed to return home. *National Archives*

CQ.70f 1493   May 4
Maka Te Hutu
Patea.
    Requests permission for this
    tribe to return home ...
    Ngatiporou ...
    They are relieved.

F. Young
Translator Native Office   Patea, April 27th 1870.
4. 5. 70
    To Mr. Mclean,
            O my loving
    friend salutations to you
    this is a word from me
    or rather from all the
    tribe Aparun to you that
    they may be allowed to
    go during may.   Many
    letters have been received
    from home requesting us
    to hurry back. per:
    :haps there is some trouble
    at home.   Therefore I ask
    you to let us go first only
    us.   Let Ngatiporou be
    left until they are relieved.
    Let us go by steamer, but
    if you say we are to go
    overland, very well.   The year
    for which we took the oath
    has expired.   That is all.
    If you find fault with these words
    write.   From all the tribe
            Maka Te Hutu

‖Contemporary evidence also suggests that Maaka Te Ehutu's cooperation with the Government was limited and his sympathies lay with the 'rebels'; Major Noakes, who was the commanding officer in Patea, Taranaki, sent a telegraph to the Undersecretary of Defence in Wellington which read in part, 'Maka te hutu is the lieut. who left here some days ago for Wellington and about whom I telegraphed not to detain but allow him to return to East Coast being troublesome and obstructive – he got as far as Wanganui and returned – I am afraid the result of his return here will be the unsettlement of the whole of these people. He was the means of deeping (sic) the tribe from working on the roads . . .' (Telegraph No. 214, May 19 1869 AD1/70/1548). Note that these were military roads, aimed at subduing the 'rebels'.

Now
I am telling the story my Grand Father
told me about the army
movements all over New Zealand, and the
number of tribes they met
in favour of the Government forces, and
those who opposed the Army, they
stayed away for about three years
and moved Round all over the
North Island, they were all waiting for the
Day when the Maori forces are freed
from the Army, and after the Great
Battle of Gate Pa was over Peace
came, and the Government arranged
to Return all members of Maori War,
Officers and men to their own District of
Te Tai Rawhiti, word came that a Government
Schooner will take Back the Maori Officers
and men Back to Tikitiki, Hicks Bay
and Waihau Bay, and they all transferred
from the warship to a schooner¶ sailing to
East Cape vie Cape Runaway, Waihau Bay.
When they entered the ship, word came
from Army Head quarters to shell all the
Hauhau Pas on the East Coast and the
Bay of Plenty, the strongholds of the Hauhaus
at Pukemaire Pa in Tikitiki, and
Round the Bay of Plenty at Raukokore,
Moutara Pa, these were strong Holds
of Hauhau Religion, and Major
Mokena Kohere in charge of the
Tikitiki area said we have to
carry out The Government order.
They left Gisborne at night and sailing
along the coast arrived at the mouth
of the Waiapu River, opposite the
Rangitukia Pa Home of Mokena
Kohere, and Here the Government
Gave him five thousand Pounds

¶The warship was the *Eagle*, (Capt. Read), and the 'schooner' (in fact a paddle-steamer) was the *Luna* (Capt. Fairchild). (William Williams, writing in his journal, Gisborne, 31 October 1870: 'The Eagle at anchor at daylight having on board a body of Ngati Porou'; and 1 November, 'Early this morning the Luna was at anchor, and soon Captn. Fairchild was on shore . . . He gave me a letter and said he is now bound for Opotiki and Tauranga . . . Later in the day I found that Fairchild is to take these Ngati Porou back to their homes.' – courtesy Sharon Dell)

If we take the Land we'll not shoot
the People in the Pukemaire Pa

but Mokena Kohere Refused, I want my
People and my Land, Take your money
away. All the officers and men of the
Ngati Porou got off and the schooner
sailed for Hicks Bay, the old
chief Houkamau was taken ashore to
his People, and the schooner continued
its Journey to Land at Raukokore.

As the schooner turned Round Cape
Runaway, Maaka Te Ehutu arranged
with one of the Seamen to take him
ashore when the schooner anchors
to sleep there for the Night, and while
every one was asleep, the sailor took
him ashore and landed him. The Sailor Returned
Back to the ship, when they all came
up for their Morning Breakfast, they
found out one man was missing and
Major Ropata Wahawaha called
out 'Where is Maaka Te Ehutu?' The
Sailor said, 'I have put him ashore'
and Major Ropata Wahawaha said, 'Oh,
He has Gone to Save His People!' Maaka
Te Ehutu Landed at Waihau and walked

three miles to the Moutara Pa at
Raukokore, when he arrived there
the Tribes were all asleep, the three
Tribes, Whanau-a-Pararaki, Whanau-
a-Kauaetangohia, Whanau-a-Maruhaeremuri
were all in the Pa at Moutara. He
called every body young and old
to go Down to the meeting House
Te Hau-ki-Tikirau, all together with
Everything because The Pa is going
to be Blown Out by big Guns
on the warship, and the tribes
moved out of the Pa quickly and
settled all together in their meeting –
House, and in the Early hours of
the Morning the Schooner was
seen, Steaming into the Bay

and early that Morning they
turned the Guns on to the Pa,
and it was Blown to Pieces, and
after the shelling, the crew of the schooner
and men and officers came ashore
Here my grand father welcomed
them ashore, and He joined again
with his Group of Taranaki War
Leaders and Major Ropata Wahawaha.
After the Peace Terms were arranged Maaka
Te Ehutu gave a farewell Speech to
His Relations all from the Tribe of
Te Whanau-a-Rakairoa of Ngati Porou
and this is a true story told by my
Grandfather to me.

from *The Centennial of the Waiomatatini Maori School*
by Eruera Stirling, 1978

In later years my father had the farm at Moutara where the pa stood; he ploughed the pa and cleaned it up to make it look nice, and he picked up quite a lot of steel from the burst shrapnel that was shot over by the Government schooner. He set the place up, because he didn't like to see the Moutara pa all blown to blazes.

Well, that was my grandfather Maaka Te Ehutu, he was good and he helped people. People said nothing against him, and when he stood up to speak they listened. I know Apirana Ngata himself told me that when his grandfather Ropata Wahawaha died, Te Whanau-a-Apanui came to the tangi at Waiomatatini and different chiefs stood up to speak, and the last speaker from Te Whanau-a-Apanui was Maaka Te Ehutu. He said farewell to Ropata Wahawaha and this is what he said:

'Ropata Wahawaha, kai toa koe kia mate noa atu! Porokai-a-whanako ki nga whenua o Ngati Porou!'

In other words, you know, 'Ropata Wahawaha, good job you died! You did a lot of dirty work stealing the lands of Ngati Porou!'

Ropata Wahawaha had been appointed a Member of Parliament and an assessor in the Land Court, and he beat my grandfather to the title of some land. That's why Maaka stood up on the marae and said, 'Kai toa a koe kia mate! Porokai-a-whanako ki nga whenua o Ngati Porou!'

The people were shocked and one woman, a cousin to Ropata Wahawaha, was so wild that she started to stand up on the marae. The people howled her off and told her, 'You sit down! You can't talk against the old man!'

Then Te Houkamau stood up and said,

'You are quite right, Maaka Te Ehutu, I am supporting what you have said.'

The whole crowd started shouting at him,

'E, why don't you sit down, why didn't you stand up and say that before!'

They howled down Te Houkamau and he had to sit down too.

Major Ropata Wahawaha's tangi held at Waiomatatini. The figure striding across the marae in the middle photo is probably Maaka Te Ehutu. *Gisborne Museum and Arts Centre*

When Apirana Ngata told me about it he said, 'By joves, your grandfather was very strong, he was a man of his own word! When he stood up on the marae he had the crowd with him all the time.'

And Doc Wi Repa* told me, 'If your grandfather had started working plans, he could have taken away all the Whanau-a-Apanui lands, but no, he was not that type – he was humble and he worked with the people.'

I will say this, though, even if my grandfather said those things at Ropata Wahawaha's tangi, Ropata Wahawaha was still a great man; he saved all the land of Ngati Porou from being lost in the landslides of confiscation after the Taranaki Wars, and he was a great leader of the Ngati Porou people.

My grandfather Maaka Te Ehutu and his wife Ruiha Rahuta had three children, and they were all girls – Te Wharau the eldest, Keita Horowai, and my mother Mihi Kotukutuku. My grandfather was born in the senior male line of descent right down from the ancestors, but when it came to his children it changed, they were all girls. Jealousy grew among the tribes because instead of men taking control of the area, the women were coming up, and in the Maori custom that's bad luck! Some of the people organized a makutu, a curse, and first of all Te Wharau the eldest daughter died. She was drowned in the Raukokore River, and when she disappeared my mother's aunty, one of the old ladies who still had that mana, told the parents that Te Wharau would be brought back by the ancestors in the early hours of the morning. In the morning when the old people went down to the Wairuru beach just below the graveyard, they found Te Wharau lying on a big flat rock under a kotukutuku tree, washed up by the tide. They brought her back to the marae for the tangi, and the next girl was named Keita Horowai, 'Keita Lost in the Water', in memory of her sister Te Wharau. When Keita grew up and was going to get married, she took sick suddenly and died, and at the tangi one of my mother's relations, the old man Akuhata Kaua from Ngati Porou, stood up and said,

'That curse is going to clean up the whole family! We're going to take Mihi Kotukutuku away from here and look after her, because she is the only one left.'

They took my mother away to Reporua in Ngati Porou, and after she was there for a while she got very sick. They took her to the tohunga Nukunuku from Te Whenua-a-kura, but he told them,

'No, I can't touch this curse, it's too strong. You'll have to take her to the old lady Miriama at Maketu . . .'

They took my mother to Maketu and her relations, the Pokiha family, took her in. The old lady Miriama te Manu† took my mother to the sacred wai and fixed her up and then she said,

'When you go back home, Mihi Kotukutuku, you are not to marry any Maori from there – you must marry someone from outside!'

*Dr Tutere Wi Repa studied at Te Aute and went on to Otago University to take a degree in medicine; he practised in Te Araroa for many years (*Te Kaha Maori District High School Anniversary, 1875-1955*, p. 27).

†The genealogical links between Miriama te Manu and Mihi Kotukutuku (through the children of Te Ehutu and Rukahika) are recorded in Apirana Mahuika, *Nga Wahine Kai Hautu o Ngati Porou*, p. 121.

The Te Kaua family brought my mother back to Ngati Porou and told the story, and the people started to make arrangements. My father Duncan Stirling was building a church for the people at Te Horo and the people liked him, and because he was a half-caste from the South Island, that was all right. One day they asked him,

'Would you like to marry our cousin Mihi Kotukutuku?'

He answered,

'I'd be quite agreeable!'

The Te Kaua family arranged a time, and they brought my father down to the marae at Raukokore along with quite a big crowd of people. When they arrived at the marae it was packed out, all the tribes were there, and my father told me he could see the old man Maaka Te Ehutu sitting by himself in front of the old meeting-house.

All of a sudden a big man came running on to the marae, dressed up in a piupiu and a feather hat and carrying an axe in his hand! He came along swinging his axe, pointing to the sea and yelling out at my father,

'We don't want that taurekareka pakeha coming here! He's not the man for Mihi Kotukutuku! Take that taurekareka away to the sea and kill him!'

This man was cursing and all sorts – Dad didn't understand, but the elders told him what was happening, and then this fellow came straight over to hit my father with the axe! Dad told me that he had a revolver in his pocket, and if that man had come any closer, he'd have shot him. Just then a big strong voice from the marae rose up, it was Maaka Te Ehutu calling out,

'No! Stop! It's finished!'

The man with the axe stopped in his tracks and turned away, and then he went back and sat down. Dad told me,

'I'd heard about the Maori people, but that day I saw it. I was going to be killed, and only the voice of your grandfather from amongst hundreds of people could prevent it!'

The people had a talk on the marae, and the old man Te Kaua told them,

'When we took Mihi to the tohunga Miriama at Maketu, this is what she said to us: "If you marry a Maori from your own people, Mihi Kotukutuku, your days will be over!"'

When the people heard that they agreed to the match, and Mum and Dad were married by Bishop Williams in the Raukokore Church in 1896. Mum married my father to get away from the blood, and the result of the marriage was nine of us, and my mother lived to a good old age.[18]

> Mihi Kotukutuku
> was born on the 30 Day October 1870
> at Raukokore on Pohaturoa the
> Great Sacred Grounds of Te Aotata,
> to Bring out and teach all the Great
> ways and Traditions and Tribal
> Leadership of men and women. She is
> the Last of the Three Sisters Left after

the Curse of the change from the male
to a female line, to take the title, in which
women are not allowed from the trees
of Genealogy from Hawaiki, and
Mihi had to be taken to many tohunga
to be saved, she was taken to East Coast,
Waiapu, the Tohunga there could not cure
This case, and she had to go through Maketu
in the Bay of Plenty, travel on foot with
Her People and on Reaching the Maketu Pa
the faith Healer Miriama Temanu Cured
Her Witch Craft sickness at Maketu Pa. She
was warned by the Priest, not to marry any Maori
from Her District, and through arrangement my
Mother's People of the East Coast, Saw my father who
was a builder for Thomas Sidney Williams built all
the churches in the East Coast, Akuhata Kaua asked
my father Duncan Stirling to marry Mihi and he
agreed, and Mum and Dad Got married at
Raukokore by Bishop Williams in the Raukokore
church 1896 and mother Brought out my Brother
Taikorekore, first Born of male line Back
again to the Line from Hawaiki, and the
curse have been lifted and mother was
saved. Blessed All mighty God for His Saving
Mum's life.
Amine

by Eruera Stirling, 1978

2
THE BOOK
OF MY LIFETIME

Mihi Kotukutuku. *Te Kaha Carving Centre, courtesy Roka Paora*

CHAPTER ONE
BORN TO THIS WORLD OF LIGHT

Tihere – mauri ora!
I sneeze – it is life!
Tihei uriuri, tihei nakonako
It is darkness, blackness
Ka tau, ha, whakatau ko te rangi i runga nei
Lay, ha, set in its place the sky above
Ka tau, ha, whakatau ko te papa i raro nei
Lay, ha, set in its place the earth below
Ka tau, ha, whakatau ko Te Matuku mai i Rarotonga
Trace back to Te Matuku from Rarotonga
Koia i rukuhia manawa pou roto
Who dived to the spirit within
Koia i rukuhia manawa pou waho
Who dived to the spirit without
Whakatina kia tina, Te More i Hawaiki
Fix firmly, Te More from Hawaiki
E pupu ana hoki e wawau ana hoki
Rising and falling
Tarewa tu ki te rangi
Rise and stand up to the sky
Aua kia eke, eke panuku, eke Tangaroa
Up, up together, rise Tangaroa
Hui e! Taiki e!
Bring them together! It is done!

a patere or chant

The first of my mother's children was Taikorekore, the matamua, the eldest in the senior line. When the time came for his birth my mother was in Maaka Te Ehutu's house, a pakeha house given to him by the Government after the Taranaki wars. She lay in her father's house and laboured for a long time but the baby wouldn't come, and after a while my father thought,

'Ha! I wonder what is the matter?'

He went off to see an old lady named Hiria Te Rangihaeata, who was well known to everybody for seeing signs in the heavens and listening to the owls and all these things; she was related to my grandfather and she lived about three miles into the bush. When he got there the old lady already seemed to know what had happened and she told him,

Pohaturoa Point in the foreground, showing the Church of Jesus Christ at Moutara; Waikoukou to its right; Maruhinemaka Point behind with the school buildings; Orete Point behind that; and in the distance, Tihirau-mai-tawhiti. *Jane Wordsworth*

'Go back and wait – in the morning when the star Poututerangi* rises in the sky, carry your wife to the sea's edge – she will give birth there.'

Early in the morning they took my mother to that place and Taikorekore was born, and my mother had an easy delivery.

I was Mihi Kotukutuku's second son and when the time came for my birth it was just the same. My mother started to labour in the house and all her older relatives came to sit with her, but somehow the baby wouldn't appear. They carried her outside to a place about a hundred yards from our house, but still the baby didn't come, and some of the old people said,

'Let's take this woman to the papa pohatu, the rock pile by the sea . . .'

My mother was moved to the place where Taikorekore had been born – there was a big pile of stones from the seashore my grandparents had put there to mark the spot, and it still is there today. She stayed there for a while but no, the baby wouldn't come. My mother's aunties got a bit worried because they knew that something must be wrong, so they sent word again to Hiria Te Rangihaeata. The old lady looked up to the stars and noted the ebb and flow of the tide, all those signs on the spiritual side, and she sent a message back to say that they'd have to move my mother, I wasn't meant to be born at that place. So the people took my mother

---

*Poututerangi (also the name of Eruera's great-grandfather) was the star that marked the advent of autumn.

to an old-fashioned hut in the bush on the Kapongaroa block. Mum started to labour again and then the pains stopped, and Hiria came and said no, the child should not be born there, and she told them to take my mother across to the Kaikoura block and lay her under a big karaka tree planted by my great-grandpeople years back. She looked up to the sky and said,

'Engari kia haramai nga tai o Kirieke, a kia paepae mai hoki a Poututerangi ki runga o Tihirau, koina te wa ka whanau a ia – When the tides of Kirieke begin to flow and the star Poututerangi rises above Tihirau mountain, that is when this child will be born.'

The people carried my mother to the Kaikoura block and laid her under that karaka tree in the hills, near the cultivations of my ancestor Te Ao-o-tata. The stars were bright beneath the karaka tree and as the tide flowed in her pains grew stronger and at three o'clock that morning I was born into the world. It was on the thirtieth of March in the year 1899.†

After everything was finished they took my mother back to her home at Pohaturoa, that special place where she had been born and all of my great-grandfather's family before her. Pohaturoa was a point near Raukokore – when the ancestors came in their canoes from Hawaiki, somewhere round about Raiatea or Rarotonga, they saw this reef of rocks pointing out into the sea just like a point way back in Hawaiki so they called it by the same name; and that was where the people carried us that morning.

Just at that time a group of Ngati Porou people had gone to Whakatane for a meeting called 'Te Kotahitanga o Nga Kaunihera o Te Iwi Maori', 'The Union of the Councils of the Maori People'. They were under the leadership of Eruera Kawhia, and after the meeting they came back to Raukokore to talk about it and slept there on the marae, and that was the morning when I was born. When the Reverend Eruera Kawhia heard that Mihi Kotukutuku had just had a son he said,

'I will christen this baby with my name, Eruera Kawhia,' and all the people agreed.

One old lady, though, one of the Rakuraku family from the Waimana Valley and a relation of my grandfather's, called out,

'You people have just returned from Whakatane, so let this child be named Whakatane! He will carry that name in memory of his ancestress Muriwai!'

That is how I got my name, Eruera Kawhia Whakatane Stirling. My mother always called me 'Whakatane', and I am the only one left today with that name; its story goes right back to the time of the ancestors when Toroa, his brothers Puhimoanaariki and Taneatua, and their sister Muriwai came to New Zealand in the Matatua canoe. As the canoe approached the New Zealand coast it headed for a point on the East Coast called Tihirau – the real name of that place is Tihirau-mai-tawhiti (a hundred summits from the far-off land)‡ but they made a mistake in the survey and put it down as Tikirau, eh. All the big canoes headed there first, Tainui, Te Arawa and Matatua, and they stopped at a spot called Ratanui in front of the mountain at Cape Runaway. The Matatua canoe moved on

---

†We apologize to readers of *Amiria* for some unavoidable repetition of material in this chapter.

‡ Moana Waititi gives the story of 'Tihirau-Whangaparaoa-mai-Tawhiti' in an article in *Te Ao Hou*, No. 30.

Whakatane Harbour. *Alexander Turnbull Library*

and turned west along the coast, and as the canoe approached Whakatane they could see a beautiful mountain and a harbour with a good landing-place, so Toroa said, 'We'd better go and inspect that place!'

They left Muriwai and some of the people on board the canoe, and went ashore. As Toroa and his men scaled the rocks a mob of men came out from a pa nearby and these were Te Tini o Toi, the people who had arrived in New Zealand before the Great Migration – they were coming to kill Toroa and Puhimoanaariki. The sea was rising and the current carried the Matatua canoe close to the rocks, and Muriwai was sitting there but she couldn't do a thing – in those days women couldn't give orders to the men. In the end Muriwai thought, 'I'll have to do something,' so she stood up in the canoe and started chanting special prayers, asking the gods to give her the right, and open the way for a woman to talk. When she finished her sacred chant she called out,

'E-i! Tena, kia whakatane ake au i ahau! – Now I shall make myself a man!'

She called out to the crew and ordered them to start paddling quickly, and they just managed to pull the canoe away from the rocks – that is how Muriwai saved the Matatua canoe for her brothers. It was after that that Puhimoanaariki stole the canoe and took it away up north to found the tribal peoples of that area. From that day right down to now, there has been a 'kawa wahine', a women's etiquette amongst the tribes descended from Muriwai, and high-born women in the direct line from Muriwai have held the right to speak on the marae. My mother Mihi Kotukutuku was one of those women:

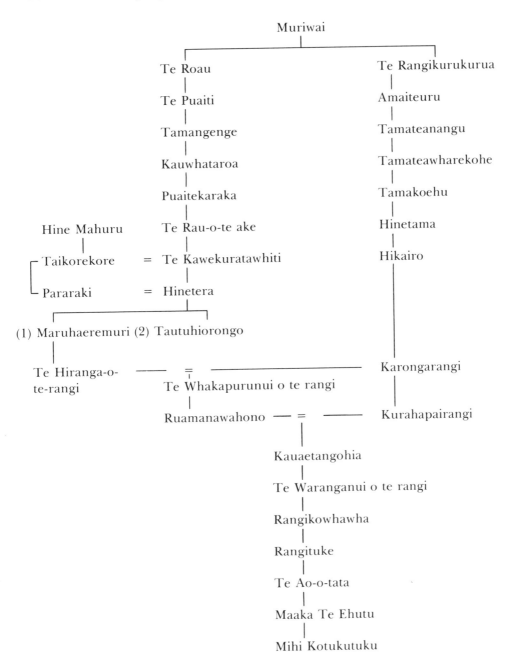

Muriwai

Te Roau — Te Rangikurukurua

Te Puaiti — Amaiteuru

Tamangenge — Tamateanangu

Kauwhataroa — Tamateawharekohe

Puaitekaraka — Tamakoehu

Hine Mahuru   Te Rau-o-te ake — Hinetama

┌ Taikorekore   =   Te Kawekuratawhiti — Hikairo
└ Pararaki   =   Hinetera

(1) Maruhaeremuri (2) Tautuhiorongo

Te Hiranga-o-
te-rangi ——— =̄ ——————————— Karongarangi

Te Whakapurunui o te rangi

Ruamanawahono —— = —— Kurahapairangi

Kauaetangohia

Te Waranganui o te rangi

Rangikowhawha

Rangituke

Te Ao-o-tata

Maaka Te Ehutu

Mihi Kotukutuku

Nowadays some people§ say that it was Wairaka, the daughter of Toroa, who rescued the Matatua canoe instead of Muriwai, but she was only a kid at the time –

§For example, Rongo Halbert in *Te Tini o Toi*, p. 73, and H. D. London, 'Traditional History of the Eastern Bay of Plenty', in McCallion *et al*, *Their Greatness*, p.8.

A descent line from Muriwai, written by Eruera Stirling in his whakapapa book.

how could a kid give the order in a big thing like that? That is why I heard my own great-grandpeople saying, 'No, it was Muriwai, all right!'[||]

If you look at Muriwai today, she is a woman known right through the East

[||] The writer of the *Omarumutu War Memorial Hall opening booklet* agrees: 'A voice called out, "Oh Muriwai, the canoe is being battered by the waves." Muriwai then rose and said, "Kia tu Whakatane ahau i au," meaning "Let me stand to as a man." '

Wairaka meeting-house, Whakatane. *Alexander Turnbull Library*

Coast, something was shown out of her and her descendants were all born chiefs, from Kawekuratawhiti to Taikorekore on the East Coast, down to Te Houkamau and the Potaes, right on to Gisborne with Te Eke-tu-o-te-rangi, and even to the Metekingis at Whanganui-a-Tara.

One time when I went through to the tangi of Te Hurinui Apanui at Wairaka, Whakatane, they were arguing about whether Muriwai or Wairaka saved the Matatua canoe, and one of the leading elders there was Kepa Tawhiao, a cousin of Te Hurinui. I was there representing my mother, and the old man said to me,

'We wanted your mother to be here, but since you have come, I want you to pick up the ashes at the graveside and throw them onto your uncle. You are the right man to do it.'

At the burial I threw the ashes onto my uncle Te Hurinui Apanui, and that afternoon when the elders began to argue about Muriwai and Wairaka, they asked me to speak about it. Of course I said it was Muriwai who saved the canoe, and afterwards Kepa Tawhiao stood up and said,

'I support my mokopuna, Eruera Stirling – he's right! When I went to Te Kaha, way back, the Ngati Porou people led by Kaka Tarau Kohere were attacking Te Toka-a-kuku pa. My people of Ngati Awa at Whakatane organized a party and went down to help Te Whanau-a-Apanui, because we were their relations through Muriwai. We defeated Ngati Porou and killed Kaka Tarau, and it was on this trip that I heard all about Muriwai. That is why I support my mokopuna Eruera – he's right, and I don't want anybody standing up to say anything more about it!'

He closed the ceremony off. There was an old man from Tuhoe there, though, sitting in the marae in an old cloak, and I was frightened of this old fellow. He was the only man at the tangi dressed like that, and I knew he wanted to fight about my talk, but Kepa told him,

'Sit down!'

Later on that afternoon when the sun was going down over White Island I felt very funny. I was feeling giddy and I couldn't eat, and my head started to spin. I knew that something was wrong, so after my kai, I went down to the beach to bless myself with the water because the old people always told me, if something goes wrong, go straight to the sea and bless yourself. The sun was setting and I could hardly walk, but I got into the water and just as I was coming out, I heard footsteps behind me. I turned round and saw a very elderly man. He said,

'I have seen your trouble, Eruera, I have seen what is happening to you and I have come here to help you. But it won't affect you now, as soon as you touched the water and blessed it, your ancestors were beside you.'

He blessed the water for me and then we went back to the marae. This old chap was a Ringatu¶ and he told me, 'In three days' time we'll hear the news – that makutu fellow will pay for his curse. His work will turn back on himself, you'll see!'

I went back to Raukokore, and three days later I heard that the old man from Tuhoe had died. You see how true it is, eh – very strong! That's why I will protest with anybody about the Muriwai case. I am the only elder living today with the name Whakatane, and so I am behind my name, and I support my ancestress Muriwai!

As soon as I was old enough and able to look after myself, when I was about two or three years old and finished with my mother, the old lady Hiria Te Rangihaeata came to her and said,

'We're taking him as our mokopuna, Mihi, we want to take him away from you. We can see all the signs on him, he will be the one to hold the mana and the traditions of his ancestors in the Kirieke School of Learning.'

I had two moles, one on my lower lip and one on the chin. The first was the sign of te kauae runga, the upper jaw which holds the prestige and the mana of everything, the tapu and the sacred power; and the second was the sign of te kauae raro, the lower jaw for the modern college, the knowledge coming from below. Those were the signs that I was going to take both the top and the bottom, that I should be put through the rituals of the whare wananga.

The whare wananga in the old days was a house of learning, a special place set aside for the priests to talk about the treasures from Hawaiki, the journeys of the canoes to these islands, the settling of the ancestors, the prayers for each district and all of the tribal genealogies. Only certain people were allowed to enter the whare wananga and they were trained to carry these treasures until they died, with the blessings of their ancestors upon them.

¶A member of the Ringatu Church, which bases its belief upon the teachings of Te Kooti.

The nikau hut where Eruera spent his early childhood in the bush, sketched in his whakapapa book.

The whare wananga of our area was up in the Kirieke pa, and my tipuna Pera Te Kaongahau, Hiria's husband, was the last of the old men who had been trained there; he was the one and only survivor from the Whare Wananga of Kirieke.

When Hiria Te Rangihaeata came and asked for me my mother agreed, she had to, and the old lady took me to her whare nikau in the bush. I lived there with Hiria and Pera until I was about seven years old. Pera was a first cousin in the junior line to my grandfather, but he was the one who'd been through all the channels of the tapu side, holding onto the history of Te Whanau-a-Apanui and Ngati Porou. During the Taranaki wars he had joined up with Ngati Porou under Major Ropata Wahawaha and travelled around with my grandfather, and that's how he met Hiria Te Rangihaeata of Ngati Awa and Ngati Raukawa and they decided to get married; Hiria was another person who'd been trained in the school of Maori studies.

Our toetoe hut was pretty nice. It was warm and well-kept, made out of nikau and ponga and toetoe, with plaited mats, a special place to light the fire, and a window and two holes at the top to let out the smoke. There were special experts in our tribe for building these huts, and that old-fashioned type of house was very comfortable. At night after the fire was kindled I lay on my sleeping-mat and Pera and Hiria lay on theirs, and I watched the smoke lift and rise through the air to the outside.

I enjoyed staying with the old people because I got plenty to eat, they gave me the best of food. We ate berries – taraire, tawa, karaka and miro cooked in the

Fishermen near Te Kaha, catching schnapper as they come to feed on crayfish at low tide. Photo by Canon Pahewa. *Auckland Weekly News, 20 June 1912*

hangi; pigeons, tui and parrots cooked in their own fat and kept in calabashes; wild pigs and fish, but one of the special delicacies my grandparents liked was the kiore, the grey rat – that was their special. When it's cut up and cooked it's something like the bird, eh, it tastes very sweet, and I just followed their way and ate up the meat and everything. There were big grey rats in the bush that fed on berries, and my grandfather snared them and put them in the calabash; and when we were hungry he'd just take them out and skin them.

Some of our other foods were fern-root and pikopiko – fern shoots – and the streams were full of eels. When my grandfather took me eeling to the deep pools of the river he'd catch just one or two of the big black ones and carry them home to hang in the sun to dry – we'd be eating eel for weeks after that! Sometimes we went to the sea and fished with a baited net; we'd let our net down into the water and when the fish were feeding we pulled it up and dragged the fish to shore. Pera taught me how to snare pigeons in the trees and the parrot, too – he'd call the parrot and it would hop right into the snare! He knew the songs of all the birds in the bush, and he could call a pigeon down into the tree and catch it with his hand. Sometimes we set up a waikaha net in a taraire tree when the berries were ripe, and when the birds flew down to the branches to feed, my grandfather pulled on a rope that closed the net and caught them all.

We had plenty of kumara and that was one thing about the old people, they always liked you to eat; if they saw that you weren't eating they'd get worried and try to find something that you wanted.

There were a lot of birds in the bush around our hut, and one of the most important birds to the old people was the owl, the ruru koukou. Sometimes an owl would come outside our house at night and talk, and Pera would say to me,

'Did you hear that owl? He's telling us that somebody has died.'

He knew all the cries of the owl, some brought good news and others brought a warning of death and danger, and if the owl started to talk at night my grandfather stood up in the whare puni and he'd growl at it, calling it all sorts of names.

'Who is this talking outside? You get away from here, you . . .'

The owl would speak more softly then, and the old man would talk back. Pera taught me to listen to the owl, and he told me,

'If you hear the owl talking in a bad way, e tama, don't go outside the hut – you stay inside!'

If someone had died Pera always knew about it before the messenger came to our nikau hut and he had pet parrots too, he taught them how to speak Maori. They could talk and sing and whistle, those parrots could do anything.

That was my life with the old people out in the bush, there were no other children living nearby and the birds were my friends. The pigeons, parrots, fantails, tui and the shining-cuckoo sang and talked in the trees around our hut, they were not afraid of us and as they flew about calling, I stood down below talking to them, and I listened to my grandfather echoing their cries.

As I grew a bit older the old man started to teach me history; now and again and little by little he'd try to teach me, and then he'd go on to talk to me about genealogy. He had been one of the tohungas in the Kirieke School of Learning and now he was the only one left. He told me about the mana on the land, how each ancestor came to own the land and how it was passed on in history right down to now. He taught me about all the big blocks around Raukokore – Tawaroa block, Matangareka block, Pohueroro block, Whangaparaoa block, Maraehako, Kapongaroa, and the boundaries around each one, then he showed me the places where the ancestors collected food, cultivated the ground and where they built their fortified pa. The main blocks were divided amongst different hapu through different ancestors, but it all came back to the one ancestress, Hine Mahuru, and Pera gave me all these lectures about it. He taught me the days of the month, the good days for planting and the bad days, the good days for fishing and the days to go out and catch eels, because the old people had a proper day for every kind of work in their calendar, following the stars and the moon.*

I suppose I was about four years old when I began to understand and when I got further, somewhere about six years old, I'd sit together with the old people and they'd ask me, who are the ancestors of Pohaturoa block, of Kapongaroa and Tawaroa, and what are the boundaries for the Otaimina block and so on. I would

*Elsdon Best discusses Maori calendrical systems in *The Maori Division of Time*, Dominion Museum Monograph No. 1, 1922.

answer, and in the end it was automatically in me. If I got something wrong I'd feel the hair of my head starting to pull, and then it would come back to my right mind.

The old man took me back through the genealogies little by little, he didn't hurry, but we went right back to the canoes – Horouta, Tainui, Te Arawa, Matatua, Takitimu and the rest.

Last year I heard a Rarotongan man talking about those canoes at the Holy Sepulchre marae in Auckland, and he said that the Maori people are taina, junior in descent to the people of Rarotonga, because the chiefs of Rarotonga kicked out their low-ranking relations years back and forced them to migrate on the canoes to these islands. Well, that was not the story that my grandfather Pera taught me in those early days. He taught me that the crews of those canoes were carefully selected from people of high rank and given special sacred chants to guide them, because it took the chiefs to open up the pathway for the people. The commoners were left at home and they were the ancestors of the Rarotongan people – that is why I say that we, the Maori people who came on the canoes are the tuakanas and they, the Rarotongans who stayed at home, are our juniors in descent!

Pera always taught me in a special part of our hut, a little room set aside on its own where no food was allowed to enter. Everything in there was tapu, the family heirlooms and the talk of whakapapa, and we only entered that place at certain times. The old man took me in there at night-time and he would start to chant; spiritually he seemed to know when it was time for us to go through the right channels of karakia, and we always opened up by praying to the gods. I sat there in the darkness, listening to him talk and the mana and the tapu of our ancestors came upon us.

One day the old people called me, and the two of them sat together, then Pera said, 'You go and sit over there.'

He went back on these things all over again, and the old kuia asked me questions too – I answered the whole lot. When I had answered everything Hiria said to the old man, 'Well, I think it's about time you should take him to the wai tapu.'

My grandfather held me by one hand and the old lady held me by the other and they started chanting. After the karakia Pera said to me,

'Tomorrow morning when the star Poututerangi comes above the mountain we will take you onto the waters of Te Wai-o-puru-whakamataku.'

There is a sacred pool near the Wairuru marae where the water springs out of the ground, and it is still there today. I felt myself ready and I wanted to get it over; I slept well that night, I was happy.

In the early hours of the morning we all got up and had our karakia, then we walked a long way out of the hills, past the marae and up into a gully. The pool was there by the cliff, with the water running from the cliff into a basin in the rocks. When we got there my grandfather started his special chants, and when his ceremony was finished he and I both had to go into the water. He took off our clothes and the old man went in first, then he took hold of me and said,

'As we dive you must grab a stone from the bottom.'

He put his hand on my head and we both dived down, but that first time, oh! it was too cold, I just went down a little way and I didn't get to the bottom. He kept his hand on my head and he was still praying, then he said,

'You *must* bring up that stone.'

The second time it was still too cold, and I was shivering and scared and the old man knew I hadn't caught a stone. He called out to me,

'Tupou, karakia – dive and pray!'

When we went down for the third time, he kept his hand on my head so I couldn't come up, and the stone came automatically into my hand. As soon as we came up he said,

'Have you got the stone?'

'Yes.'

'Give it to me!'

I passed it to him. Then he started with all the karakias to the moon and the stars, and the heavens above, and all the waters of the earth, calling on the gods to support me, to let me take the mana of history and carry on for the rest of my days; and when he was finished he put the stone back in the pool to the rising sun. We came out of the pool and went home without our clothes on, but I didn't feel cold at all. The old man dressed me and lit a fire, and he said to me,

'E tama, now the mana and the mauri rest upon you; I have given you the power of your ancestors, and it will lead you for the rest of your days. No one will ever come across your way. You have been through the faith and you go in light, with the knowledge I have passed to you; one day you'll be helping your people.'

After that ceremony I still lived with my grandparents for a while and I was happy, I was getting the best in the food line and I was having my good sleep, I enjoyed those years with them. But when I was about seven, word came from my mother that I had to go home to attend the Native School; that was in 1907. My father came to ask the old man to send me home, and that was one sad day for us. I saw the old people just sitting there and I knew that it was a big shock to them, my parting away. My grandmother pulled my hand and said,

'Oh well – haere e tama . . . Go, child, but we have given everything to you, and it will stay with you for the rest of your life.'

Then the old man wept over me, and I was very sad, too. I will always remember those good years with Hiria Te Rangihaeata and Pera Te Kaongahau in our whare puni way out in the bush.

CHAPTER TWO
YOUNG DAYS IN RAUKOKORE

When I arrived at the home of my father and mother, I wasn't happy with the pakeha way. Our father was a builder and he had built a big home for us with a piano and everything, but I missed our little nikau hut in the bush. I couldn't speak any English, and when my father spoke English to my brothers, I didn't know what he was saying. Every time he spoke to me, my brothers had to tell me what he wanted. One thing though, my mother was very good to me. She really looked after me and she always talked to me about the old people.

The first day I went to school at Raukokore, I wasn't interested in the other children and their games. I walked away from school into the paddocks and I was talking to the seagulls and the sparrows in Maori. Those were the sounds of my young days, the singing of the birds and the noises of the bush. In those days though, if anybody was found speaking the Maori language at school they'd get a hiding for it, and on my first day at school I was taken inside and the teacher gave me a warning. I didn't know what he was talking about so they had to get my brother Tai, and Tai told me not to talk Maori at school any more. The trouble was, I couldn't speak anything else and school life was not very happy for me at the start. I kept away from the other children, I wasn't interested in playmates and I got worse and worse, my mind kept going back to that other life and I didn't like school – I was more interested in the past.

Pretty nearly every day I'd get a hiding, and one morning I got so wild I refused to come into the classroom, I stayed outside talking Maori to the birds. They had to come and get me, and the master gave me a very strong thrashing. The marks showed on my hands and feet, and I cried and cried and cried!

When I arrived home my mother saw my face and asked me what was wrong, and when I showed her the marks she cried too. My father was building at Cape Runaway at the time, and when he came home my mother said to him,

'Go and look at Dick!'

He looked at the marks on my hands and feet, and he was *wild*. He said to Mum, 'I am not going to work tomorrow, I'm going to see that headmaster!'

The next morning Dad took me to school, and when the bell rang Dad went over to Mr Mulhern, the headmaster.

'Don't you ever give my son the strap again, you *bloody* Irishman! If you touch him again I'll give you a hiding – you leave him alone!'

They had a few words about it but after a while they calmed down, and Dad said,

'This son of mine is the only one in the whole school who has been through the channel with the old people, in the real Maori custom way. You've got to give him time to pick up, I don't want you to punish him again; their way is different and you have to help him and be good to him, so that he'll forget about the life of his grandparents . . .'

The next day when I went to school, Mr Mulhern's daughter Kathleen came to me and took me away, we had a little room to ourselves and she started to give me special lessons. I didn't like her at first, but she kept on with it and gave me a pencil, and started to point out the writing to me, and in the end I listened to her. She taught me the a b c at our little table and she was nice. Within a few weeks I was really interested in schoolwork, and when I went home after school I'd get out my books and sit in the corner of our house and study. My mother helped me too, she really nursed me into it, and one day she said to my father,

'This son of ours is doing good study, and I think we'd better put him in a room by himself so he can work.'

Dad agreed and I moved into a room of my own. I kept on with school, and I advanced and I got away, and when they had the test at school, they found I was progressing quicker than the other children. After that Mr Mulhern and Vincent and Kathleen really started to pet me. I had this belief that my work with the old people was helping me with my studies, and when we started reading our books on Maori history, I looked at those histories and I thought, I've got a more important history behind me than anything written in these books. When we came to the

Raukokore school-children, 1916. Back row (left to right): Mihi Eruera, Mavis Walker, Mary McDonald, Kate Stirling, Te Oraiti Ahuriri; front row: Mona Tangira, Ivy Saunders, Te Kaihi Collier, Urikore Wikuki Waititi, Rahera Parapara, Evelyn Saunders.
Raukokore Maori School Jubilee Booklet

Raukokore & District

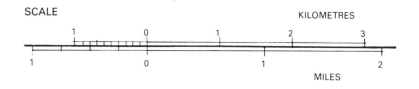

SCALE

KILOMETRES

1   0   1   2   3

1   0   1   2

MILES

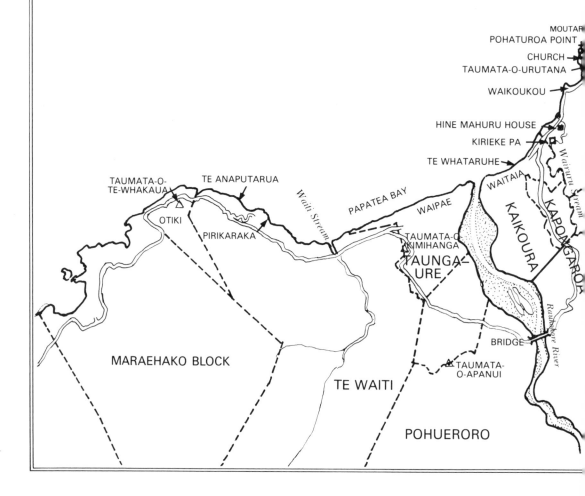

MOUTAR
POHATUROA POINT
CHURCH
TAUMATA-O-URUTANA
WAIKOUKOU

HINE MAHURU HOUSE
KIRIEKE PA
TE WHATARUHE

Wairuru Stream

TAUMATA-O-
TE-WHAKAUA
TE ANAPUTARUA

WAITAIA
KAIKOURA
KAPONGAROA

OTIKI
PIRIKARAKA

Waiti Stream

PAPATEA BAY
WAIPAE

TAUMATA-O-
KIMIHANGA
TAUNGA-
URE

Raukokore River

BRIDGE

MARAEHAKO BLOCK

TAUMATA-
O-APANUI

TE WAITI

POHUERORO

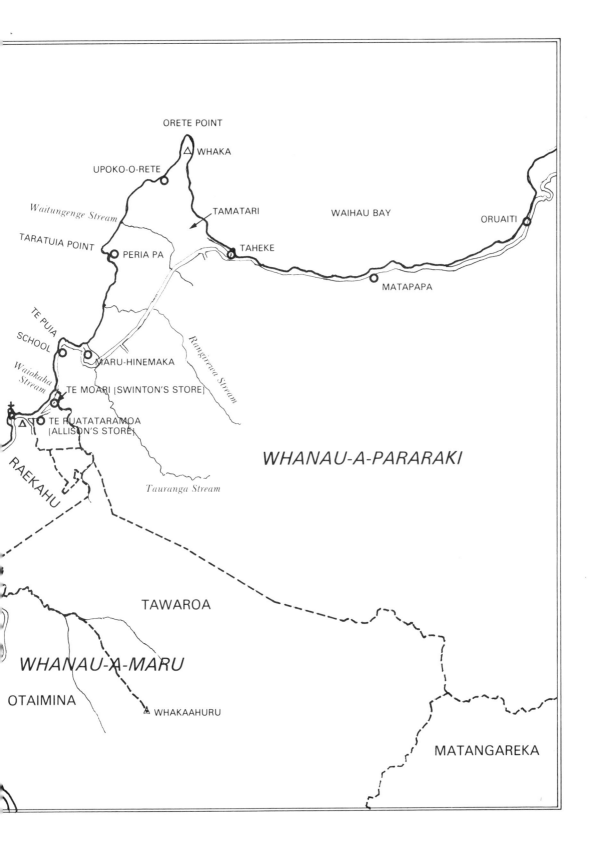

canoes I thought, by Joves, my grandfather knows the background of all these stories – Tainui, Te Arawa, Matatua, Kurahaupo and the rest! I enjoyed history because it tied up with Maori history in my mind, and I learned it without any trouble – the history of 'The Battle of Waterloo', 'The Battle of Trafalgar', 'The Battle of the Nile', 'The Boer War,' 'The Landing in Canada', even 'The Battle of Bannockburn' and 'The Fall of Stirling Castle'. My father was surprised when I got top marks in composition and history for school and he was proud, but it was all through my programme of life with the old people, learning in the way of the Maori university.

As soon as I started my schoolwork in a proper way I settled down at home with my family, and life was very nice. When I was about eight though, the old lady Rakuraku came back to Raukokore. She was the sister of Tu Rakuraku and Taua Rakuraku, very prominent people in the Waimana Valley, and she was related to my grandfather. She came to my mother and said,

'Well, Mihi, I was the one who named this boy "Whakatane", and now you people have had him to yourselves for long enough. I want to take him home.'

The trouble was, I was old enough to know my own mind by then, and I didn't want to go; if the old lady had come to get me when I was very young it would have been different. My mother said to me, 'Oh, you'd better go.'

I said, 'No, I'm not!'

I ran away and hid in the kumara pit. Mum was so wild she was calling me all sorts, but my father came and found me in the pit, and he said,

'It's all right, son, I'll tell her.'

'Oh Dad, I don't want to go!'

'Come on then, I'll tell the old lady.'

He took me back and the old kuia was crying, and Dad said to her, 'Oh well, it's no use, he doesn't want to go.'

After a while the old lady calmed down, and she decided to go back to the Waimana Valley. A few years later, when I was about eleven, word came to say that old lady Rakuraku had died, so my father, my brother, Moana Waititi and I rode on horseback to the tangi at Waimana. When we got there the marae was packed out, and Taua Rakuraku stood up and said to me,

'Well, Eruera Kawhia Whakatane, if you had come back to Waimana with your tipuna, you would have been a rich man today. She died without issue, and all that beautiful land over there would have been yours!'

I looked at that farm and I thought to myself, what a fool I was, I would have had a great start in my life with that 100 acres of beautiful land.

Never mind, I was still very happy at home with my own people.

One of the great things in our district in those days was the whaling,† and sometimes at school we'd look out of the windows and see the whaling boats *tearing* out to sea, chasing after a whale. There was a lookout on the hil at Oruaiti and another one on the hill behind the church at Raukokore, Te Taumata-a-Urutana; a man was posted up there all day to watch out for whales. As soon as he saw a

---

†See also 'Whaling Days, Te Kaha, Opotiki' in *Their Greatness*, p. 46.

whale spouting out at sea he'd light a fire, and when the people saw the flames rising on top of the hill they'd say, 'Hallo, it's a whale!'

The boats rushed out from Raukokore and Orete and Waihau Bay to meet the whale, and if they managed to harpoon it, three or four boats would tow it ashore to the nearest place and cut it up and share out the meat and the oil and everything. When they started to strip the fat off the whale in the station at Moutara, all the blood flowed into the channel, and when the tide came in hundreds of blind eels would come to drink the blood. The old people caught the blind eels because they're very sweet to eat, just like ordinary eels, eh, and straight after school all the children would rush down to Moutara for a feed. The men in charge of the trypots cooked the eels in the boiling oil, then they'd pick them out and give them to us to eat. We had some big feeds of kumara and bread and fried eels down at Moutara whaling station, and by the time we went back home kua ki nga puku i te kai, we were full up and we couldn't eat our tea.

In those days the Auckland merchants paid about £70 for a ton of whale oil, and all the people from Opotiki right around the Coast had their own whaling stations, with boats built by two boatbuilders from Omaio, Ta and Savage, trypots for boiling out the oil, and special storage tanks supplied by the merchants in Auckland. Herewini Te Moana had a boat at Waihau Bay, Te Kani had his boat, and Moana Waititi had a boat called *Tauira* at Cape Runaway.

My grandfather's boat at Raukokore was named after his daughter, *Horowai*. Some of the people had been sailors on the big whaling ships in the early days, and they even knew some of the whaling songs:

> Come ori tiori sailor boy
> *Come all ye jolly sailor boys*
> Ana Listen ana to me!
> *And listen unto me*
> Oh Mangahanea kia tika ra
> *We're bound for*
> To me go through!
> *Mangahanea*
> Oh the ship may go! The wind may blow!
> *The ship may go! The wind may blow!*
> Ona board ona *Kangaru*!
> *On board of the* Kangaroo.

In my young days the womenfolk used to sing these songs on the marae, and the old women used to stand up and do a sort of a dance – hard case!

The whaling industry was good money for the people, and when the whaling season was over, the schooner came down from Auckland to pick up the tanks, and the people were paid hundreds of pounds. That's how the Maori people paid their accounts, and when the shopkeeper asked, 'How are you going to pay for this?' – for maize seed, or sugar or a plough – they'd just say, 'Oh, kia mate te wera – as soon as we kill a whale!'

It was a dangerous job though. My father told me that one time when he went out on our boat the *Horowai*, they saw a right whale. The right whale is a very hard

Whaling days in the Bay of Plenty. These photographs by Canon Pahewa show a 'right' whale, caught off Cape Runaway. From top, the whale is beached, the blubber is cut off, and then is tried-out in the trypots. *Auckland Weekly News, 8 August 1912*

one to catch because it will fight back, even worse than the sperm whale or the killer whale, but in those days the merchants paid a big price for its oil. The *Horowai* had a hard job to chase this whale but in the finish they caught up with him, and the harpoonist speared him in the chest. Instead of running off, though, the whale dived down, then it turned round, came up and jumped, and *crashed* down its big tail on the boat and cut it in half! My father said he saw one old man who had been sitting in the middle of the boat, and all the flesh was sliced right off his leg. The other whaling boats came and picked up the crew, and the right whale got away.

Another time the old people took some of the children out in the *Horowai* to see the whales, and I went with my grandfather because he was the head of our boat. When we got out there the whales were splashing about in pairs, chasing one another, and one or two of them had calves beside them. As we came closer and closer we got very frightened and we hid behind our grandfathers. The old people told us that if whales get into a shoal like that they can be very dangerous, they will turn and fight the boat, and jump right up with their tails in the air like that, and *bang* the boat and break it to pieces.

The next time my grandfather said to me, 'Come on, we go!'

I said, 'No, I'm not going out again!'

I was too frightened – even elderly people get frightened when the whale starts playing around.

Another big industry in the Bay of Plenty in my young years was growing maize and wheat. In our area the people were very strong on growing maize, although they did grow wheat as well; when it came time to harvest the wheat they'd form up a special tent and thrash the wheat in there and put it all in bags. Dad grew oats and wheat on Raekahu farm and Kapongaroa block, and seventy acres of maize; we did all the fencing and ploughing and harvesting ourselves. We did the ploughing with a team of bullocks and it was a tiresome job too, very slow, but after a while Dad got two teams of horses and then we could run two double-furrow ploughs at the same time. My father bought a lot of machinery from the International Harvesting Company in Southland, because he was a building contractor and he was always busy going out, so Tai and Waha and I had to do most of the farm work after school. We had discs and harrows and a maize planter, and Dad bought a maize sheller running off the power and a machine to get out the wheat grains. We had a double scarifier, too, for cleaning out our seventy acres of maize; you just sat on it and dragged your feet behind the horses, and that was an easy job – after a day behind an ordinary scarifier you could hardly walk. You can see that life on the farm was very tedious for my brothers and I, straight after school we had to come home and start fencing, ploughing or discing, and when it came time to start plucking maize – oh-h! we'd stand in the cold all day, plucking maize, and then we had to cart it home. Dad grew all the oats and chaff for the local stables, and we used to help out on other farms around the place – there was no time to humbug around!

Growing kumaras was another way to make a living in those days, and my mother was a real expert in that kind of thing. She grew an acre of kumaras on the

Maize-growing at Te Kaha: (top) ploughing and (bottom) disc-ploughing, harrowing and planting in one operation. Photos by Canon Pahewa. *Auckland Weekly News, 1912*

same patch of ground every year near the old homestead at Raukokore and she stored the tubers in a pit called 'Te Rua Kumara a Te Ao-o-tata' (Te Ao-o-tata's kumara pit), dug by my great-grandfather Te Ao-o-tata. After each harvest Mum selected seed tubers from the best kumaras, nice-shaped ones with plenty of eyes, and she stored them to one side of the pit. She watched the moon and at the right time of the year, somewhere near the end of August, she'd prepare the seed bed, always in the same place. She laid the kumaras on the bed side by side, then she'd get good clean sand from the beach and cover them over. After that, some fine grass was cut and put on top, then Mum buried the bed with fine soil, and put a little bit of gravel over it. The sand gave warmth to the kumaras and they'd shoot out quickly. While she was preparing the seed bed she was always working on it, and nobody else was allowed to touch it.

As soon as the people saw Mum on her kumara bed they'd go home and say, 'Oh, I saw Mihi on her seed bed today,' and they'd start to get theirs ready too. Within a month all of the shoots were sprouting out of the ground, and Mum would start watching the moon for the right planting day. When planting day came in September or October, all the people in the district came to our place first as a working-bee, and all the kumaras were planted in one hit. After that we went around all the other homes in Raukokore, planting the kumaras for each family. The people worked together in those years because they had that feeling in them, eh, a tribal feeling – and the way of getting together in those days was very nice.

To plant the kumaras, the people pulled the shoots from the whakaika kumara bed and put them into bundles, then at sunrise they started to plant the shoots, with the roots curved up and facing east to the sunrise. The soil was pressed gently around the roots, facing to the warmth of the sun, and then you moved on, facing the sun with your body all the time. My mother always told us,

'Never turn your back to the sun, Tama-nui-te-ra!'

She would plant from sunrise until the sun was high in the sky, but never when the sun was setting in the west. The sprouts began to grow and after a while, when they were about nine inches high, you had to mound them up; and when harvest time came, the kumara pit would be packed out! My mother used to give away kumaras to people with no kai, and she supplied kumaras to all the gatherings at the marae.

One time a Japanese agricultural man‡ came to New Zealand and he wanted to know how the Maoris planted their kumara; Tipi Ropiha was the Undersecretary then and he said to him,

'You'd better go and visit Mrs Stirling at Raukokore, she runs one of the top plantations of kumara anywhere in the Bay of Plenty!'

After that Tipi got in touch with my mother and he told her,

'There's a Japanese expert coming over to see you.'

A few days later a strange car drove up the road, and it was the Japanese expert coming to our house. The kumaras were growing then and he said to me,

'How many tons of kumara do you get here, Mr Stirling?'

I showed him the ground and I told him, 'We get quite a few tons out of this patch, it's pretty good.'

'And how long have you been planting kumara here?'

'Well, my great-great-grandfather started this plantation, and after him my great-grandfather Poututerangi. My grandfather Maaka Te Ehutu is eighty now, and my mother is sixty. If you put all those years together, that's how long the kumaras have been growing on this ground!'

He could hardly believe it, and he asked me, 'What manure do you use?'

'Oh, the Maoris don't use any manure. We go by the phases of the moon, and the sun and the moon give the light to the kumara, not manure!'

He dug up a bit of the patch and he found some big kumaras, and he said he hadn't seen kumaras like that anywhere in New Zealand. He looked at them and he said,

'Well I never! I can't believe it – no manure!'

Then I told him, 'The manure is from Nature! God gave us the land, God gave us everything. He goes by the light, the life, the moon and everything, that's how the manure comes up! If you go to manured areas, you won't see kumaras like this. That's the best of no manure, its natural, Nature! It's the Man up There who gives the manure.'

‡ This was Douglas Yen, of New Zealand-born Chinese extraction, who carried out extensive research into kumara cultivation in the 1950s.

An East Coast rua kumara. *Auckland Weekly News, 2 June 1910*

He was really surprised. After that I took him over to the kumara pit and opened it, and there you are, the kumara were just as good as the day they were put in. He said to me, 'Wonderful!'

And then I told him all about the rua kumara and how it was made.

Years back my great-great-grandfather Te Ao-o-tata found a spot where the hill comes down near our house, and he dug the pit into the slope. He made a proper roof for it, like a house, but with eaves sitting on the ground, built out of ponga logs with the soft parts or huru stripped off and laid in the gaps, and a layer of toetoe reeds on top. After that it was covered with earth, and all these layers kept the pit dry and warm. Our pit had its own door, with a gap over it to let out the steam, and inside the floor was lined with special fern from the bush or anything soft – rarauhe or toetoe, and the kumaras were stacked on top. My mother wouldn't trust anybody else to stack the kumaras so she did it all herself, because if you knock one kumara the bruise starts to rot, and it spreads right through the pit. Mum was also very careful to keep out of the pit when she had her period, and she seemed to know exactly when to stop the other women in the family from going there too, because that's another way to make the kumaras go rotten. She stacked the big kumaras at the back of the pit and smaller ones near the front, and the seed kumaras were picked out and put to one side. Every year we changed the toetoe reeds and the ferns on the floor to keep the pit clean and dry, and kumaras would last forever in Te Rua Kumara a Te Ao-o-tata. All these things were passed from my great-great-grandfather Te Ao-o-tata down to my mother, and from my mother down to me.§

§ For other accounts of kumara cultivation on the East Coast see Arapera Blanc, 'Ko Taku Kumara', *Te Ao Hou* No. 24, Oct. 1958, pp. 6-8, and Koro Dewes, 'The Growing of Kumara', *Te Ao Hou* No. 25, Dec. 1958, pp. 41-5.

Raukokore in 1912, with Callaghan's store and Post Office in foreground, Swinton's house at Te Moari in the bay behind, and Maruhinemaka Point in the background. *Auckland Weekly News, 5 September 1912*

In those years we did sell some of our crops, but money wasn't the big thing that it is today. We had to pay for our flour and sugar and machinery for the farm, though, and in every Maori settlement on the East Coast there were bound to be some pakeha businesses. In Raukokore we had Swinton or 'Piripoto' (they called him 'Short Billy' because he was just a little fellow), an accountant from England who ran a shop and a pub; Allison, a naval officer from the Shetland Islands who kept a shop, and Te Karehana or Callaghan, an Irishman from Invercargill who was our local blacksmith. The shopkeepers got their supplies from Auckland, and Captain Skinner brought them down to the Bay of Plenty on his schooner the *Kaeo*, taking back tanks of whale oil, kumaras, maize and wheat to the markets in Auckland. That was our living in those days, but as I have said, most of our kai came from the land and the sea. The people used to go into the bush and snare pigeons, kaka, and tui, and they hunted the wild pig too. They collected hinau berries and taraire berries and karaka berries, and we'd cook the karaka berries at home, then dry them, and take them to school to eat. The kiekie tree was used a lot, there was a part called the ure that was very sweet, and some of the old people also collected fern-root from the hills.

One of our great delicacies at Raukokore was the mutton-bird; my grandfather John Stirling sent barrels of mutton-birds from the South Island on the schooner every year, and they were beautiful – 300 big birds to a barrel. My mother would call all the people of the district to our house and she gave mutton-birds to every one of them! The Raukokore people were so thrilled with those birds that they used to plait the finest of kits and whariki mats out of kiekie to send to the South Island as a gift. When I visited my cousins in the South Island they showed me a special room in their house full of the most beautiful kits and whariki that the old people had carefully preserved, and they may still be there today.

We had plenty of kai moana, too in our times, food from the sea. My grandfather made crayfish pots – taruke – for our family, and we'd set them at a special place; when you pulled them up in the morning they'd be packed with crayfish, big and young! Each district had its own mussel beds, and they were reserved for the owners of that place. If the people saw a stranger picking their mussels, look out! He'd be a dead man if he came ashore. Fishing was very tapu and each family had its own fishing grounds, no one else could fish there or there would be a big fight. The old people were very particular about the sea, and nobody was allowed to eat or smoke out on the boats. If a man took food with him when he went fishing, he'd sit there all day with his hook and line empty and the fish would stay away. Sometimes if the fishing was very bad the people would start asking questions, and if they found out the guilty man he'd get into a hang of a big trouble for breaking the Maori sacred law of tapu. The people would just about knock him to pieces because he had spoiled the day for everyone and he wouldn't be allowed to go out to sea again for quite a while. If a thing like that happened at home, you were well marked by the people!

Women were not allowed to go out to the fishing grounds either, but they were the best at diving for crayfish, better than the men. I know my mother-in-law was a wonderful diver, it was nothing to her to fill a bag with crayfish; she knew exactly where to go, even in deep water. At some places the crayfish would come out at high tide, and Ani Kahutawhiti would go out there and dive. I went out with her one day at high water, and I was frightened! I was standing on a rock with the waves *booming* up, and she just dived and brought up a crayfish every time, and threw it to me to put in the bag. By half tide the bag was full, and I floated back to shore. The fishermen at Tuparoa paid her £3 or £4 for a bag of crayfish, and she kept them supplied, no trouble. If a woman had her periods, though, she was not allowed to enter the water or cook food or go near a kumara patch, she had to be very careful not to break that rule.

Our family was involved in everything in the district, and the people were very nice in those years. We had the marae at Wairuru with the meeting-house Hine Mahuru, and Mum used to get all the people together, because she was in the senior line of the tribal people of the district. When it came to the time of the moki fishing down at Cape Runaway, Manihera Waititi would go to open up the fishing grounds, and the first fish always came to my mother, but she never used the fish for herself, she distributed them to everybody because she was very kind-hearted. Manihera Waititi lived at Cape Runaway near to the fishing grounds, and he was the most talented moki fisherman in the district, and a real expert in tribal histories of the Cape. When he was ready to catch the first moki each year he'd send word to my mother, and Taikorekore and I had to ride on packhorses to the Waititi homestead at Whangaparaoa, and old Mrs Waititi would make us a good cup of tea while the old man loaded the moki into our saddlebags to carry home to Mum.[||]

[||] For more information on moki fishing in the area see Lynne Owen, *School at Cape Runaway*, p. 51; 'The Story of Moki' in the *Whangaparaoa Maori School Golden Jubilee Booklet*, pp. 8-11; and W. Bird's account of going moki fishing with Manihera Waititi in McCallion *et al, Their Greatness*, p. 12.

Going out to the fishing grounds at Maraehako, just south of Raukokore. *Auckland Weekly News, 19 September 1912*

One year my mother said to us, 'Well, boys, the moki season is just about to start; you two had better go over and see Manihera.'

We loaded all our fishing gear on the packhorses, and rode together over the hills to Whangaparaoa. When we got there the old man came down and unpacked our saddlebags and put all the gear away, and that night we slept together in a small meeting-house near his home. The old man welcomed us, and then he told us about the moki fishing, how to go out and how to use the lines, all those things, and he said,

'I am going out tomorrow morning to the fishing grounds, and I'll take you both out there.'

We woke up early the next morning before sunrise, and as the sun came up a strong wind was blowing from the land. Manihera said,

'This is the best time to go out to the grounds because you don't have to use the oars, just put the sail up and the wind will take you there.'

We went up the Whangaparaoa river to the sea and put up the sail, and within a few minutes we were on the spot. The fishing ground was at Ratanui, where the canoes landed in the Great Migration, and when we were about one hundred yards offshore from the cave at Ratanui, the old man called out to my brother, 'Drop the anchor!'

Taikorekore let the anchor go and Manihera got our lines ready with the special Maori hooks – the moki hooks were made of whalebone in the early days but these ones were bent out of ordinary wire, the old man had that talent. He told us,

'When the moki jumps onto your line, you let him pull first, and then *yank* him into the boat.'

As soon as we dropped our lines, there you are – I pulled up a moki, my brother pulled up a moki and the old man pulled up two! He said,

'That's enough from this ground, now we'll move on to the next spot.'

We took the boat a bit further out to sea, and the old man showed us the points of land that marked the second fishing place, and we caught a few more moki there. Manihera told us,

'These two places are special, I keep them secret and I don't let *anybody* know about them. There are plenty of moki here, but if people come and fish without knowing the proper use of the moki, all the fish will leave and in the end there'll be nothing. If you want to come out to these grounds, sail out early in the morning before anybody else is on the sea; and if you see any boats coming, drift away and don't show the spot to anybody!'

Finally he took us about half a mile out to the reef that marked the general fishing ground, and we caught a few moki then the old man said,

'Oh well, we'd better go home now.'

When we went ashore his wife came and cleaned up the moki and packed them together, and she said to us,

'Tomorrow morning you two can ride home and take all the moki with you.'

Well that was that. Whenever Tai and I wanted to go out fishing for moki we knew exactly where to go.

One time though, I looked out at the sea one morning and it was very calm, so I said to my mother, 'Well, Mum, I think I'd better go out fishing today.'

She asked me 'Why don't you get your brother to go out with you?'

'No, this time I'd like to go on my own. I'd like a trial by myself.'

I got all my fishing gear ready, and my clothes for sleeping in the big cave at Ratanui, and by the time I got to the sea there was a whistling wind blowing out to White Island, and that's a good sign. Dad was an expert sailor, he was really a master on the sea, and he had cut out the sails for our boat himself and taught my brother and I the art of sailing. I put up the sail and there was a strong land breeze, and within an hour I was well out on the water; then I caught the westerly wind and sailed round Orete Point, and landed at the mouth of the Cape Runaway river. When the people at the Cape saw my boat sailing in from the west they got suspicious, and they wondered,

'Who is this early man coming in to land?'

They thought I was a pakeha or something so they all came down the river to have a look. When Manihera Waititi and the Waengas saw that it was me they called out,

'Hey, Eruera! Did you come by yourself?'

'Yes.'

'Oh well, bring your gear into the marae.'

'No – I'm camping in the cave tonight!'

Not long after that two more boats sailed in from Waihau Bay, with Parekura Brown and Tom Collier and Tuhi Puru on board, and they were surprised to see

me. We all got together and went to the Ratanui cave and slept there for the night.
I remembered what the old man Manihera had told me,

'If you want to go out to those special moki grounds, get up very early before
anybody else is on the sea, and don't show those spots to anyone!'

So next morning I woke up very early and sneaked out of the cave, and when my
mates got up they couldn't find me anywhere.

'Ha! Dick has already gone!'

I had already caught quite a few moki when I saw their boats coming on the sea,
so I hid my moki and drifted away from that special place, and when Parekura
Brown came over to talk to me I told him,

'I've only caught one moki – there's nothing here!'

The other boats went out to the main fishing grounds then I went to the second
secret spot and caught a few more moki and sailed out to join them on the reef.
The moki came in abundance that day and everybody was hauling them up, and
by late that afternoon all the boats were full. I had caught seventy moki altogether
and they weighed between thirty and fifty pounds each, so my fourteen footer was
really loaded! When I went ashore my mates looked in my boat and said,

'Joves, Dick, you've got a lot!'

We decided to sleep in the big cave that night, and early next morning we got
into our boats and headed back to Waihau Bay. There was a good strong land
breeze blowing so I lifted my sail and left all the others behind. I sailed out into the
deep water way past Tihirau Point, and a funny thing happened that day; when I
got right out to sea the wind turned to the north-east and the waves came up, and I
could see that the sea was white everywhere. I remembered what my father had
told me,

'If a storm blows up, the farther you go out to sea the better; go to the deep
ocean because the rolling waves out there don't break, and stay right away from
the reefs.'

I kept sailing out to sea and when I was about three or four miles offshore the
wind was really roaring and the waves were starting to break, and I was frightened.
My boat was loaded with all those moki and I thought, if the sea gets into this boat
it'll sink! I sailed on until I was about four or five miles out, my boat was being
tossed about by the current and the seas were mountainous, but they weren't
breaking. Then the wind changed to a westerly and I thought, I'll never get back
with this wind! I had to sail out farther still but when I sighted Otiki Point and
Okawa Point, I decided that was far enough, and I turned my boat in towards
Raukokore with my sail half-way to the sea. The wind was whistling past and I
could see the church at Raukokore with the hill coming down and my boat came
singing in on the the waves! I thought, well, I'm not going to worry, I'll hold on to
my faith in the teachings of my grandpeople; Tangaroa the sea god and the
taniwhas will help me in this time of trouble. If the boat capsizes, the reef is there
and the current is coming in, not going out, so I'll have a chance to swim in on the
waves. . . As I came in to Raukokore it was a Sunday and all the people were in
church, but someone at the Bailey's house up on the hill looked out to sea and saw
my boat going up and down, up and down on the waves. As the boat was tearing in
towards Moutara Point, I remembered what my father had told me,

Waikoukou Bay today – 'Stirling castle' stood just to the left of the house in this photograph. *Jeremy Salmond, 1976*

Raukokore Church, built by the Savage brothers from Opotiki. *Gisborne Museum and Arts Centre*

'Look for the eighth wave, that's the big one!'
I counted the waves, one, two, three. . . right up to seven, and then I saw the

eighth wave coming like a mountain, not roaring but just rolling along. At that moment the church service finished and Canon Pahewa came outside, and he saw this mountainous wave pick up my boat in a cloud of spray. He called to the people,

'That's the Stirlings' boat out there!'

The wave crashed and it started to break, and my boat was tossed into a sort of lagoon right by the landing place at Moutara.

My mother ran crying down the beach because she thought I wouldn't make it and when she saw my boat sitting on the lagoon she called out,

'Oh, your tipuna and Almighty God have worked together to save you!'

My brother and Dad came out to my boat and it was still loaded down with moki, not one of those seventy moki was lost. All the other boats capsized when they landed at Oruaiti beach, the people got ashore but they lost all their fish. That was a real history in the district for months afterwards, and the people reckoned it was a miracle that my small boat sailed ten miles to Raukokore in a raging storm, and landed safely at Moutara with seventy moki still on board. Well, I did that! and I believe it was my ancestors that saved me, and my faith in Almighty God.

My father was very active in our district; he started up the Stirling Family Band, and he and my two sisters Kate and Matemoana, my two brothers Tai and Waha and I travelled on horseback to all the dances at Te Kaha, Omaio, and even as far as Opotiki, Hicks Bay and Te Araroa. The roads were real pig tracks then, and to go to Omaio or Opotiki you had to ride up hills, down gullies, on to the beach and all sorts! We had a small organ that we carried with us on horseback; you could see the Stirling Family Band riding along the beach with all their musical instruments. My father was the real musical man, he played the piano, the clarinet, the violin and the flute; the girls played the organ, I played the banjo and the mandolin, and we had accordions as well. Those dances were pretty good, and we had a lot of fun. On a Saturday night the people all dressed up neatly to come to the marae, they didn't come in any old clothes or the M.C. at the door would tell them,

'Sorry, you're not allowed in here!'

The women were all in their long dresses, and we played 'The Lancers', the 'de Albert', the 'Mazurka', the 'Valeta' and waltzes, and the people did Scottish dancing too. The M.C. was very strict, and if there was any rough dancing he'd go and warn the people,

'Any more of that and out you go!'

That was the Stirling Family Band – we did all the catering for band work in those years.

In my young days Dad kept very busy with his building, and he built a big house for us at Wairuru with a sitting-room and a piano, that the people called 'Stirling Castle'. Crowds of people came there to see my mother, they were always coming and going, and she gave them a lot of help. One time my father had to mend the tower of the Raukokore church, built by the Savage brothers, because it was just about falling down. He called for people to help him put the iron on the belfry and no one would come, because it was too high. In the end Dad did it all by himself, heights didn't bother him at all. Even when he was a very old man he'd climb onto

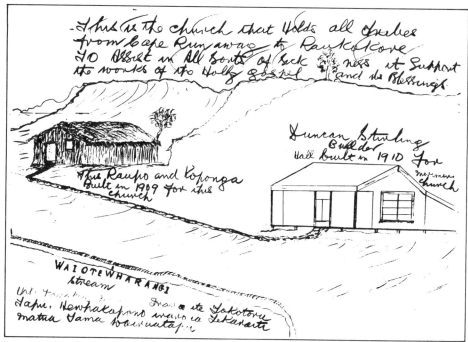

The hall built by Duncan Stirling in 1910 for the Merimeri Church, sketched in Eruera Stirling's whakapapa book.

the roof of a house and walk along the ridge just like that!

When it came to rebuilding our meeting-house, Hine Mahuru, that was a very big job. The tahuhu or ridge-pole was a big long timber, very weighty, and the people wondered, 'How is he going to get it up?'

First of all Dad built all the walls, floor and everything, and then he leaned some big planks at each end of the building and in the middle, and fixed them on top of the main posts. After that he got the people to tie big ropes on to the tahuhu. They hitched a team of bullocks to each rope and when the time came, my father gave the signal, the bullocks pulled on the ropes from the other side of the house, and the tahuhu slid up the planks and dropped neatly on top of the main posts. In 1910, Dad also built a hall for the Merimeri church, and I have drawn a picture of that building in one of my books.

On Sundays we had services at the Raukokore church and Dad was the lay reader; after Bishop Williams married my parents way back in 1894 he appointed my father a lay reader for the Te Kaha district, because in those years all the people in Raukokore believed in the Ringatu religion. Dad started off a Sunday school and the people came from Waihau Bay and far and near, and he held competitions for the juniors and the seniors in scripture work; by the time I was at school, the Raukokore church was full every Sunday. After church everybody went down to the beach and had a big kai, with a big fire blazing, and the women went out to get crayfish and pupus and kinas. That was the beauty of those days — the unity of the people!

CHAPTER THREE
COMING UP IN LIFE

E kore i te mea
Love
No naianei te aroha
Is not a thing of today only
No nga tipuna
It comes from the ancestors
Tuku iho, tuku iho
Passed down, passed down

a song

I kept up with my schooling and I advanced, and in the sixth standard I sat the Proficiency examination. After that some students from our school were selected to sit for a scholarship to Te Aute College, my brother Tai and I and quite a few others; and when it came to that examination in 1915 I took top marks in history and beat my own brother, and I won the scholarship for four years of free education at Te Aute College! I believe it was the schooling from my old people that gave me the strength to go through.

I was glad to go to Te Aute College because I wanted to be a lawyer; my mother was a very large landowner in the tribal areas of the Whanau-a-Maru at Raukokore, and I knew we would need someone to look after her interests in the Land Court. During my time at Te Aute College I was doing very well in my education, I got through my Junior Civil Service and my Senior Civil Service, and I was just stepping up to the Matriculation class when this marriage business came along – my people wished me to get married to their tribal history, and that ended the whole programme. I know that if I had gone through all the stages of College I would have reached my aim – to be a lawyer . . .

Anyhow, I enjoyed my two years at Te Aute, the life there was very, very good. Students from all parts of New Zealand came to the College to learn how to study and go in the Christian way of life; every morning we had chapel, and when chapel was finished we had kai, and after that we went to school. There was a farm at Te Aute and the experienced students did a lot of farm work, sheep-farming, cattle-farming, milking cows, haymaking and all those kind of things. Every morning my duty was to go to the butcher shop and cut the meat into forequarters, and take it over to Mr Baker in the kitchen. If you were interested in farming you learned a lot of that work at Te Aute, and it was a very clean life.

Apirana Ngata was one of the important graduates of Te Aute College, he was the first Maori to graduate LLB and master of arts, and while I was at school he came to talk to us. He said,

'When I look at you children of today, I see you are having an easy time – in our days it was a big hard job to go to Te Aute College, but you people can travel in just like that!'

He talked to us about working hard and not wasting our time at school and then he told us,

'If you want to be something, a doctor or a barrister, the thing is to make up your mind about it. But don't forget your ancestors and always remember your Maori side! If you go that way I'm sure that some of you will reach the heights of education in times to come.'

He was right, too. One of my best friends at Te Aute was Waipaina Matahe and we had the same ambition, to study law. In the end he graduated master of arts and bachelor of laws, and he invited me to his graduation. When I arrived at the university he told some of his friends,

'Well, if Eruera had been able to stay at school, he'd be graduating with me today!'

Another of my schoolmates was Apirana's son, Purewa Ngata, and he was very clever but he was the same as me, he wasn't allowed to stay at school. When we came home from Te Aute in 1916 Purewa and I travelled with the Tikitiki boys, and we landed at Tokomaru Bay. My cousin Addie Haerewa came to meet me, and we all went over to Te Ariuru pa because they were having a farewell there for the soldiers, they were moving overseas the next day. The old people said to us,

'Oh well, you young schoolboys can take a little bit of drink, it won't do you any harm, just as a memorial to the soldiers going overseas.'

We stood there and I had drunk mine up, and Purewa was just going to drink his when Apirana came in. When we saw his son with a drink in his hand he got really *wild*, and he said to Purewa,

'You're not going to Te Aute College any more! You're going overseas! No son of mine is going to drink – you go!'

Apirana was the recruiting officer, and that is why he had to tell his son to go to war. Purewa left school, and he went overseas and he came back unhurt. He is the elder at home now, and if he'd stayed at Te Aute he would have been another man like his father, because he is a very clever fellow.

We were all young chaps in those days, and we liked to have our bit of fun. We played a lot of football at Te Aute, in Napier and Palmerston North and Hastings, and after a game generally we'd go around to Hukarere School to meet the girls. One time I went to Hukarere to see my own cousin, and my schoolmates at Te Aute gave me a lot of letters to pass over to their girlfriends. Well, when I arrived at Hukarere there was a big mob of girls waiting so I passed over the letters, and someone must have been watching us. That afternoon the principal of Hukarere School rang up our headmaster and said,

'Some Te Aute boys have been here today, and they passed over love letters to my girls!'

She gave the headmaster our names and he called us in, then he asked me,

'Where you there, Stirling?'

'Yessir!'

'Why were you at Hukarere?'

Te Aute College in 1901; Eruera's dormitory was in the top storey of the central house.
Auckland Weekly News, 17 October 1901

'Well, I only went to see my first cousin!'

'Did you pass letters to the girls?'

'. . . Yessir.'

'Well, Stirling, you are going to be punished. I'm giving all of you boys black marks, and you will have to do hard work all day on Saturday.'

That's what I got for playing around.

When I came home for the school holidays in 1917, a big thing happened to me. One of the old rangatiras in our district, Parekohiwi Te Kani, died at Orete Point and all the tribes came to the tangi, Ngati Porou, Whanau-a-Apanui and Tuhoe. Moana Waititi took his big launch the *Royal Irish* to pick up the Ngai-te-Rangi people from Tauranga, fifty or more of them, and everybody was waiting for them at Peria marae. Suddenly somebody spotted the sails of the launch coming around Orete Point, and while we were watching the sails were dropped and the *Royal Irish* turned slowly, crashing through the waves into Waihau Bay. It was a very rough day and the wind was whistling over the water; and the next minute the boat stopped moving and we heard the foghorn. Moana Waititi was calling out for the people ashore to take a big whale rope out to the launch, because it was wrecked on a rock! We could see the *Royal Irish* sitting out there with the waves crashing around her, and nearly the whole district was gathered on the marae, but nobody offered to go. Moana Waititi sounded the foghorn again and he yelled out to the people ashore,

'Hurry up and swim out with the rope! As soon as the tide turns the boat will tip over, and we'll all be drowned!'

Suddenly the thought came into my mind, 'I'm going to swim out there!'

I stood up, and my mother was sitting next to me, she asked, 'Are you going?'

'Yes, Mum, I'm going to swim out there.'

'Well, go then with the help of your tipuna, your ancestors.'

She was happy about it. The men of the district fetched the big whale rope and dragged it onto the rocks of Orete Point, then I tied a little rope around my waist and dived into the sea. I swam out to the *Royal Irish* and when I got there Moana Waititi called out,

'A haramai rawa ko koe ko te ariki hai mau mai, kei whea nga iwi ra? – Well, it took you of our ariki family to bring us the rope – where is the rest of the tribe?'

He was wild with the people, but he said to me,

'A kati, kai te pai nahau ano i haramai, a, i ora ai enei o ou tipuna, nahau! Now that you have come, you have saved the lives of your old people!'

He grabbed the rope and tied it to the launch, and he took the foghorn and called to the people on shore,

'Pull! When the wave comes, pull!'

A big wave came and the people heaved together and they pulled the *Royal Irish* off the rocks. We came ashore with the people of Tauranga, and later on that day, Moana Waititi stood on the marae and *told* the people off.

'Fancy you people sending the descendant of Poututerangi into the sea! He should have been the last person to come. I can see a few of you grown men over there who should have been sent! But anyhow, he came out and we were saved.'

The old people of Tauranga stood on the marae and greeted me. That was the biggest thing that happened to me in my young days, when I was still going to school.

In my school days naturally I had a few girlfriends myself; one of my girlfriends was called Nellie, she was a really fine-looking girl, and I had another girlfriend in Omaio, we were running around together for years. Her father was very strict and if she went out with anybody he'd give her a hiding, so I thought I'd play something, and I went up to him and said,

'I wonder, would you allow your girl to come with me to the dance tonight? I want your consent.'

He said to me, 'Well, don't you humbug around with my daughter!'

He agreed because he liked our family, so I went off with her to the Omaio football dance, and after that I courted that girl for a long time. I was quite happy to enjoy myself because I was still at Te Aute and I didn't want to get serious with anybody, but in the end the father tried to insist that we get married. After that he told all the people at home,

'If I get hold of that Stirling boy I'll kill him! Playing around with my girl like that!'

But I was only eighteen, eh, and I didn't want to settle down at such a young age. That was the trouble in those days, the parents always wanted to pick the husband or the wife for their children, and sometimes it was very hard on the young people. I know there was one girl at home called Te Pare Herehere, and the parents of her boyfriend didn't want her because of the difference in rank between them, they wouldn't accept her into their home. She was so sorry about it that she composed this song:

Oku nei matua
My parents
Kihai rawa i riri mai
Are not angry with me
Ko Takopeka kua riri
It is Takopeka
Taikaha e
Who is so angry

Kore au e mutu
I won't stop
Kore au e rongo
I won't listen
Ka tohetohe au
I will persist
Mohou ra e tama
In wanting you, my love

He tira mokemoke
It is a lonely travelling party
Te tira i a Pouhana
That rides with Pouhana [his horse]
E huri mai ki
Turning down
Te Kaha i raro e!
Towards Te Kaha!

The Te Kaha pub, where Te Pare's lover rode down on his horse Pouhana. *Whakatane Museum*

Mate koe i te waiunu
When you are drunk
Me huri ki Hirere
Turn to Hirere
Anei to waiunu
Here is drink for you –
Ko aku roimata e . . .
My tears . . .

I was very happy at Te Aute, I enjoyed my schoolwork and that year I won the gold medal for the senior 100 yards championship; the life was very good. Towards the end of my second year at Te Aute, though, my mother wrote me a letter – she wanted me to come home and get married. She told me that the old people of the two tribes Ngati Hinekehu of Ngati Porou and Te Whanau-a-Apanui had arranged a marriage for me in the old Maori custom way, a taumau marriage to carry on the links between the tribal histories. I wrote back to my mother and said,

'No, I am not coming home – I want to study to be a lawyer!'

When my letter arrived at Raukokore my mother talked to Apirana Ngata, and Apirana wrote to the headmaster of Te Aute College, and explained the whole position to him. He told the headmaster that my mother wanted me to come home because the court would be sitting soon to investigate her land titles, and she wanted me to represent her, because I had all the genealogies of the tribal area given to me by my great-grandfather Pera Te Kaongahau, the last of the tohungas from the Whare Wananga of Kirieke. The headmaster called me into his office and said,

'Well, Stirling, it looks as though you'd better go home.'

'No! No, sir, I want to stay on at Te Aute!'

'I want you to think deeply about this, Stirling. Which is more important to you – to stay on here at Te Aute, or looking after your mother's land titles? You'll inherit land from your mother in days to come, but if she loses the case, you will get nothing! I think you had better go home.'

Well, when the headmaster said that to me I just looked at him and I couldn't say anything. I knew that if only I could stay on at school, I would get somewhere in my life and I would reach my ambition to be a lawyer. I was very sorry to leave Te Aute College.

When I went back to the Bay of Plenty in December 1917 I travelled on the boat from Napier to Tokomaru Bay and stayed with my cousin Addie Haerewa, and then I rode home to Raukokore. My mother was very pleased to see me and she said,

'Well, Eruera, you are going to get married very soon.'

I said to my mother, 'No, Mum, I don't want to get married yet!'

'Now boy, you listen to me. We have already arranged a wife for you, and she's coming here today, too! You *have* to marry this woman, because if you don't, I'll have to pay very heavily for it.'

She explained to me that if I cut back the taumau promise, she would have to

Eruera Stirling (far left), with Tom Collier (front) and Wahawaha Stirling. *Stirling family*

give those people a lot of land to pay for it, and she didn't want to do that. I tried to say something but it was no use, Mum just flared up at me and said,

'If you don't listen to me, you go! Get away! There'll be no land for you!'

So I agreed, I had no choice. My mother took me to another part of the house and opened a room,

'There you are – this is your bedroom for the night.'

There was a bed for a couple in there, all made up and ready. I couldn't argue with my mother, and the day after I got home old Hakopa Haerewa arrived with my cousins Addie and Kareti, and they brought Amiria with them. When I looked at her, I thought she was a fine-looking woman, and Mum said to me,

'There's your wife!'

The only trouble was, Amiria didn't like me at first, I think she preferred my elder brother Tai. Tai was a fine chap and very good at everything – singing, carpentry and carving – and he was the senior son, but the old people had made up their minds and that was that. After tea they took us to the room and told us,

'Now you two – there's the bed!'

Of course it didn't take place then, because Amiria tried to run away. She found out that I had been playing around with Susan, the girl who helped my mother at home, and she asked Susan to get the horse ready for her so she could ride away from Raukokore. Kareti and Addie heard them talking though, and they hid Amiria's horse somewhere else, and Susan couldn't find it. After a while Amiria had to go to bed, and in the finish of course, we came together.

Amiria (centre) with the Haerewa family: (back) Hakopa Haerewa, Bill Butler; (front) Areta Haerewa, Amiria O'Hara, Kareti Haerewa. *Stirling family*

That was on the 20th December 1917.

Once Amiria and I were settled, arrangements were made for the wedding. Ours was one of the last big taumau marriages in our tribal area and about a thousand people came to Raukokore. The people had to sleep in the different meeting-houses around the place, and our sitting-room at home gave bedding to quite a lot of people. It was a very customary wedding. We were married on the 8th of May 1918, and it was a beautiful day. All the different tribes attended – Te Whanau-a-Apanui, Ngati Porou, Whakatohea and Ngai-te-Rangi from Tauranga; the best men from Whakatohea were Warakihi Waiapu, Tane Tukaki, Waikura Tautuhi-o-rongo; from Te Whanau-a-Apanui they were Te Aranga-a-Moki and Tohi Koopu; and Hoani Retimana was the best man respresenting the Ngai-te-Rangi. The Ngati Porou chiefs were Hakopa Haerewa, Tamati Kaiwai, Ani Parata, Keriana Tupaea, Whaka Parakau, Hukarere Taitua, Waikohu Waenga, Ue-ana-te-whare Waenga, Te Huna Houkamau, Te Hati Poutu and Henare Ahuriri, and the Whanau-a-Apanui chiefs were Manihera Waititi, Paerau Te Kani, Hohepa Karapaina, Kanarahi Pururangi, Rawinia Ropiha and Mihi Kotukutuku.

The other people present included James Swinton, Duncan Stirling, William Allison; the local pakehas James Walker, Frank Walker, Mr and Mrs Rutledge, J. S. W. Neilson, W. S. Saunders the schoolmaster, and Jack and Ernest Kemp; Moana Waititi, Sid Waititi, and Hirini Puha, Kahu Puha, Wi Pahuru Heremia, Marama Paraone, Hauraki Tawhai, Paratene Hia Takimoana, Paretio Tupaea and Wi Tupaea, Parekura Brown, Tumau Koria, Tame Koria and Hinekino Koria.

Only one or two of all these people are still alive today.

A lot of things happened on our wedding day. I had a favourite aunty called Te Waena and when I was a boy she used to carry me around on her back, and if she caught my brothers hitting me she would give them a hiding. She adored me more than my brother Taikorekore. Te Waena was a nice woman but very powerful, no man could talk to her and she would fight anybody. On the day of the wedding she heard someone say that Tai was going to the church to ring the bell, so she sneaked out, and long before the proper time we heard the church bell ringing like mad! Tai galloped off to find out what was happening, and there was Te Waena hanging onto the bell. He told her,

'No aunty! You're not supposed to ring the bell yet – it's not time!'

'You get out of here, Taikorekore! I'm the one to ring this bell, nobody else; I brought him up, not you!'

She wouldn't let go of the rope, and in the end, Tai had to give her a hard knock, and the people took her away crying.

After that, when we left our house to walk to the church, suddenly we heard someone wailing and cursing up on top of Te Taumata-a-Urutana, the hill behind

Church of Jesus Christ at Raukokore, with Te Taumata-o-Urutana hill in the foreground, where Ani Kahutawhiti wailed for her daughter. *Jeremy Salmond, 1976*

Mika and Eva Eruera in later years. *Eva Eruera*

the church. It was Amiria's mother Ani; the marriage had been arranged without consulting her, and she opposed it. That was why she was up on the hill, farewelling Amiria and cursing everybody.

Another thing happened in the church, when it came to the time for blessing the ring. When I put my hand in my pocket, I found that I had left the ring at home! Archdeacon Williams said,

'Oh well, I can marry you with an ordinary ring for now.' Straight away after the ceremony I went and fetched the ring, and he blessed it. These were all the things that happened at our wedding.

Another couple were married with us, Mika and Eva Eruera, and that caused another big fight. I had been to Opotiki weeks before to order our wedding-cake, but Mika and Eva's cake was ordered close to the day, and the icing on it wasn't quite set. When the women were setting the tables in the dining-hall Wikitoria, Mika's cousin, saw that the icing on Mika's cake had cracked a bit, so she changed it over with ours. Some of the women started to argue about it and Wikitoria got all upset, but when I came into the hall I went straight over to the tables and changed the cakes back again.

There were even two sets of wedding clothes for our wedding; my mother had brought a dress for Amiria as a present, and the Ngati Porou people brought her a set of clothes as well, and of course they had a scrap about that. That was the trouble with our wedding, the two sides were fighting each other all the time, and there was no unity in the people . . .

After the wedding Te Huna Houkamau stood up in the dancing-hall and invited the wedding party to visit Hicks Bay, and Reweti Kohere invited us to Te Araroa, so the old people agreed that after a few days' rest, we should travel around all the maraes of the East Coast. On the 10th of May the schooner *Mako* arrived with two tons of potatoes, fruit, tinned meat and all the sweet drinks for the wedding, sent by the Ngati Hinekehu people of Ngati Porou, and that made my mother wild all over again. She said to me,

'I suppose they think we haven't got any kai here at Raukokore!'

We waited a while, and on the 15th of May I called Wirihana Tatai to come back and take us along the Coast in his big buggy. We set off from Raukokore with a big crowd of people riding behind us on horseback; on the 19th of May we stayed at Hicks Bay with Te Huna Houkamau and his people, and on the 20th we were given a reception in the old meeting-house Tumoana-Kotore by the old chief Wingara Houkamau, Te Huria's uncle.

When we went on to Te Araroa, all the people from Hicks Bay joined us, and we were welcomed at Hinerupe meeting-house in Te Araroa by Henipepi Houkamau, Henare Ahuriri, Ani Kaniroki and Wi Taotu, Dr Wi Repa and Reweti Kohere.

At Te Araroa, Watene Waititi invited us to call at Kiwikiwi for a while, then we moved on with all the people from Hicks Bay, Te Araroa and Kiwikiwi to Rongomaianiwaniwa meeting-house at Tikitiki, where we were welcomed by Rauhuia Tawhiwhirangi, Te Koroneho, Maraea Te Iritawa and others. By now there was a very big crowd of old people travelling with us, and at every marae the people put down a koha, a gift of money for the marriage.

Materoa Ngarimu, at the Moana-nui-a-kiwa Ngarimu VC Celebrations in 1943.
Alexander Turnbull Library

That night Pene Heihi, known as Te Kai Rakau, invited us to his marae at
Reporua, and at Reporua James Heihi and Mata Nuku told us that Kereama
Aupouri wanted us to go to Tuparoa. When we went on to the marae at Tuparoa
you could hardly move, it was packed with people. The speakers were Te Hati
Pakaroa, Awatere Ahipene Mika and Ruka Haenga, and they gave us the highest
of home greetings, and delivered the last invitation from Materoa Ngarimu, to
visit Te Poho-o-Materoa at Whareponga.

The next morning we all set out, some by way of the beach and the rest on
horseback across the hills to Whareponga, and when we arrived there all the
people from Waipiro Bay and Hiruharama were already assembled, the marae
was chock-a-block! Tuta Ngarimu, Tuhere Maraki, Piripi Te Awarau stood to
greet us, and Materoa Ngarimu was the last speaker. She recited the genealogies
that linked us together and said to us,

'Well, Eruera and Amiria, we are very pleased that you have come together, and
I am glad that all the tribal people are supporting you – welcome to this marae!
Now that you have come, here is the koha of Ngati Porou for your marriage – 500
breeding ewes, fourteen dairy cows and one jersey bull! When you have settled
down, come back here and pick up the stock to start you off on a farm of your own.'

That big gift was the finish of our travelling around the East Coast maraes, and
we returned home to Raukokore in Wirihana Tatai's buggy.

CHAPTER FOUR
SETTLING DOWN

In January 1919 the Maori Land Court sat to investigate the land titles at Raukokore; the judge was Judge Brown and I was there to represent the interests of my mother. I had no fear of the old people, Manihera Waititi and the Te Kanis and all those people; I knew they were great orators on genealogy, but I was sitting on top of the world with the knowledge my great-grandpeople passed on to me.

When the court opened at 10 o'clock, there were three elderly kaumatuas, all grey-haired old chaps who were going to oppose me for the land titles. Te Kani, Waititi and the Waengas all put claims on the ancestral rights to our land. My tipuna Pera Te Kaongahau had told me in the days of our teaching,

'Your great-great-grandfather Te Ao-o-tata was the man who controlled all of this area, and your ancestors occupied this land right from the time the canoes came until now.'

Then he taught me all the whakapapa.

When Judge Brown opened the court he saw me sitting there, and he knew that I was only young to face those old chaps, so he explained what the court was going to do, and how we should make our claims, then he held off the proceedings until 2 o'clock. After that he said to me,

'Are you going to act for your mother?'

'Yes.'

'All right. Now, I'm going to get the clerk to give you the minute books of the title investigations into this land. You have a good look, and make sure you write down everything important.'

When everybody had left the meeting-house the judge told me I could stay in there and take my notes. When I looked at the minute books, ha! The first thing I saw was the first sitting of the Maori Land Court in Opotiki 1886* – Maaka Te Ehutu had established his claim for the whole of our district by way of tribal occupation or papatipu, and the original ancestor was Kai-a-runga-te-rangi. I took all those records and wrote them down before the court opened. After a while the judge and the clerk came back, and the judge said to me,

'Have you taken the evidence of your grandfather?'

'Yes, I've got it here.'

'All right. Let the other people make their claims, and then I'll call you to come into the box. You ask them where they were born, and whether they have ever

---

*I have been unable to locate this case, but there is a map in the Lands and Survey office of Gisborne (ML1110) with the following caption written on it: 'this is the Sketch Map of the Raukokore Block referred to in the attached application to the Native Land Court Dated fourth September 1895'. The guides for the surveyor were Maka Tu Hutu (Maaka Te Ehutu) and Timora Tuke.

lived at Raukokore. Can you give the genealogy of the Te Kanis and the Waengas and the Waititis?'

'Yes.'

So at 2 o'clock the judge called out to Waititi and he put his claim – finish. Then Te Kani, then Waenga – finish. After that the judge called out to me,

'Well, Mr Stirling, have you got any questions?'

I asked Manihera Waititi, 'Where were you born?'

'At Whangaparaoa.'

'Have you ever lived on this land?'

'No.'

That was the end of those questions. Then I asked Te Kani the same, and then Te Waenga. The judge said,

'Well Mr Stirling, are you objecting to these people claiming ancestral rights?'

'Yes. They have no rights here whatsoever, their ancestors have never had permanent occupation on this property – only my great-great-grandfather.'

'Oh. And on behalf of your mother, can you give the genealogies of this tribal area?'

I gave him the genealogies of all the descendants of Maru-haere-muri – there were seven in the family, and I brought it right down to Te Kani, Te Waenga, Manihera Waititi and my mother.

Then the judge said, 'According to the minutes of the Maori Land Court at Opotiki in 1886, no one contested the claim of Mr Stirling's grandfather to this land at that time. You people have no right to come from Cape Runaway and claim this land. I will vest the title of all this area in Mihi Kotukutuku, and if she wishes to divide the land, it's up to her.'

When the court was over I said to my mother, 'Oh, we'll claim the whole lot, never mind about giving it to those other people.'

'No, we can't do that. You must give aroha to the people, they're part of you too. If your grandfather was alive today he'd give that land.'

'Oh Mum, we had to fight today for our land, otherwise they would have taken it from us!'

But my mother still said, 'No! If you go back in your whakapapa, Manihera, Te Kani, they're yours, your own.'

I was disgusted with Mum. In the end she was the one that put so much for the Te Kanis, so much for the Waengas and so much for the other families. She told me,

'The main thing is to love your people. You have to look after them, because they're your *own*.'

When I look back now, I can see that Mum was right, and those people from Cape Runaway were very close to our family.

Not long after that I had a big fight with some of the other people from Cape Runaway. My grandfather Maaka Te Ehutu had given permission years back for Te Hata Moutara and some of the Te Kani family to come from Cape Runaway and live on our land near the Raukokore church; they buried their dead in the graveyard there and used our big meeting-house on the point called Te Hau-ki-Tihirau, built for my grandfather by his relations from Ngati Porou. In later years, though, some of the Te Kanis decided that they would like to shift the meeting-house back to Cape Runaway, and they came to see my mother about it. Mum didn't want Te Hau-ki-Tihirau moved and she said, 'No!'

Then these people started to fight with her about it. My mother didn't like to cause trouble and she would have given it to them in the finish, but I decided well, it's time for me to butt in. I stood up in the meeting and said,

'No! Te Hau-ki-Tihirau is *not* going to be shifted! It is standing on my mother's property, it was built for my grandfather by Ngati Porou, and if anyone comes to move it off they will get into big trouble!'

Mum came over to me and said, 'Oh, let them have it! Let them have the place!'

Those people kept on arguing and fighting, and in the end I got really wild with them. I said,

'All right, if you want to take Te Hau-ki-Tihirau away from here, take it! But first you can shift *all* your people out of the graveyard, or that meeting-house won't move an inch!'

Do you know what those people did? They came and dug up all their bodies from the graveyard by the church where they were buried in my grandfather's soil, even their old chief Te Hata Moutara; and then they came and took the meeting-house away. Mum tried to get me to take back my words, but I told her,

'No, they're doing the wrong thing! They can dig up the bodies, I don't give a hang!'

In the finish it all went back on them – those people came to nothing, their houses tumbled down and Te Hau-ki-Tihirau rotted and fell to pieces. That was the cheek of those young people, coming to interfere with my mother.

Towards the end of 1919 my mother got very sick, she had a big lump in her breast and the doctor said it was cancer, she would die within a matter of months. In those years Wiremu Ratana was faith-healing at Ratana Pa, and people were going there by the hundreds, pakeha, Maori, mission people and everyone! He was doing wonderful work for the people and his power was very strong. My father decided to take Mum to Ratana Pa and he asked me to go with him, and near the end of 1919 we left Raukokore. We travelled on the boat to Opotiki, on the coach to Rotorua, and then on the train to Whanganui, and when we got to Ratana Pa I saw a lot of people from the East Coast there, Ngati Porou, Whanau-a-Apanui and even Ngai Tai. There were sick people everywhere, on crutches and all sorts, and some of them went to be blessed by Ratana and walked away carrying their crutches just like that – it was a miracle. When we were on the marae at Ratana Pa, word came that a sick woman was being flown from Nelson to see Ratana, a doctor's daughter who was paralysed from the waist down, and the rest of the crowd was asked to wait. The doctors had done everything they could to help this girl but she still couldn't walk. We saw the van arriving at the marae and a stretcher was made ready, and the girl was carried in to see Ratana. I saw it with my own eyes; Ratana prayed to the Lord Jesus Christ to help her as the stretcher came closer, and then he called out to the crippled girl,

'Get up!'

She got up from her stretcher and walked towards Ratana, and then they

The Ratana Tabernacle Church, Temepara o te Hahi Ratana. *Alexander Turnbull Library*

walked together to the meeting-house. Ratana prayed over her, then she walked back to her father and mother – she was cured! Her doctor father gave Ratana a cheque for £5000 but Ratana said, 'No, I do not take money for this.'

The father insisted and in the end the money went to build the Ratana Tabernacle Church, still standing at Ratana Pa today.

Shortly after that my mother went up to be blessed, and Ratana saved my mother's life. From that day the lump in her breast started to go down and she lived from 1919 until she died in the 1960s. Ratana told my mother she'd be all right, and as soon as she got home she got an old man to give her a Maori herbal remedy, he scraped the ponga to get a sort of slime, and she boiled that and put it on the cancer, and she lived on for many, many years.

Not long after that, Ratana decided to go overseas, and before he went he toured around the maraes of New Zealand, and he came to visit the Bay of Plenty. The night that Ratana's party arrived at our marae, I had a dream. I dreamed that I saw the twelve Apostles standing there with collars around their necks, and then a white hand came down from Heaven and took all the collars away from the twelve – finish! The next morning I told my father about it, and he gave me his interpretation. He said,

'Well, Ratana has still got the mana upon him, but as soon as he goes overseas, that power will automatically be taken away!'

It was quite right too, because as soon as Ratana left New Zealand his faith healing started to go back, and the mana was taken away.

After Amiria and I were married we lived in Raukokore for about a year, and I started to think deeply into farming. The stock that Materoa Ngarimu had given us as a wedding present arrived from Whareponga, but I didn't have any land of my own and I thought to myself,

'What's the use of having this stock, I don't know much about shearing, crutching, wool-classing, earmarking stock or anything like that! No good holding on to something like this without experience!'

I put my stock to run on my father's farm and I said to Amiria,

'We'd better go and live at Tuparoa for a while with your mother, and when we arrive there I will go and work at Pakihiroa Station for Mr Williams. I don't know anything about stock work, and that's the only thing to do.'

T. S. Williams. *Gisborne Museum and Arts Centre*

Pakihiroa Station. *Gisborne Herald*

Thomas Sydney Williams ran the Pakihiroa Station and he was one of the outstanding men on the East Coast, he was Maori at heart! He used to lease land all about the Coast and when the lease expired he'd say to the Maori owners,

'Well, if you want sheep, you come to me.'

Most of the prominent farmers of the East Coast started out with T. S. Williams; the Reedys, the Ngatas, the Mahuikas and many other people, and he trained most of the young men in the proper ways of farming – Te Warahi Tako, Watene Waititi, Raana Waaka, Tuhaka Pokiha, Pene Heihi, Hirini Heeki, Pine Heeki, Hoone Reedy, Wi Pepere, Rauhuia Tawhiwhirangi, Piniha Maru, Henare Makarati. T. S. Williams also helped my father a lot, and when Dad took over land development in Raukokore, Williams supplied him with his stock.†

† On one occasion when Ngata was Member for Eastern Maori, the Williams family were attacked in the House for profiteering, and he spoke in their defence: 'No family in this country . . . has done so much for any group of people as the Williams family has done for the Maoris of Waiapu County. The Native Minister and other members of the House who have some acquaintance with the district know that the assistance they have rendered to the Maoris has been far more than any businessman in the ordinary way of business would have given. No bank dare make the advances they made to the Natives . . . In many cases the security was that which the old chiefs gave to their fathers and grandfathers – just the bare word, nothing on paper. I know in one year Mr T. S. Williams had lent to Native tribes and individual Natives in various portions of Waiapu county, as much as £30,000, and with regard to £10,000 or £15,000 of that, his security was the word of the chiefs – nothing else . . . That was either sheer foolishness or it was the height of philanthropy, as you please. I call it the very height of philanthropy!' (*N.Z. Parliamentary Debates*, Vol. 174, pp. 616-7)

Amiria was happy to go to Tuparoa, and when we arrived there I told my mother-in-law my intentions, and she said,

'Oh well, that's quite all right.'

I rode over to Pakihiroa Station to ask for a job; the manager at that time was Mr Bennett who used to manage Matangareka Station at the back of Raukokore and when he saw me he said,

'Ha, what are you doing here, Dick?'

'Well, I want to get a job – I want to study sheep-farming!'

'Oh yes, that will be all right. Are you going to stay here for long?'

'Yes, as long as I can stay.'

'All right, you can start here right away – go and see the gang-boss.'

I went to the workers' quarters on the station and when I walked in, I saw that the gang-boss was my own relation, Wi Maraki– he was related to my mother, and he was in charge of the fencing work and everything. Wi Maraki said to me,

'Ha! I thought you were in Raukokore!'

I told him the reason I had come to Pakihiroa Station, and he said,

'That's good – you come with me.'

He took me around the station and showed me all the work, and I started to help him and that's how I got a job at Pakihiroa Station. In those days the wages were 5/- a day, 30/- a week, but you learned all about the proper ways of farming with T. S. Williams.

One day Wi Maraki and I went fencing over the hills, and when we got to the top of the hills in the back country he said to me,

'Would you like to see Hikurangi?'

'Yes, I would, Wi!'

The next Saturday after work he took me right to the top of Hikurangi mountain, and he showed me the little lake up there, Te Puna o Tinirau, that marks the spot where Maui-tikitiki-a-Taranga was buried. Maui‡ was the ancestor who hooked the North Island (Te Ika a Maui, Maui's fish) and pulled it out of the sea; the old people say his canoe got stuck on Hikurangi mountain as it rose from the water and it is up there still, turned into a rock.

It was beautiful on top of the mountain, the sun was shining and white clouds circled round us, and I looked to the west and saw Whanokao mountain standing in Whanau-a-Apanui country. Wi said to me,

'One day we'll cross over to your mountain, Whanokao.'

We looked right out over the countryside and then we went back to Pakihiroa Station.

---

‡An East Coast tradition says there was a time when the waters covered the earth; that at that time, Maui and his three sons floated upon the waters in a canoe, fishing; that presently Maui hooked the earth, and with great labour he drew it to the surface with the assistance of his sons. Then their canoe grounded upon what proved to be the top of a mountain. As the earth became bare, the sons of Maui took possession but Maui himself vanished and returned to the place whence he came. The canoe remained upon the top of the Mountain (Hikurangi), where it may be seen in a petrified state at the present time.' (P. Harrison *The Traditions of the Ngati Porou Tribe*, p. 3).

Hikurangi mountain, where Maui's canoe still lies. *Alexander Turnbull Library*

My uncle Wi Maraki was one of the fastest shearers on the East Coast, he could shear about 300-400 sheep a day and he was a clean shearer too. He showed me how to hold the sheep and how to look after my machine, and when crutching time came around he taught me how to crutch. In my second season at Pakihiroa I was starting to improve, and at shearing time that year he made me a clerk of the scale. He said to me,

'Your job is to keep the tally of the wool bales, and you've got a chance to learn about wool-classing too.'

I tallied the bales after they were pressed and weighed them on the scales, and my uncle told the wool-classer to explain his work to me, because I was going to be a farmer myself. Amiria worked in the shearing shed too, she started as a fleece-o but she gradually worked up and in the finish she became a very good wool-classer, working on all the big farms around Ruatorea. She could touch a fleece of wool and she knew the class exactly, A1, B2, C, D, E, F or G, from the softness and the silky brightness of the wool.

We really enjoyed our time at Pakihiroa, and at the end of four years I had learned a clear and progressive way of farming. After that we went back to Raukokore and lived at home, and my father started me off on Pohaturoa block with the 500 head of sheep, the fourteen milking cows and the jersey bull given to us by Ngati Porou. Ngata had recently started up the development scheme on the Coast, milking cows, and a lot of people had to borrow money to get themselves going but we were lucky, we already had our own stock. Those were the fruits of the arrangement of our marriage in the old tribal way, and we settled down after that and lived happily together on the farm at Raukokore.

CHAPTER FIVE
RAISING OUR FAMILY

Our first child Lucy was born while I was still working at Pakihiroa Station. In those days we delivered most of the babies ourselves and to my way of thinking it was a good thing, everybody should learn how to bring their own family into the world. A man and his wife should be No.1 when the baby is born, they help one another to get it out, and that brings them closer together. When Lucy was born at Taumata-o-mihi I had no experience in that kind of work, so the local nurse Heni Pokino came to the house to look after Amiria. She said to me,

'This is going to be an experience for you – this is your first child! I want you to get a basin and boil some water, and fetch something sharp to cut the cord, and when the baby is born, I want you to watch exactly what I do.'

Amiria had a hard time with Lucy because it was a breech birth, and Heni explained to me that when the baby is coming feet first, you have to watch that the hands stay close to the body or one of the arms might get caught; and she told me the difference between the way a boy comes out and a girl, all those sorts of things. In the finish Lucy was born, and I washed her and wrapped her up, and gave her to Amiria to feed. In those days we thought that breast-fed babies were the best, because they didn't get sick and it was less work for the mother. After that we managed the confinement of most of our eight children by ourselves, and we had very little trouble.

When we went back to Raukokore, we lived for a short time on Pohaturoa block and then we spent a year on Kapongaroa block, but those blocks were not big enough to carry all our stock and in the end we settled at Otaimina. Around that time, in 1924, Sir Apirana Ngata called a meeting in the district to talk to the people about setting up a dairy factory at Te Kaha, and in those years the main incorporation around Raukokore was Tawaroa Incorporation, founded in 1917. The main shareholders in Tawaroa were the Waititi family, the Brown family, the Swintons and my mother; they had leased the land, 2,800 acres, to Barker and Neilson from Gisborne who turned it into one of the most beautiful farms on the Coast, with a big homestead and woolsheds and everything.

The capital value of the property rose to a very high amount and the Maori owners had a good security, so when Apirana Ngata wanted support for the Te Kaha Dairy Factory he talked to the Tawaroa Committee members about it, and they decided to ask for a loan from the Maori Land Board in Rotorua. Of course we were very lucky that we had one of our own men there, Tiweka Anaru; he was a resident of Raukokore who became Registrar of the Maori Land Court and later they appointed him a judge. The loan came through the Maori Trustee on the security of Maungaroa blocks 1, 2 and 3, and it paid for all the materials for the factory. The local people built the Te Kaha Dairy Factory themselves, led by

The Te Kaha Co-operative Dairy Factory. *Alexander Turnbull Library*

Hoani Pirini of Te Kaha, a qualified building contractor. Once the factory was established a lot of the families around Raukokore started on the job of milking cows.

Most of the people started dairy-farming with assistance from the New Zealand Loan Co. and Dalgetys, and a few years afterwards Apirana Ngata started a Maori land development scheme at home for milking cows. I joined the scheme to get a loan to build us a house at Otaimina and a milking shed, and Amiria and I worked hard to get the farm in good order.

When we first came to Otaimina the land was very rough and I had to clean the place up, 120 acres of stumps and scrub. One old man called Marama Brown showed me how to train teams of bullocks to do the heavy work, hauling out stumps and all that sort of thing, and in the end I had four teams of bullocks. I tied a little rope to the leader, and I'd call out to him,

'Reddy – *tiia! e huri!* Come on Reddy! Turn!'

Our head bullock Reddy was very smart, although at times I had to curse him and call him all sorts, and he kept the other bullocks straight on the line.

We taught our children to help with the work on the farm, and the boys and girls worked together just like that! The boys learned to milk cows and fence and keep the kumara gardens clean, and now and again they'd come and help the girls in the house. Lucy was our eldest and she knew how to cook and wash the dishes and scrub the floor, she taught her younger sisters to keep the place tidy, and she was pretty good on the farm work too; George was the eldest boy and he looked after his brothers, and they did a lot of work outside. Our son George went on to school at St. Stephen's and he was a very clever fellow; he was born on the 3rd of June and when I looked up his birthday in the Bible the psalm said,

'But thou, O Lord, art a shield for me; my glory and the lifter of my head!' (Psalms 3, verse 3).

Marama Brown and his bullock team.

I thought, well, he's going to be one chap; he is born on the 3rd, the same day as Apirana Ngata, and he will be another man like him. George went through his schooling at Raukokore and he did very well, then he went through St. Stephen's and he won *everything* at St. Stephen's – Boxing Champion, Senior Athletics Champion, Head Prefect, he was the scoring man on the football field and he was the top boy right around. Our son George was the top man everywhere he went, and in the end he won a place at Feilding Agricultural College to learn the modern ways of farming.

Waha our next son was a merry chap and always full of life, you could hear his voice singing around the farm, and the other children, Lilian and Kiwa, Marama, Tama and Kepa were all very good; we had to work hard on the farm, getting up early in the morning to milk the cows, and there was no rest for the children but they were a big help in keeping the place going. I taught my children what my father told me, 'If you're going to do a thing, do it properly,' and we followed the example that he had set out for us.

Every year at Otaimina I grew a big patch of kumaras, and I followed the way of planting that my mother had learned from her grandfather and her great-grandfather Te Ao-o-tata before him on their land at Raukokore. When I first started growing kumaras on the farm I ploughed up about four or five acres for my patch and some of the other farmers around the place, Jack Nyman and Parekura Brown, laughed when they saw me planting a big lot of kumaras and said,
'Huh! Look at this man, he won't get anything out of it!'

When my kumaras were just about ready though, I went on a car to Taneatua and travelled on the railway to Auckland; I wanted to see the Auckland markets for myself. When I arrived at the markets Frank Turner, one of the directors of Turners and Growers, showed me around; I looked at the kumaras that the Chinamen and the Hindus were selling there and I said to Mr Turner,

'D'you know, I've got better kumaras than those at home!'

Mr Turner said, 'Well, Mr Stirling, when your kumaras are ready, send us a consignment; or bring them up to Auckland yourself and I'll take you to the auction.'

He explained to me exactly how to pack the kumaras, with the big kumaras and the small ones in different bags, and I had a good look at all the sacks of kumaras packed up by the Chinamen and the Hindus.

When I arrived back at Raukokore my kumara patch was ready, so I asked Moana Waititi to come in with his tractor and plough it up, and then Marama Brown and all the other men helped our family to pick the kumaras out of the ground and pack them in sugar bags, so many sacks of big kumaras and so many sacks of the smaller variety. When Jack Nyman and Parekura Brown rode down to look at my stacks of kumaras, they laughed and said to me,

'You're wasting your time! Who's going to buy your kumaras?'

I took no notice of them and when Sam Hayes came to Otaimina with his big truck and loaded up my kumaras, eight tons of them from my four-acre patch, I rode with the consignment on the truck as far as Taneatua and then I hopped on the train. The train arrived in Auckland and a big Turners and Growers truck was standing at the station; they loaded up my kumaras and gave me a message from Frank Turner to be at the markets the next morning at 10 o'clock.

When I arrived at the markets the next day Frank Turner sat next to me while the kumaras were being auctioned, and the Chinamen's kumaras were sold and the kumaras grown by the Hindus, and then the auctioneer said,

'Well, ladies and gentlemen, the next lot is eight tons of kumaras grown in the Bay of Plenty. Bring out one of those sacks of Mr Stirling's kumaras, please, and put them out on the table!'

One of the men brought a sack to the big table in front of the auctioneer and cut it open, and the auctioneer said,

'There you are! Some of the finest kumars ever to come on this market. Now, what am I bid?'

The bidding started, and went up and up, and the buyers all went for my kumaras, forgetting about the stuff put in by the other growers. In the end the eight tons were sold, and I got £45 a ton.

When Sam Hayes got back to Raukokore Jack Nyman and some of the local farmers pulled him up and asked,

'Is it right that Stirling sold all his kumaras in Auckland?'

Sammy Hayes said, 'Yeah! He topped the market in Auckland and he beat all the Chinese and the Hindus; he got £45 a ton!'

They had a hang of a big shock about it. The next year Jack Nyman and Parekura Brown and all the other farmers started growing kumaras in Raukokore, they had the women out working and they put in very big kumara patches. Jack Nyman was the Postmaster and he saw all the telegrams that came to me from Turners and Growers, telling me the prices of kumaras at certain times, and he and Parekura Brown decided to beat me to the markets. They lifted their kumaras and sent them away before my crop was ready, and straight after that Turners and Growers sent me a telegram to say that the price of kumaras had dropped. Nyman and Brown's kumaras arrived at the markets that day – the price had flopped way down and they had to pay out money for the freight and everything; they tried to cut across me and they lost. I held on to my kumaras for a while and when they arrived at the markets I got a good price for them.

After that I started selling kumaras in a big way, I was appointed an agent for Turners and Growers and I bought all the kumaras from Te Kaha, Torere, Te Araroa and Tikitiki, right round. My opposition was Lou Gow, a Chinaman from Gisborne who came round the Coast in a big truck, buying up supplies, and one time somebody from Opotiki said to him,

'It's no use you coming around here, Lou Gow – Stirling is buying our kumaras now.'

Lou Gow told him, 'Hà! Stirling's got no money! I've got money!'

This chap answered, 'Oh, he's got the money all right, he's got a big man from Auckland behind him – you can't go on beating Turners and Growers forever, you know!'

So Lou Gow put his price up, and the people said, 'Oh well, if you give us more than Stirling, we'll sell.'

That year I didn't buy any kumaras, and Lou Gow went around the Coast, Tokomaru Bay, Rangitukia, Te Araroa and Hicks Bay, buying up tons and tons of kumaras. I had a telegram from Turners and Growers that season telling me not to buy any because the price had gone right down. Lou Gow sent two trucks full of kumaras to Wellington and he couldn't get rid of them, he had to sell them for nothing and he went broke. He lost his job and he got pushed out of his firm, and after that the Maoris on the Coast called him 'Pakaru Me', meaning 'I went broke.'

Not long after that I went out eeling one time, and I caught the biggest eel I've ever seen in my life. There was a special pool in the Raukokore River called Kopungawha, and it was the custom of our great-grandpeople in the tribal area long before my time, that only the sons and grandsons of the senior line of chiefs could go to that pool to catch eels. My great-grandfather and my grandfather caught eels at Kopungawha, and when it came to our generation the old man Maaka Te Ehutu showed the pool to my brother Taikorekore and me. There was a big rock standing in the river at Kopungawha, and that was the special place in the district for catching really big eels, not any other part. When the old people wanted eel for a tribal feast or a hui, they'd ask my grandfather or Taikorekore to go to Kopungawha and pull out two or three eels and hang them up, and that was a feed for the big crowd at the marae.

That year a few days before Christmas I decided to go to the pool and catch a big eel for our Christmas dinner. I rode up the river to the Kopungawha basin with my line and baits, and when I came to the big rock I got off my horse and threw some pieces of liver into the pool. The small eels all came swarming out and they had their show, then some bigger eels came along and the little ones took off. I

Children on horseback outside the Wairuru marae, Raukokore. *Auckland Weekly News, 9 April 1941*

waited and waited until I saw a very big eel hanging around, then I put the bait on my line and dropped it in. Of course the eel *went* for the bait and he grabbed it, and I had to play my line like anything in case the big eel broke it. In the end the eel got tired and drowned himself, and when I hauled it out, hika! it was about seven feet long, and twelve inches across, it was the biggest eel I've ever seen! It was very heavy so I tied it to my saddle with a rope, and when I rode home it was dragging on the ground. A lot of people heard about this eel and they came to see it hanging up; a local pakeha called Mr Warrington told the *Herald* about it and they came and took a photo, years ago. On Christmas Day we had a big crowd at our place, and we cut up the eel and put it in the hangi, and it fed the whole lot! Everybody enjoyed it because it was a big fat eel, one of the biggest that's ever been caught in the pools of the Raukokore River.

CHAPTER SIX
SIR APIRANA NGATA

Aue! Ta Apirana
Alas! Sir Apirana!
Ahakoa kua ngaro koe
Although you are lost
Ki enei ra
These days
Ka tarai kia tutuki e
We are trying to carry out
O tumanako, e koro e, aue!
Your hopes, e koro – alas!
Aue! Ta Apirana
Alas! Sir Apirana,
Kore rawa koe
You will never
E warewaretia
Be forgotten
O tohutohu kia mau
Nor your advice, to hold fast to
Te mauri e
Our spiritual power
Kai te aroha ra, e ta!
We still love you, our friend!

a lament for Sir Apirana Ngata (Ngati Porou)

One of the best things in my life was working with Sir Apirana Ngata. He was the finest leader that Ngati Porou and Te Whanau-a-Apanui have ever had, and he came to the end of his days a poor man, because all his time was given to others. Apirana stayed at home to help his people, he was that type of man. Right from the beginning of his life he was blessed; he was conceived according to the sacred rites of the old priests, and he was a chosen man.

Paratene Ngata and his wife Katerina had no children, and after some years Katerina went to see a tohunga called Hakopa and asked him to help them. Hakopa agreed, and he began by chanting some of the ancient prayers to make a woman tapu, and then Katerina was taken to the sacred water and blessed. The expert women weavers of the tribe made a takapau wharanui, a special

Paratene Ngata (right) sitting on the verandah of the Bungalow at Waiomatatini, talking to Elsdon Best (centre). *James McDonald*

sleeping-mat woven from kiekie and pingao,* and when it was ready Hakopa blessed it and said to Katerina and Paratene,

'Good, it is over to you two now – but before you lie on the takapau wharanui, take this kawakawa leaf and place it beneath you.'†

The next morning Hakopa came to them and they all went to the river's edge; he placed some embers in a paua shell there and began to pray, and as he chanted a rainbow rose up in the sky! That was a kai-arahi, a guide come to meet them. When Hakopa had finished his prayers he kicked the paua shell with its embers out into the water, and then he said to Paratene and Katerina,

'Your prayers have been answered! Before long you will have a child and it will be a boy, and a second son will follow. Your first-born son has taken all the power of my mind and my spirit from me, and on the day that he is born into this world, I shall die! Why did you come to me for this blessing – why didn't you go to somebody else?'

Well, the old man was quite right. Before long Apirana was born, and on the day of his birth, Hakopa died. About a year later Katerina and Paratene had a second son, and they named him Hone.‡

---

* Kiekie is a supple white leaf from a bush plant, and the pingao leaf is yellow.
† Kawakawa leaves are often used in tapu rituals.
‡ For Paratene Ngata's account of these events, see J.P.S. Vol. 59, pp. 280–85.

Well, we can all see that Apirana was given everything through his life by the blessings of that priest, the last of the old men of Tapere-nui-a-Whatonga and Te Rawheoro, the very, very high schools of learning in Maori history on the East Coast. Apirana grew up with that spirit upon him, the understanding of Maori history and genealogies, and in his later years he wrote *Nga Moteatea* and the *Rauru-nui-a-Toi lectures*, those articles passed on to him by the old man of the Tapere-nui-a-Whatonga School of Learning. The blessings of Almighty God were upon him too, and the greatness of his future life was predicted in the psalm for his birthday, the 3rd: 'But thou, O Lord, art a shield for me; my glory, and the lifter up of mine head.' (Psalms 3, verse 3).

Once Apirana started to go to school all the people at Waiomatatini could see that he was very talented, so they decided to send him to Te Aute College.§ He did

§ Ngata wrote an account of his childhood at Reporua Village and his travels to Te Aute in *History of the East Coast Native Schools*: 'Tu Fox was barely 10 years of age, Keiti Pokiha and I a month or two this side of nine . . . – we were sent to what seemed to be a foreign land, banished from home and parents for eleven months of the year – for no Coast boy was ever allowed to come home for the winter holidays . . .'

Apirana Ngata as a graduate. *Alexander Turnbull Library*

very well at Te Aute and he carried off all the prizes, then he went down south to Otago University College and graduated LLB and master of arts, he was one of the top students of the day along with Rhodes and Rutherford. Rhodes passed, Rutherford passed, and Apirana passed, the whole lot of them had degrees, and after their graduation Rhodes said to the other two,

'Well, I think we'd better go overseas – we'll be rich men when the time comes!'

Rhodes and Rutherford both decided to go, but when Apirana went back to Waiomatatini and spoke to the old people about it, his grandfather Ropata Wahawaha said to him,

'You're not going overseas, Api, you must stay here! We need you to fix up the lands and everything. We went to fight with the Government forces to hold on to the mauri of our lands, we have done our small part, and now it's up to you to carry on the job. You stay!'

> After the Taranaki Wars,
> from Rangitaiki, Paeroa, Waikato
> thousands of Land went under through
> the Maori People Joining to Help
> Te Whiti and Rongomai in their fight
>
> for their land in Taranaki and Round
> Parihaka and Wanganui. Their claim
> was Just, and their Lands were Taken
> by the Crown for Turning against
> them, forming their Groups to fight
> Led by Te Whiti and Rongomai. All tribes
> Respected Te Whiti's Land Claims, that is
> why they all assisted, He tangi na te
> nuinga nei o nga iwi Maori kua
> murua i nga whenua e hia ke nga
> miriona eka, all the tribes of New Zealand
> Deeply felt that Great Loss of their Lands
> Those who Happened to be Lucky to
> come out of these Land Slides of
> the turn in the Early History of the
> Settlement of the Country I may say
> that all mighty God moved in
> Some How, and inherited that Spirit
> to the Leading Chiefs, and officers
> of the Government at that time who
> Paved the way for those who have
> Joined with the Government forces
> and from those movements it certainly
> moved on to the District where the
> Maori Officers were appointed, I have
> mentioned the Chiefs, Major Ropata
> Wahawaha, Major Mokena Kohere

> Captain Pine Tuhaka Captain Houkamau
> Henare Potae, Maaka Te Ehutu, Wiremu Kingi
> all these chiefs Represented the Ngati Porou
> and Whanau Apanui Tribes. They saved
> the Tribes from losing their Lands,
> and from Torere, Ngai Tai Tribe to all
> East Coast Whanau Apanui No Land
> was taken. The people of Tai Rawhiti
> District were very Lucky in the
> Land Slides of that time.
>
> by Eruera Stirling

Ropata Wahawaha was quite right, if he and some of the other chiefs had not gone to fight with the Government forces all the lands of Ngati Porou and Te Whanau-a-Apanui would have been confiscated; the Government took the Rangitaiki Plains, they took Whakatane and thousands of acres away from the Whakatohea people, and only the lands of Ngai Tai, Te Whanau-a-Apanui and Ngati Porou were saved. That's why he said to Apirana,

'You stay here and help us. If you go away to Africa or somewhere else, who will put things right for us?'

So Apirana went back to his friends Rhodes and Rutherford, and said,

'I'm not going, my old people will not agree to it. I'm staying at home.'

His friends went overseas and they both became famous men; Rhodes was a lawyer and he went to Africa and headed up a government there and died a big chief, and Rutherford carried on with his research and he did very well at that. Ngata told me one day,

'I'll die a poor man, Eru; when I die I'll leave nothing behind me – not like Rutherford and Rhodes!'[||]

After his graduation Apirana decided to go and work in Auckland for a while, and he got a job with Cooper, one of the leading barristers there.[¶] When he told his people about it they said,

'Well, Ngata, is that what you're going to do – go and work in Auckland as a lawyer for the pakehas! By Joves! We thought you were going to stay here as a lawyer for your own people!'

Apirana replied, 'Never mind, it's only for a year or two, I want to get some experience as a barrister and solicitor, and then I'll come home. When you need me, you call me back.'

He stayed in Auckland for a while, and in 1905 the people of the East Coast decided to put Apirana in the House of Parliament to sort out their land problems. Wi Pere was the sitting member for Eastern Maori and he'd been there for years;

[||] Apirana Ngata and Ernest Rutherford, the nuclear physicist, were contemporaries at Canterbury College; Ngata graduated BA in 1893 and Rutherford graduated MA in the same year. There were several 'Rhodes' among the students of that year but the reference to South Africa is a mystery.

[¶] Ngata was articled to Theodore Cooper in Auckland 1894.

it's very hard to turn a man out of office when he's been there for so long, and Ngata had to go round the East Coast, talking about it. When he came to the Bay of Plenty he called a meeting of Te Whanau-a-Apanui at our marae in Raukokore, and when the people gathered they decided unanimously to stand behind him. My grandfather Maaka selected my father Duncan Stirling as one of the organizers for Ngata's campaign, and he sent him with a group of old people to his relations in Tuhoe, Te Arawa and Ngai Te Rangi. When the people of Tuhoe saw my father coming onto their marae with Te Whanau-a-Apanui they all said,

'Ha! What's that pakeha coming here for?'

They looked at him, but afterwards when they found out that he was Maaka Te Ehutu's son-in-law they said no more about it. The campaign party travelled right through Tuhoe, Ngai-te-Rangi, Te Arawa and Te Whanau-a-Apanui, and when the time came for the Election in 1905 Ngata won the Eastern Maori seat; he entered Parliament and started to carry out the work that the old people had passed on to him. He and Maui Pomare battled to build up the health of the Maori people, they set up the land incorporations and founded the first Maori councils, and always Apirana held fast to the mana and the mauri of his people, and fought to give them a living on their own lands.*

One of the hardest things that Ngata did was to set up the land incorporations, because there was a lot of opposition within the government and they said to him,

'Oh, the Maori people can't run all that land! Who's going to supervise the farming, and who can we trust to look after the money? Oh no, we won't agree to that!'

But Ngata kept on going, and he got his people to put their shares in a certain block into an incorporated company, with an incorporation committee to run the land, and then they raised money from the banks with the land as their security. The incorporations were just like other incorporated businesses – Farmers Trading Company Incorporated, Dalgetys and N.Z. Loan Incorporated, and Ngata was a very clever man to think of that. Today there are incorporations of Maori owners all over the country, running their own land, and the biggest one is Mangatu near Gisborne – 500,000 acres!

During World War I Apirana worked hard to establish a battalion of Maori soldiers, and towards the end of the war when the soldiers were about to come home he decided to buy some farming land and put it in trust for the men of the Pioneer Battalion. He went fund-raising all over the Coast, and he travelled to Gisborne and Hastings and Rotorua, right around the island. When he came to the Bay of Plenty he went to see my mother and asked,

'Well, Mihi, can you give me some of the rentals from your land to support our scheme?'

'Yes, Api, and not only that – put it down that the money came from the whole of Te Whanau-a-Apanui people.'

When the money was ready we sent it to Tiweka Anaru, the Registrar of the Maori Land Court, and in the end there were thousands of pounds in that special

---

* For a detailed discussion of Apirana Ngata's career, see Graeme Butterworth's thesis, *The Politics of Adaptation*, 1969.

Sir Apirana Ngata, 1940. *Alexander Turnbull Library*

Tiweka Anaru and Sir Apirana Ngata sitting outside Tukaki meeting-house, Te Kaha.
Te Ao Hou

fund. Anaru and Ngata worked together and they managed to buy two farms with
the money, Hoia Station at Hicks Bay and Hereheretau block in Hawke's Bay, and
they put the land in a trust for the soldiers. Some people said that Apirana was
spending all the money on himself, but that was just jealous talk, eh, and when
Apirana died years later it came out in their eulogies on the marae. When Tipi
Ropiha heard them talking like that, he stood up at Waiomatatini marae and
presented the balance sheet for the Soldiers' Trust showing the running of the two
stations and everything, and he told them,

'When Apirana helped Te Arawa claim Lake Rotorua, Lake Rotoma, and Lake
Rotoiti, they won the case and the lakes came back to the Maori people, and Te
Arawa came to Waiomatatini and presented Ngata with a cheque for £6,000! If
you look at the balance sheet you can see that Api gave that £6,000 to the Soldiers'
Trust – how many of you would give away £6,000?† That was Apirana, he never
thought of his own pocket and yet you people are calling him names!'

The people looked at the balance sheet and they saw that Tipi was right, and
then they cried; they agreed that some of the money should be set aside for a
Ngata Scholarship, and in later years our new Archbishop, Paul Reeves, was one of
the first to win that scholarship and travel overseas to university. You can see how
the fruits of Apirana's work keep coming on, and still the memories linger.

In all his movements around the East Coast, Apirana would come and visit my
mother whenever he was in the Whanau-a-Apanui district, and he talked to her
about the work he was doing. Ngata and my mother were very close and they were
related on the background of our genealogy. I remember Apirana visiting at
Stirling Castle in my childhood days, and when I went to Te Aute College I heard
the teachers talking about him and the other old boys of the school.

† In 1918, Ngata fought hard to claim the Rotorua lakes for Te Arawa, and the Government finally
paid Te Arawa £6,000 a year to compensate them for taking the lakes for the Crown.

I started to get close to the old man when I went to work at Pakihiroa Station; now and again I'd meet him at one of the maraes and he'd ask me,

'How are you getting on Eruera?'

'Oh, I'm doing all right.'

One time he asked me to come and see him at his place, and we talked about his work and the lands and the teachings of the old people. After that he rang me up a few times to say,

'If you're free, come over to see me at Waiomatatini.'

Apirana had gone through the school of learning in the old way, and that was a bond between us; once the old priests have given you the tribal training you can pick another person with that spirit upon them, and it makes you very close. The feeling comes to you as a sign, and you know that the other man is really genuine.

In the finish Apirana went to Raukokore and asked my mother if I could be one of the men to help him in his political campaigning, and Mum said to him,

'Oh yes, Api, he'll do that work for you.'

That was in 1924, and after that I worked to support Ngata in the Eastern Maori electorate for more than twenty years, and I visited the different maraes from Te Whanau-a-Apanui to Whakatohea, Tuhoe, Ngai-te-Rangi at Tauranga and Te Arawa. Apirana would send me the pamphlets about his work with Maori land, incorporations and development work, and I'd go around to the maraes and have a talk with the people. When Apirana visited those pas where the pamphlets had been left there would be a large gathering, young and old, and the people would say to him,

'Don't worry, Api! We'll be behind you, it doesn't matter who else comes here!'

When election night came, sure enough Apirana always flowed in, and he'd be back in the House of Parliament.

Back at home when there was something urgent to be done, the people would send word to me and I'd telegram him down in Wellington, oh, so-and-so wants this to be done in a hurry, and that's how I supported Apirana in his work on the Coast.

Apirana was always very good to me, and he called me in on a lot of the big

The Bungalow, Apirana Ngata's home at Waiomatatini. *Alexander Turnbull Library*

things that he did. When the *Nga Moteatea* book was being printed he showed me a waiata that came from my grandpeople, and it gave the whakapapa of my great grandfather Poututerangi. Apirana called me to Waiomatatini to look at this waiata, and I saw that the whakapapa of Poututerangi was wrong. Ngata said to me,

'What do you think, Eruera?'

I said, 'Well, if you go that way it's not a bad mistake, it would just take a little bit to get it right.'

'It's a big job to correct it now though, it's right through all the books.'

'Oh well, my great-grandfather died in the wrong way, so his whakapapa can stay wrong too! Anyway never mind, there's only one thing missing.'

Apirana said to me, 'As long as you're satisfied, we'll leave it there. It will be all right, because you and I are the ones to growl about it if it's like that!'

So we left it that way, and when the first issue of *Nga Moteatea* was printed, Ngata called me at Raukokore and asked me to visit him at the Bungalow. I went to Waiomatatini and stayed there for the night, and that evening Apirana presented me with one of the first copies of *Nga Moteatea*, printed in Maori.

One time in 1927, Apirana called a meeting of the people to talk about consolidation or 'whakawhitiwhiti', and we all went to Mangahanea. When we arrived at the marae the whole of Ngati Porou was assembled and there was a welcome in the usual custom, then the old man stood up and said,

'This is the beginning of the scheme of consolidation. Consolidation is a good thing, because little interests can be brought together into big areas and that's better for the owners. Without consolidation you'll have little blocks here and there but the owners get nothing out of it, their interests are uneconomic and that type of land stays there untouched, with no value! I want to start our first consolidation right here, to bring some blocks into a good understanding, and to bring benefits to the owners.'‡

The people just sat there and said nothing. Ngata continued,

'I think that Tapuwaeroa 1B, 2 and 3, and the land down on the beach at Tuparoa are ready to be consolidated. People from the beach can move their interests to the back country or whatever, and this is the time to talk about it.'

Nobody spoke. Apirana turned to me and said,

'Well, Eruera, you are here from the Bay of Plenty representing the interests of your mother Mihi Kotukutuku, and I'm asking you, are you in favour of this scheme?'

I waited for a while, and then I stood up and answered him.

'Well Api, I want all of my mother's interests in Reporua, Tuparoa and around the beach shifted back into Tapuwaeroa B5! I want the whole lot to go into B5!'

All the people sat quietly, nobody said anything, and the old man said, 'Right! You are the first claim for Tapuwaeroa B5, so all of your interests will go back there.'

My cousins the Haerewas stood up and moved all of their interests into B5 too, and then Apirana asked me,

'You have no other wish for your mother, Eruera?'

'No, I want B5, that's finished.'

'All right, it's settled; but I warn you, if anybody finds their mistake in years to come, they can't go back – you will have to stay as you are.'

I made no mistake though, because I saw that the valuation of the land down at the beach was £40 to £50 an acre, and the valuation of the land in Tapuwaeroa B5 was £4 an acre. I swapped our small interests at Tuparoa for a big lump of land and my cousins joined me, and we claimed 1,500 acres altogether. The people didn't see it at first but afterwards they said,

'By Joves, you were the only one that saw it! After studying your point we can see that you gained a good block of land, and it's all in farming country!'

That was one of the first consolidations on the Coast, settled by Ngata at Mangahanea in 1927.

Early in 1927 Apirana rang me at home one day and said,

'Eruera, I want you to lead a group of old people to Rotorua with Lady Arihia, Rutu Tawhiwhirangi, Tamati Kaiwai, your uncle Hakopa Haerewa and a few others, for the visit of the Duke of York. I'll be coming the day after you people with Wiremu Potae and the rest of the people from the Coast.'

I agreed, and when the time came I went back to Taumata-o-Mihi to gather the old people and get them together on our little bus. Apirana said to me,

'You please yourself how you organize your people, Eruera, but go slowly and we'll meet you on the way up to Rotorua.'

‡'Consolidation: a system of exchanges of interests of Maori land which aimed to concentrate each owner's share in one block,' Graeme Butterworth, *The Politics of Adaptation*, p.iv. The very first consolidation on the East Coast was the Waipiro block, 1911 (*The Politics of Adaptation*, p. 72).

'All right, Api.'

I decided that we would stay the night at Whakatane so I rang up the old man in charge of the marae there, Tunoa Lawson, and told him that a crowd of people was coming to stay overnight at Wairaka marae. He sent the people out to the sea and they caught maomaos and all sorts of fish for us. We went right through and when we arrived in Whakatane at about 2 o'clock in the afternoon, boy you should have seen that set-up inside the meeting-house at Wairaka! All the beds were made with pillows embroidered with flowers and silk quilts on every mattress, and after Tunoa welcomed us we went into the dining-hall and had a beautiful kai. That night, though, Lady Arihia and Rutu Tawhiwhirangi decided to leave the marae and when I looked around I couldn't see them anywhere. I said to myself,

'Ha, I wonder where Rutu and Lady Arihia have gone?'

Someone told me that they had gone to sleep at the pub that night and I was really wild with them, but I thought, all right, I know the regulations at the Whakatane Hotel and they don't allow any Maoris in there. We had our evening prayers, and when I had finished the service one of the local people came over to me and said,

'Someone outside wants to see you!'

I went outside and there were those two old kuia standing on the marae. I told them off and said,

'Well, fancy coming to a beautiful marae like this, with everything prepared, and you decide to go and sleep in a pub! Why didn't you stay at the pub and sleep there?'

They didn't say a word and when they came inside all the people looked at them.

While Ngati Porou were on the road from Gisborne, Captain Pitt's car went over a bank and they were delayed, so Apirana didn't meet us at Rotorua. When our bus arrived at the marae there the people were having their lunch and Tai Mitchell came out to see us. He asked me,

'What is the name of this tribal group, Eruera?'

'This is part of the Ngati Porou tribe, Te Whanau-a-Ruataupare.'

'Yes, all right.'

He went back to the marae, and all the people came out and welcomed us, and then they sat down. An old man stood up to speak and said,

'Who are these people? I don't know who they are – we know Apirana Ngata, but we don't know those people over there!'

That was all the welcome they gave us. After he sat down I stood up and said,

'Well, this is a nice way for you to greet us, instead of greeting us in the right manner you are treating us as if we're nothing! This is Te Whanau-a-Ruataupare and all the top people of Ngati Porou are here, and you say that you only know Apirana! Here is Rutu Tawhiwhirangi and all the queens of Ngati Porou, the senior lines of descent from the East Coast – they are here, and you don't recognize us!'

I gave them the genealogy of Rutu Tawhiwhirangi and all the other leaders, and then I sat down. The next day when Apirana and Wiremu Potae came with the rest of Ngati Porou, that old man stood up again at the marae to greet Ngata, and he mentioned my speech. Ngata said,

The Maori welcome to the Duke and Duchess of York at Rotorua. *Auckland Weekly News,*
10 March 1927

'Well, you have said something about the whakapapa that Eruera Stirling
recited on this marae; Eruera Stirling spoke for us and whatever tribal genealogy
he has given to you, that's us, Ngati Porou! I sent him ahead with the high chiefs of
Ngati Porou to open the way for the rest of us, and whatever genealogy he has
given to you I support it, it is the true figure of our tribal area. Finish!'

Apirana just put his hand up and walked away, and he came and shook hands
with us. This happened on the marae, and afterwards we went down to the
meeting-house where we were staying, the one below Tama-te-Kapua called Te
Ao Marama, and when Apirana saw it he said,

'Well, I can see you're all right in here! They have given you a beautiful house
and everything fitting for the high chiefs of Ngati Porou!'

Apirana was happy about that and when the time came to welcome the Duke of
York they had all the hakas and entertainment in the park and Ngata arranged for
me to be one of the speakers when the Duke visited Tama-te-Kapua marae. You
can see how good Apirana always was to me, he was a generous and humble man.

Not long after our trip to welcome the Duke of York, Te Puea of Waikato
brought her people around the Coast§ raising funds for Mahinarangi, the big
meeting-house at Turangawaewae in Waikato. When Apirana heard that Te Puea
wanted to build a house called Mahinarangi he said,

§This was in 1928.

'That's good – bring your people to Ngati Porou, and we will raise money for our ancestress!'

Apirana put it that way because Mahinarangi was descended from Ueroa the youngest son of Porourangi; she was taken to Waikato to marry Turongo, and all the chiefs of Ngati Maniapoto, Ngati Raukawa and Waikato are descended from that marriage:

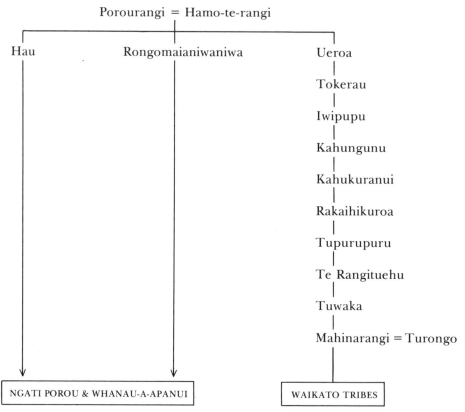

Porourangi = Hamo-te-rangi

Hau	Rongomaianiwaniwa	Ueroa
		Tokerau
		Iwipupu
		Kahungunu
		Kahukuranui
		Rakaihikuroa
		Tupurupuru
		Te Rangituehu
		Tuwaka
		Mahinarangi = Turongo

NGATI POROU & WHANAU-A-APANUI   WAIKATO TRIBES

So Te Puea brought her people to Ngati Porou and they gave concerts at all the different maraes and raised £2,000, then they came on to Te Whanau-a-Apanui and raised £500, and that's how Mahinarangi meeting-house was started. Even today when Waikato hold their huis at Turangawaewae marae Ngati Porou go there, because of the link made between the tribes when Mahinarangi married Turongo.

Sometime around 1932 Apirana Ngata came to Wairuru marae and told us that Lord Bledisloe was presenting a cup for the best Maori farmer of the year; the prize was to be presented at Rotorua and there would be haka competitions as well. My father had started to develop a farm on the Taungaure block during the First World War, 257 acres of land in scrub with about seventy acres of swamp; he raised a loan of £4,000 to cut the scrub and clean the swamp, but after the war there was a big depression and he was unable to repay the loan. Bill Swinton came

Above
Mahinarangi and Turongo as pou tokomanawa (centre-pole) figures in Te
Tokanganui-a-Noho meeting-house at Te Kuiti, 1969. *Photographic Archives, Department
of Anthropology, University of Auckland*

back from the war and took over the lease of Taungaure, because his farm was
leased to Barker and Neilson when he went away to fight. He finished developing
the land and built up a beautiful dairy farm, and Apirana told him,

'Well, Bill, I think you'd better enter Taungaure for the Ahuwhenua Cup!'

There is a stream running through that land called Waiwhero; Ngati Porou
came to battle with Te Whanau-a-Apanui and they were defeated in a big fight on
Taungaure, and the blood of those on the spot flowed into the stream so it was
named 'Waiwhero' – 'Red Water'. Bill Swinton started to prepare his farm for
inspection, and when we all went to Rotorua in 1932 he won the Ahuwhenua Cup
for the best Maori farmer in New Zealand!

My brother Taikorekore was the leader of our haka team, he was the best man
for haka and patere and singing in our district, and I composed our haka for the
Lord Bledisloe competitions in Rotorua:

William Swinton is presented with the Ahuwhenua Cup by Lord Bledisloe in 1937 (Sir Apirana Ngata behind Swinton). *Auckland Weekly News, 7 March 1933*

Hakas during the Ahuwhenua Cup celebrations.

Takahia rawatia te takutai e takoto nei
Whakaheke kau taku haere ki Rotorua!
Ki te tiki i te kapu a Te Kawana
Ko wai te toa? Ko wai te toa ki runga?
Ko Winitana!   Ko Winitana!
Ka uira i te rangi, ka kanapa ki te whenua!
Hi a ha! ha!
Mate atu he toa, ara mai ra he toa!
Mate atu he toa, ara mai ra he toa!
I a ha!   ha!
Ko kokoma, kokoma!
I ko te hautapu e rite ki te kai na Matariki
Tapa reireia koia tapa, Tapa koia nuku
Koia ra tukua, i aue!!

When the old man Hirini Puha was teaching our team he told us, 'You must learn the haka until it is settled properly in your minds!'

Then he said to Taikorekore, 'Well Tai, you are the leader of the haka party – make sure you have a mate to back you up, because if you break the chant in a haka that's a bad omen, it foretells big trouble for the people!'

Tai and I learned the words together, and when we stood on the marae at Ohinemutu in front of hundreds of people, I heard him chanting the first part of the haka and then his voice faded away, as if he was going to miss something. I took up the words and we carried on the haka together, right through, then Apirana called out to repeat it and we did a good show. In the finish the Whanau-a-Apanui team, with the Swintons and the Callaghans and everyone, won the Lord Bledisloe haka competitions in 1932.

In the same year Bishop Bennett was appointed the Bishop of Aotearoa[||], and the people brought him on a tour right around the East Coast from Napier to the Bay of Plenty. All the people of Raukokore met at Wairuru marae and we had a big day there, but that night it started to rain, and it kept on raining, raining, raining, for the next four days until the creeks were all flooding and the Raukokore River had burst its banks. Of course Bishop Bennett was worried because he had to go right up north for a big celebration, and on the fifth day he stood up at the marae and said,

'I'm really worried about my timetable! We can't go back to Gisborne and there are big slips in the Waioeka gorge, the only way we can leave the Coast is through Opotiki. Can anyone think how to get us across the Raukokore River?'

When Bishop Bennett had finished talking Moana Waititi stood up and said,

'Well, Bishop, I think I can get you across! I can collect a whole lot of empty drums from around the district and lash them together to make a pontoon, and I'm sure we'll get you across all right!'

[||] According to W. Rosevear in *Waiapu: Story of a Diocese* (p.128), Frederick Bennett was consecrated Bishop of Aotearoa in 1928.

Bishop Bennett by his car at Karetu. *Dan Munn*

Moana got on his truck and went to the Cape and gathered about twenty or forty big drums, then the men at the marae sealed them and laid them together and tied them up with wire, and they made a barge big enough to carry the Bishop, his wife and his son and their motorcar across the river. They pushed the barge into the Wairuru creek and drove the car on to it, then Moana Waititi said,

'Well, it's ready now, but the only thing is – we want somebody to swim across the river and take the ropes over to the other side.'

Bullocks towing a truck across the Raukokore River. *Whakatane Museum*

The river was in full flood, it had swept away the banks at its mouth and you could see big logs roaring along in the current. Moana stood up at the marae and asked the crowd,

'Does anybody want to cross the river? Otherwise, we won't get across for a week!'

It came to my mind, well I'll do it. I looked over and saw my mother sitting on the porch of Hine Mahuru, and I put up my hand and said,

'Yes.'

'Oh-h-h, you're going to cross again, Dick!'

'Yes.'

The team of bullocks dragged the barge up the creek to the Raukokore River, then Moana asked me, 'Where are you going to swim across?'

There was a big rata tree hanging out over the river where we used to go in our childhood days; we'd climb up the tree and hang on to a rope tied to the big branch, and we'd jump and swing *way* out, then dive into this special pool! I said to Moana,

'Let's drag the barge to the jumping-pool.'

When we got there I tied the rope around my waist and climbed to the top of the rata tree, and then I jumped into the river with the rope tumbling behind me. Well, when I was swimming in that big river I had no fear with me, the current took me and I swam along, no trouble, and I landed on the other side where Benny Harrison was standing with his team of bullocks. He took the rope and tied it to the bullocks, and Moana Waititi and the other men cut the barge loose, then Harrison's bullocks pulled the Bishop, his wife, one of their sons John Bennett and their motorcar right across the Raukokore river.

Later on that year I was ordained a lay reader in the church at Raukokore, to follow in the footsteps of my father.

The first bridge over the Raukokore River. The tree (left) is Te Putiki; Eruera swang out from its branches to make his crossing of the river. *Whakatane Museum*

When I started milking cows at Otaimina our milking shed was four miles away from the road, we had no access to the place and our children had to go up and down on horseback, carrying the cream cans to the stand. Every now and then the horse would stumble and the cream can crashed to the ground, we lost gallons and gallons of milk that way but you couldn't help it, the track was too rough. In the finish I got really fed up about it and I made an application to the New Zealand Roads Board in Wellington to survey a road through my place. I asked Apirana to help me and he tried his level best but he couldn't do anything, the Highway Board wouldn't look at it, and when I tried to get up a petition locally, the other people around Raukokore just laughed at me and said,

'Oh, Dick Stirling is just trying to better himself!'

After that I decided to see if the Labour Party could put the road through. I formed a small branch of the Labour Party in Raukokore, just Swinton, myself, and one or two others and when the rest of the people heard about it they said,

'U-uh! *We* are not going to turn to Labour! Fancy that, Stirling has been supporting Apirana all these years and now he's a Labour!'

My mother got very wild with me and she wouldn't let me have the hall for dances or anything, she said,

'No! All these halls belong to Ngata! You go to the Labour Party and ask them for a hall!'

I thought to myself, well it's not a sin, I just want this one thing for the farm, so we started raising funds and I was the president of our little branch and Swinton was the secretary. We had sales and auctions, I killed sheep and cattle and the people came to buy meat, and after a while we had quite a bit of capital. There were some Ratana maraes in the Bay of Plenty and they helped us, and other people supported the branch because I had been an organizer for the Shearers' Union in the Bay for years.

When Apirana heard that I had joined the Labour Party he called a meeting at Wairuru marae and when all the people had gathered he said to me,

'Why have you turned away from me, Eruera?'

He wasn't wild, he just asked me straight out like that. I explained to him about the road, and he said,

'That is true, the Government wouldn't listen to me about that. Well, that's all right then, I hope your road goes through. Just as long as you still keep in touch with me, that's all I want.'

That was one thing about Apirana, he didn't hold grudges like other people – there was no ill-feeling at all. That night he slept at the marae and the next day he went back to Wellington.

In 1937 I went to the Labour Party Conference as the Bay of Plenty delegate, and I presented a petition to the Conference to bring the highway through my land, and quite a few of the other delegates supported my case. In those years the highway went down to a bridge across the Raukokore River near the beach, but the river was always flooding and three bridges had already been swept away. If they shifted the highway onto my land, the bridge would cross the river higher up, and that would be safer for everybody. About a month after the Conference, on Christmas Eve, I received a telegram from the Minister of Public Works to say that the Highway Board had agreed to shift the highway.

The engineer came from Tauranga shortly after Christmas and they surveyed the road, and recommended that the new bridge should be built on my mother's property because the river wouldn't interfere with it up there. Some of the people thought that the bridge should be named after my mother Mihi Kotukutuku but she was still wild with me and she said, 'No!'

The Public Works Department gave me the fencing contract, and I brought some people in to cut down puriri trees on Otaimina and split them into fence-posts, then I built the fences with gates opening into my mother's property, and when I came to the farms of those people who had fought with me I shut them off the road, I didn't put in any gates at all!

When the next election came I turned back to Apirana Ngata and I was very happy to be working with him again. A few years later when the Raukokore bridge was opened Apirana said to me,

'Well, Eruera, I'm glad to see you got your wish.'

You can see what type of man he was, he was good, and all the people liked him.

Opening the Raukokore Bridge: Sir Apirana Ngata answers the local greetings at Wairuru marae, Raukokore. *Auckland Weekly News*

CHAPTER SEVEN
THE WAR YEARS

When the 1939 War came the Government called for recruits and the Maori
Battalion started to form, but some of the people didn't like it and the men from
Waikato refused to volunteer to go overseas. Apirana Ngata turned around and
told his people on the East Coast that they had to go away and fight, and everybody
at home was talking about the war. Apirana nominated me as a recruiting officer
for the Whanau-a-Apanui; my job was to travel around the maraes telling people
about the Maori Battalion, and after a while my place was full of young people
coming from all over, Hicks Bay, Tolaga Bay and right around the East Coast. One
of the first recruits from our district was Marama Brown, he was a man of the First
World War, 1914, and one day, he came to my place and said,

'Look, Dick, I want to go overseas!'

I told him, 'You can't go now, Marama – you're too old!'

'Well, you and I can change my birthday around . . .'

We dropped his age to thirty and he went away to fight. Noel and Mark Stirling
both joined up from our family and all of the Swintons, and my son George was
training as an officer at Massey. Quite a few young men from the Coast wanted to
go overseas but their parents opposed them, and when they arrived at my place,
I'd ring up their parents and say,

'Your son is here and he wants to join the Battalion.'

Some of the parents got angry, but others said to me,

'Oh well, if he has gone all that way to enlist, let him go!'

So then I'd sign him up.

I did all the recruiting work for our district and after a while the people at
Raukokore started to talk about it, saying,

'Look at Dick Stirling, he's a recruiting officer but *his* boys don't go to war!'

I thought, blow that, so I signed up my own papers to go into the Army and sent
them down to Wellington. The next thing Apirana rang me at home and said,

'You're *not* going overseas, Eruera – you are doing good work on the Coast and
I've written to Wellington telling them to strike you off the list. Who is going to
look after the interests of your mother if you go overseas? You stay home!'

My parents were feeling very lonely at that time because my elder brother
Taikorekore had just died, and we all missed him; he was the matamua, the first
born in our senior line, and he was going to be a great leader for the district. He
was far ahead of me in singing and hakas and he was a very good carpenter too,
and if he'd lived I know he would have been one of the best carvers in the country.
He was training with Te Wheoro Puni, Piri Munroe's uncle, in Rotorua, and Te
Wheoro told my uncle that Tai was going to the top in that type of work.

One day at home in Raukokore Tai got a very bad toothache and he went away

Soldiers leaving Te Kaha, 1944. *Alexander Turnbull Library*

to Opotiki to have some teeth extracted; when he came home in the bus it broke down at Waikawa, and Tai had to sit there all night in the freezing cold. He caught pneumonia and they took him to hospital, but he didn't survive. Tai would have been a great leader because he really knew how to pick up things – I have a book at home of all the songs he'd written down, and he could sing the whole lot too! Now and again I look through it, but there was nobody like Taikorekore for that kind of work, so I put the book away again.

I listened to Ngata because I knew the old people needed me now that Tai was dead, and I stayed; after that George and Waha decided to do something about all the gossip at home. George said to Waha, 'I'm going to join up!'

Waha didn't want his brother to go away to war so he told him,

'No, boy – you stay and go on with your studies, I'll go for us!'

When Waha came and talked to me about it I said,

'Look Waha, you are *not* going to fight, you're far too young!'

'But Dad, all those people are saying that our father is a recruiting officer, and none of his sons are going overseas . . .'

'That's my business, and you're not going – finish! I don't want to hear anything more about it.'

After that Waha started watching and listening whenever I was filling out the warrant papers for a new recruit, and one day when I went to the tangi of an uncle of ours, Pehikuru Awatere, Waha pinched some of my papers and signed them, and sent them off to the recruiting office in Opotiki. When the card came for him

Waha in uniform (second left). *Stirling family*

to go to Opotiki Waha got on the bus and went there, and while he was having his
medical examination the doctor asked him,

'How old are you, Waha?'

'Oh, I'm twenty-one.'

The doctor had a look at him and said, 'I don't think so – you're still a teenager!'

This doctor knew me quite well though, and he thought I had signed Waha's
papers so he let him through, and a few weeks later Waha got a notice in the mail
saying that he could join the Maori Battalion. When Lucy found the letter in the
pocket of Waha's pants she came to me,

'Dad, did you know that Waha has joined up with the forces?'

'No!'

I went to Waha and said, 'I told you that you are too young to go away to fight!'

'Well Dad, if you won't let me go, George will go – we had a talk about it and
that's that!'

Amiria asked me to stop Waha from going but I told her,

'No! Our son has done this for his brother, and we must let him go . . .'

That is the story of how Waha went away to war at the young age of fifteen, and
he was the youngest recruit to sign up in our district.

On the day that Wahawaha went to war my father said to me, 'Tell my moko to
come over and see me before he goes.'

Waha went to the old people's place and his grandfather blessed him, and gave
him a small pocket Testament that had been passed down in the Scottish line of his
family for years; and Waha put it in his pocket and carried it with him right

through the war, at drill, in battle, and even while he was asleep at night.

After Waha had been in the Territorials for a while he applied for the Air Force and trained as a gunner, and not long after that Apirana put out a call for all the Maori soldiers to join the last batch of the Maori Battalion going overseas. Waha went with them and he fought in some of the big battles around Italy, and when it came time for the Battle of Casino he went there with three of his mates from Raukokore. Early that morning as they were setting off to fight Waha took his grandfather's pocket Testament and put it in his breast pocket, and later on that day as the Battalion was advancing they were held up by some German machine-gunners, sitting on top of a hill. General Freyberg was in charge at the Battle of Casino and he told them,

'We have to clean up those machine-guns so the Battalion can move over the hill!'

Waha and his mates went up the hill with some others and they were fighting very hard, they knocked out one machine-gun and then another, and the next minute a machine-gun on the other side of them opened fire. Waha's mates were all shot and they dropped down, and a bullet hit Waha in the chest and knocked him to the floor. He lay there for a while unconscious, and when he came back to himself he felt inside his jacket and hah! There was no blood. He reached into his pocket and pulled out the little Testament and there was the bullet, shot right through its pages. Waha's mates were on the ground dying, and as he got up they looked at him and said,

'Give our last regards to our parents . . .'

Waha held on to that Bible for the rest of the war, and when he came home he showed it to me and said,

'Well, Dad, my tipuna's Testament saved my life!'

I looked at that little Bible and saw the bullet shot right into it and I thought, 'There you are – the power of Almighty God!'

During those war years a chap called Norman Perry was working on the Coast as a Welfare Officer; he was a mission man in the first part of it and he came to Omaio and joined in with the Delamares and the Maori people there, and then he moved around the Coast with Ngata. Norman Perry was a religious man and he did a lot of private work to help the people, and at the same time he listened to Ngata and studied what the old man said. Not long after the war had started Norman came to Raukokore for a meeting one time and Ngata was there, and Apirana stood up at the marae and announced,

'I think Norman Perry is the man to look after the canteen for the Maori Battalion!'

Ngata sent in his nomination and it was approved, and Norman went overseas to join the Battalion. From that day to this he has taken the work of the Maori to heart and he has done a lot of great things in the Maori world and the pakeha world; he started off a clothing factory in Opotiki and helped with the Dairy Factory at Te Kaha, he established another factory at Mangere with Maori workers and he arranged for a reservation of the sea between Cape Runaway and Maraenui, to stop the skindivers going there to take all the crayfish, and now Norman and John

Norman Perry. *New Zealand Herald*

Waititi together have started up the Whanau-a-Apanui Trust. Whatever Norman Perry does goes through, he is moving in Apirana's footsteps and he is just like Ngata, he works for the people and not for himself. Apirana used to tell us,

'Make a careful study of anything before you start it off, and if it's not right, don't touch it!'

That's exactly how Norman Perry is moving today.*

When his factory at Mangere was set up I went to the opening, and Norman said to me,

'Dick, I'd like you to welcome the Whakatohea party – there are ten buses from Whakatohea coming to the hui.'

When the Whakatohea people arrived I welcomed them to the marae at Mangere and then I turned round to Norman and said,

'Well, Norman, I still remember the day at Raukokore when Apirana nominated you to go overseas with the Battalion!'

*Norman Perry was knighted in 1976 for his services to the Maori people.

Norman stood up to reply, he said to me, 'Well, Dick, you make me feel . . . just about like crying. How many of the people alive today still remember what Apirana said? Very few! I think you and I are the only ones talking about the old man now, because we know! We listened to Apirana Ngata and we studied what he said . . .'

Right through the war the people on the Coast were very active, the womenfolk collected seafood and other Maori kai to send off to the Battalion, and at Raukokore we had a big association called the 'Young People's Club' that raised funds for our boys overseas. Amiria was the chairman of the YPC and they were very financial, they presented a gold watch to everybody who went away to fight and they did a lot of work on the maraes around the Bay.

Ngata was very keen on building new meeting-houses and getting the maraes in good order, and in 1940 he started to think about building a meeting-house in the centre of the Whanau-a-Apanui district so that the tribal people could get together to discuss their problems. The Ngati Porou people had Porourangi meeting-house at Waiomatatini, set up by the old people years back, and Apirana wanted a central marae for the Whanau-a-Apanui as well.

One day when I was at my mother's place the phone rang and it was Apirana. He said, 'I'm coming over tomorrow Eruera, I have some very special things that I want to discuss with your mother – you'd better be there too.'

'All right Api, I'll come down in the morning.'

The next day I went over early to the old people's place and Apirana arrived with one of his drivers at 10 o'clock, and after my mother made them a cup of tea she stood up to welcome Apirana, and I supported her welcome. Ngata returned our greetings, and then he put the question to Mum:

'I have been talking to the Whanau-a-Apanui people, Mihi, and they have agreed that a carved meeting-house should be built at Te Kaha, but I wanted to come and see you first, to hear what you have to say. What do you think about it?'

My mother stood up and said to Ngata,

'E Api, I am *not* going to have a carved meeting-house at Te Kaha, I'm against it! Here is my house, Hine Mahuru, and I want Hine Mahuru to be carved! Those people at Te Kaha have got no money, their lands are all finished, we are the only people getting money and I don't want it to go for a carved house at Te Kaha. I want Hine Mahuru to be carved, that is my wish!'

Apirana sat there quietly for a while, and then he said, 'Well, Mihi, you say that you don't want a carved house at Te Kaha, you want Hine Mahuru to be carved. All right then, this is my answer – if your ancestors had let you be tattooed we would give Hine Mahuru the moko too, and the carvers would come to Raukokore! But I remember my old people telling me that when the priest for the moko went right around the Coast, from Torere to Ngati Porou, tattooing women in Tokomaru, Tikitiki, Whangaparaoa, Omaio and Te Kaha, he refused to tattoo Mihi Kotukutuku! He said,

"No, the spirits on the other side won't let me tattoo this woman. As soon as I spill her blood I will die . . ."

'So now I'm telling you, Mihi, you must remain as you are. You are not tattooed and your house Hine Mahuru is not tattooed, and that is the wish of your ancestors – finish!'

In the end Mum gave in, she had to; she chipped in her money and the Whanau-a-Apanui raised £3,000, Ngati Porou raised another £3,000 and that's how Tukaki was organized as a meeting-house for the Whanau-a-Apanui people – all through the work of Ngata.

In the early years of the war Apirana got in touch with me and asked me to help with the Tuna-pahore case, an argument over land between Te Whanau-a-Apanui and Ngai Tai that had been going on for years. Tuna-pahore is a block of land between Torere and Maraenui, and Ngai Tai were claiming that it belonged to them privately but Te Whanau-a-Apanui said, 'No!'. Both tribes were entitled to the land. The case went through the Land Court and they appealed it and sent a petition to Parliament; the two tribes were fighting over this land for more than twenty years and there seemed to be no end to it. Every time the case went to the Maori Land Court there was no decision and at last in 1939 it ended up in the Court of Appeal. Ngata called a meeting of the Whanau-a-Apanui people and they decided to let Apirana handle their case, and gave him their story of the rights and genealogies of both peoples, but he wanted an outsider to present the whakapapas in the court. Apirana asked me to do that work because he knew that my grandfather was related to the Kingis, the chiefly family of Ngai Tai, and I understood the tribal relations between the two sides but I was not involved in the case, my family had no interests in that land.

The court sat in Wellington and I went there and Ngata summed up all the action, the work and the permanent occupation of the Tuna-pahore land, and he showed how the Ngai Tai ancestors had married into Te Whanau-a-Apanui. After that he asked me to give the main lines of the Ngai Tai genealogy, and I gave my line, the tahuhu of Te Whanau-a-Apanui, and I explained the background of relations between the two tribes. When the Court of Appeal looked at my whakapapas they agreed with Ngata's case, and Te Whanau-a-Apanui and Ngai Tai were given equal rights in the property. The boundary between Ngai Tai and Te Whanau-a-Apanui runs from a hill called Te Taumata-o-Apanui across to Te Maratu-o-Torere, and from Te Taumata-o-Apanui to Tihirau at Cape Runaway it is all Whanau-a-Apanui country, on the other side it is Ngai Tai land, and Tuna-pahore block was right on the boundary – that was the whole cause of the trouble. The court's decision ended that long period of tribal fighting over the Tuna-pahore block between Ngai Tai and Te Whanau-a-Apanui.

Round about 1941 I was just finishing milking on the farm one morning when a strange taxi drove up to our house. It wasn't Len Walker's taxi, this car was a different colour and I thought, 'Ha! That's strange . . .'

When I went back to the house the taxi-driver came up to me, he was a stranger and he asked me,

'Are you Eruera Stirling?'

'Yes . . .'

'I have an important letter for you from Judge Harvey.'

Judge Harvey was one of the main judges in the Maori Land Court in those

The opening of Tukaki at Te Kaha, 1944. *Alexander Turnbull Library*

days, so I opened the letter straight away and saw that Judge Harvey wanted me to come to Taupo and give evidence in a big case that was going on there. When I finished reading the letter the taxi-man said to me,

'Well, when you're ready I'm driving you to Taupo.'

'Yes.'

I packed my bag and we drove away from Raukokore, and when we got to Taupo I stayed the night in the hotel. Early the next morning I walked around, looking at the lake and everything, and at half-past nine I went to the courthouse.

When I walked inside Judge Harvey looked up at me and said, 'Oh! Hello, Dick, there you are!'

He told me that the case was being held to establish succession to £70,000 of trust funds from lands around Taupo, and all the claimants had been giving their whakapapa to show their right to get into this money. He said,

'I have all the articles of the claims by different people, and I want you to go through this file and check all the whakapapa; if you see any doubtful genealogies in there you just put a check and mark them, and I will deal with those when the court is sitting.'

I sat down in the court room and looked through this file of whakapapa, and then suddenly I struck it – I came across a genealogy claiming descent through the Tuwharetoa woman who married Apanui's son! I knew it was strange because when Apanui's son Hika-rukutai married Ohinekohi from Tuwharetoa, they lived together at Maraenui, and all of their issue were Whanau-a-Apanui people, the Koopus, and the Ngamokis, and others. I looked around the court and there were no Whanau-a-Apanui people present; all the other claimants were claiming traditionally under their own ancestor but this one went outside the area, and there was £70,000 at stake!

When Judge Harvey opened the court he said,

'The court has been sitting for days on this case and I have not been satisfied with some of the evidence. I have invited Eruera Stirling of Te Whanau-a-Apanui to come and examine the whakapapa that have been presented and now I want to ask him – Mr Stirling, have you looked right through the file?'

'Yes.'

'I would like you to tell the court what you have seen.'

'Well, I have put a check by one of the whakapapas in the file. All the other genealogies are quite right, but this claimant is illegal – he is claiming under an ancestor of the Whanau-a-Apanui people! If his case succeeds the Whanau-a-Apanui will get a big sum of money and that is not right – we have no rights to land in Tuwharetoa.'

As soon as I had finished the judge stood up and said, 'All of you kaumatua have heard Mr Stirling's evidence, he is from Te Whanau-a-Apanui himself and he says that his people have no interests in this trust. I now declare the claimant's case out of order.'

All the people looked at that fellow sitting in the court and he was really disgraced. The money was paid out to the right claimants, and when the court was over and we went to the meeting-house the old people told me,

'It's good you came along, Eruera, because we were all surprised when that bush-lawyer started claiming, but we didn't know how to shake him off!'

Apirana Ngata was thinking about the land all the time, and in 1943 he called the tribal peoples of Ngai Tai, Te Whanau-a-Apanui and Ngati Porou to a big hui at Waiomatatini. We came to the marae and were welcomed by Ngata, and in Porourangi meeting-house that night he laid down a programme of consolidation for putting all of the East Coast lands into good order. The delegates sat there listening to him and he told us how to work it out,

'You've got to have a deputation! There are hundreds of thousands of acres amongst you people; the only thing is to consolidate your interests and bring them to a better valuation. I want delegates from Ngai Tai, Te Kaha, Raukokore, Whangaparaoa, Hicks Bay, Te Araroa, Tikitiki and right through Ngati Porou to come with me to Parliament, and we will put our case before the Government and ask them to support a scheme to consolidate all the Maori lands on the East Coast . . .'

We listened to Ngata's explanations and we were satisfied, and then he told us,

'In about October I will call you people together again, we'll have a final meeting before we go.'

So we did. We all went back to Waiomatatini and Ngata selected the delegates for the deputation, and after that meeting Apirana took me aside and said,

'There is one thing the Government will ask me – who is going to pay for the delegation and all the expenses of consolidation? I want to tell them that the Incorporation will pay for it, and from the Whanau-a-Apanui area we'll have to depend on you people in Tawaroa – do you think your mother will agree?'

Mihi Kotukutuku with J. S. W. ('Swan') Neilson, who leased Tawaroa. *Te Kaha Carving Centre, courtesy Roka Paora*

'Yes! Wherever you move, Api, my mother is always behind you.'

That was the trouble with our district in those years, all the lease-hold blocks from Torere to Hicks Bay went bung in the depression;† the lessees walked out of Maungaroa, Waikawa, Te Kaha and Omaio and Maraenui and the incorporations all went out of existence. Only Tawaroa Incorporation was left, because our stations were leased to good sheep-farmers who stayed with the land – Dr Scott of Gisborne had Orete, Barker and Neilson of Gisborne had Tawaroa, Pohueroro was leased to the Kemps, and Matangareka and Whangaparaoa 3B to the Sherratts; and the main shareholders in Tawaroa were the Waititis, the Browns, the Swintons and my mother. That's why Apirana said to me,

'I'm depending on Tawaroa, Eruera, because the rest of your Whanau-a-Apanui people have got nothing.'

Apirana arranged everything with Tiweka Anaru, the Registrar of the Maori Land Court, and on the 25th October of that year we all went to Waiomatatini. We stayed the night in Porourangi meeting-house and then moved on to Wellington, and when we arrived there Apirana said to us,

'Oh well, I think we'd better separate now.'

So Te Whanau-a-Apanui slept that night at the Barrett Hotel and Ngati Porou stayed at the International, and early the next morning the old man rang us and said,

'As soon as you people have finished your breakfast, come over to join us at the International.'

We went to the International Hotel at about 9 o'clock and Apirana welcomed us, he was standing there and he just put up his hand and the barman opened the bar! Ngata told us,

'Come on – have a little drink before we go, a shandy or whatever you want . . . we have to be in the House at 10 o'clock.'

We had our drink and everything and then we walked to Parliament, and when we arrived there the man looking after the House was standing by the door, holding the key. He said to us,

'All hats off please!'

We took off our hats and went inside and stood there waiting for Apirana; and after a while my mate Tane from Te Kaha said to me,

'There is the old man coming!'

We saw Apirana coming and he walked right through the door without interference, wearing his hat and smoking his pipe! Tane called out,

'Ah, kia ora ra e Api – Hello, Api!'

Apirana greeted us, and then Tane asked him,

'Well, it's a funny thing, when we came in here the man in charge of the door ordered us to take our hats off – and now we want to know, Api, why are you still wearing yours?'

The old man laughed and told us, 'Yes, there are only three of us now who have gone through thirty years of Parliament or more, we're allowed to come into this House with our hats on and everything!'

† Probably the 1920–21 slump in wool prices (Butterworth, *The Politics of Adaptation*, p. 95).

The Delegation for the Eastern Maori Consolidation Scheme on the steps of Parliament, 1943. Back row, second to the left: Eruera Stirling; front row, centre: Sir Apirana Ngata, Mrs H. Ngata. *Stirling family*

He put his hand into his pocket and pulled out a medal, 'The Queen gives a medal for long service, and there are three of us in there – we can walk into Parliament with a smoke and all that, but only us!'

'Ne? Hika ma!'

When we went in to the House the Prime Minister came and sat in his seat, and Ngata sat down in his seat, and after a while Peter Fraser stood and welcomed our delegation. Ngata replied to the welcome, then he passed around copies of his programme of consolidation to all members of the House and gave a speech explaining everything in the pamphlet, and in less than ten minutes the thing was finished! The Speaker said,

'I think everything is in order . . . all the articles of Ngata's work asking the Government to approve this Consolidation Scheme now lie before you; if there are any comments or objections, well, this is the time!'

He waited for a moment and nobody spoke, so then he said, 'I will now put this bill to the vote – all the ayes say "aye" and the noes say "no".'

He looked around, and the ayes had it!

When everything was settled the Prime Minister stood up and said, 'This Consolidation Scheme has come before Parliament and it has been accepted by the members of this House. Now I want to ask each of the delegates in turn if they are in favour of this scheme – please raise your right hand. Maraenui?'

'Yes.'

'Torere?'

'Yes.'

'Te Kaha?'

'Yes.'

'Raukokore?'

I raised my hand and said, 'Yes!'

He went right through the list and everybody agreed, then Mr Fraser said, 'The Consolidation Scheme is unanimously carried!'

Well, as soon as the consolidation was finished, Ngata borrowed money on 250,000 acres of East Coast lands and he bought out the East Coast Commission. At that time the Commission controlled mortgages on a lot of blocks on the Coast and Wi Pere and some of the Government people had shares in it, but Ngata pushed them right out, he told them,

'You people get out of it! Give the Maori land back – *we* will control our incorporations from now on, not you!'

That was one of the big things Ngata did, and now the Mangatu Incorporation belongs to the Maori people and Henry Ngata is its accountant. The Consolidation Scheme did a lot of good work at home, it saved all that East Coast land and it helped a lot of elderly people to exchange their interests for a better valuation.‡

Not long after the Consolidation Scheme went through Parliament it came time for another General Election, and that year Jack Ormond stood against Apirana as the Labour candidate for Eastern Maori. He was a well organized man, and by then the Ratana movement was very strong on the Coast and the people were a bit jealous of Ngata. Oliver Goldsmith and Arnold Reedy called a big meeting of the Labour Party at Tuparoa just before the Election and I decided to go; I was campaigning for Apirana but I knew they couldn't kick me out, because my mother and my uncle gave the section for that marae at Tuparoa. The evening before I left for the meeting I went to see my mother and she asked me,

'Kei te haere koe ki whea, Eruera? Where are you going to?'

'Oh, I'm going to the big meeting of the Labour people at Tuparoa.'

My mother looked at me, and then she said,

'Last night I dreamt that I was sweeping all the old dust from my house to get ready for a manuhiri coming in.'

She sat down and started to cry! I said to her,

'Oh Mum, hai aha noa i tangi ai? Why are you crying?'

My mother told me, 'Now that you have said where you're going, I know . . . that's it, my dream was for Apirana! He's going to lose his seat, your tipuna Apirana will not get back in the House, there's a new man coming in!'

Well, the next day when I went to Ruatorea the people asked me,

'Are you going to the meeting at Tuparoa, Dick?'

‡ For an account of the East Coast Commission and incorporations on the Coast, see 'Land under Maori Management', *Te Ao Hou* Vol. 2, No. 4 (1954) pp. 6-9, and *Te Ao Hou* Vol. 3, No. 3 (1955), pp. 6-10.

I said, 'Nothing is going to stop me from going there – that's *my* marae!'

I went to the marae at Tuparoa and hundreds of people were there, and when Arnold Reedy stood up to welcome the crowd he turned to me and said,

'Well, Eruera, we welcome you to your marae and to the ancestral house, Ruataupare. No one can refuse you entry here, so we give you greetings; and now we will pass on to the business of the gathering . . .'

The conference went ahead and organized Jack Ormond as a candidate to stand against Ngata. Afterwards I went to see Apirana and said,

'Look Api, I think we should go campaigning amongst the Ratana people at Tuparoa, Reporua and right round, because otherwise something is going to happen.'

He told me, 'No, it's all right – I'll be all right.'

The day of the voting in that election§ was one of the saddest occasions of Apirana Ngata's political career. Some of the Ratana people at Waipiro Bay, Tuparoa and Te Araroa turned against him and they voted for Jack Ormond, and Ngata was beaten by 246 votes! We all went to Uepohatu marae afterwards to talk about it, and Apirana was very hurt, he said straight out,

'Na toku iwi ano ahau i patu! It was my own people who beat me!'

Well, after our hui at Uepohatu that night Ngata called me and said, 'Eruera, I want you to stay behind – I've got something here for you.'

The others went out and Ngata shut the door, then he pulled over his bag and opened it, and showed me some big books all set together.

'You take these home, Eruera – they are the Hansards from all my years in the House, and I don't want you to show them to anybody else, they're just for your own use. When the day comes that you are in doubt about land business or something like that, open them up and have a look – they will give you an idea . . .'

When I came out of Uepohatu I was carrying those Hansards in my bag and the others were really aching to know why Ngata had kept me back. Peta Awatere wanted to look in my bag but I said to him,

'No – that's private! The old man told me not to show this to anybody else.'

Apirana's Hansards have been in my keeping ever since that day, and they helped me to go through my farming work, incorporations and Maori Land Court business in North Auckland, Whanganui, and the other districts of New Zealand. I think Ngata picked me to hold his records because I worked with him for twenty-four years and we were really close; we went through the same channels of schooling with our old people.

In 1945 the Maori Welfare Act was passed, and the idea was to set up tribal committees in all the different districts, to look after the maraes and the welfare of the people. Ngata was disappointed with Ngati Porou because they were not really mastering the scheme, and in the end he came to me and said,

'Will you start a tribal committee in your area, Eruera?'

'Yes, I'll do that, Api.'

I called a meeting and no people turned up, so then I went around and talked to

§Apirana Ngata was defeated for the Eastern Maori seat in the 1943 election.

Moana Waititi, Dick Waititi, Sid Waititi and Hariata Turei about it and they were interested, but they were the only ones. We started off by holding a sale at Wairuru, I had one big fat beast so I killed it and sold the meat at the marae, and all the people came to have a feed. We raised £80 that day at Raukokore, then Moana Waititi stood up and announced that there would be a sale the next week at Maraenui School, and another a few weeks later at Whangaparaoa. We formed our tribal committee and called it 'Tihirau', and I was elected Chairman. We kept on with our fund-raising and in the finish we raised over £700.

Later that year Apirana called a meeting of the tribal executive at Te Araroa and I went there on Len Walker's taxi. A lot of people came to the meeting from Ngati Porou but I was the only tribal committee delegate from the Whanau-a-Apanui, because no other tribal committees had been formed in our district at that time.

Ngata was the chairman of the executive and Charlie Goldsmith was the secretary, and we decided to call the executive 'Horouta', for the whole of the Tai Rawhiti area. When it came to the time for discussing business, Apirana announced that the Tihirau Tribal Committee had been formed in the Whanau-a-Apanui district and had raised £700, and the Government had set aside funds for the committee's expenses. Then he told us that the Government had awarded us a pound-for-pound subsidy of £700 for the maraes in our area, and we were really thrilled! Afterwards Apirana asked me,

'Do you have any expenses for this meeting, Eruera?'

'Well, I came with Len Walker on the taxi.'

'All right, the executive will pay your costs.'

Then my mate Tane Tukaki from Te Kaha stood up and asked, 'What about *our* expenses, e Api?'

'Well, Tane, you people don't have a tribal committee! That's the beauty of the tribal committee, you get your expenses paid and the Government pays a pound-for-pound subsidy on any funds you raise for your marae . . .'

The people had a hang of a big shock about it, and after that they formed their tribal committees right around the Coast and all over the Bay of Plenty. Our committee used the government subsidy to renovate our meeting-houses at Raukokore and Cape Runaway and we started to put all the Whanau-a-Apanui maraes in good order.

Later that year the news came that our soldiers had won the victory in the Second World War, and the boys of the Maori Battalion were coming home. Our son Waha had been in the Army for four years but he was still all right, and I was so happy about it that I composed a song for his return. He was only nineteen when he came back from the War after four years of military service:

> Nga rongo o te toa e hau mai nei!
> Hapaitia te Matua i te rangi
> Hei karauna i te wikitoria o te ao
> E tama i te riri mo te ao
> Na Ingarangi i awhina ra
> Na Ruhia i tukituki atu e
> Taku whakataetae ki te Tiamana!

E tama i te riri mo te ao
Tenei ka huri nei ki te riri mo te ao
Haere ra, haere ra e tama ma
Na Amerika i awhina mai
Na Ruhia i tukituki atu e
Taku whakataetae ki te Tiamana!
E tama i te riri mo te ao
Ngaro noa ra nga mahara
Ki te tangi mo koutou kua wehea nei
Whakarongo ake ra e tama
Kua mau ra te Wikitoria!
Ki te kaha o te toa!
Ko te mahi Ingarangi!
Amerika me Ruhia e!
Ki te pakanga ki te Tiamana e
I tenei ra kua hinga te Tiamana e!
Tenei ka huri nei ki te riri mo te ao!
Haere ra, haere ra e tama ma!

The people started planning for the return of the Battalion and they arranged that when Colonel Peta Awatere came home there would be a big day at the marae at Mangahanea; as the time drew near everybody knew the timetable of Peta's arrival at Gisborne and his travel through to Ruatorea and quite a few people from Te Whanau-a-Apanui went to Mangahanea marae. There was a big mob from Omaio, Te Kaha and right around, and when we arrived at the marae it was *packed* out – Waikato people were there, Tuhoe, Te Arawa, Ngati Kahungunu, Ngati Porou, Te Whanau-a-Apanui and even a few from Taranaki, the North and the South – it was a really big turn-out! The next day Peta arrived at the marae with some of his officers, and there was a tangi in front of the meeting-house for all the boys who had died in the war. Speakers from each area stood to welcome Awatere and I could see that Peta was crying, and then when he stood to give his reply he caught sight of his cousins, four big men standing there who didn't go overseas to fight. All of a sudden Peta went wild, he pulled his coat off and his hat went flying and he *went* for his cousins, he told them,

'*Why* didn't you come and help us? My young brother died for the sake of you beggars!'

He called those chaps all sorts and he started moving across the marae towards them, he was just about going to bounce them out of it when one of his aunties called out to me,

'Eruera, you go and stop your taina! Stop him now!'

I stood up on the marae and called out to Peta,

'Kati, you've said enough! Leave them alone, Peta!'

He looked at me and then he went back; he just couldn't stop thinking about all those boys in the Battalion who had died overseas, that was what made him so wild.

That night when we went into the meeting-house, after the speeches Apirana stood up and said,

'The Ministry of Defence has arranged to send a car to Mangahanea tomorrow and Colonel Awatere and I will be leaving on a tour of all the maraes from Northland to the South Island, so that all the tribes may mourn their dead.'

The next morning, though, Apirana had an urgent phone call from Peter Fraser, asking him to come straight back to Wellington for a discussion about Maori lands, so he came to me and said,

'Well, Eruera, I want you to take my place on their trip, and go with Awatere to all the maraes of the North and South Island.'

Apirana told me I could select my own man to travel with us, and I asked Kahu Puha from the Whanau-a-Apanui to come on the trip – he was only a little man but he was a great leader of haka, and when he stood on the marae he always made the crowd laugh, he was really comical! Later that day the Ministry of Defence car arrived at the marae and Peta, Kahu Puha and I climbed in and started our journey right round the country. First of all we visited the maraes of the East Coast and we had a great reception everywhere we went, then we travelled on to Whakatane, Ruatoki, Rotorua and Tauranga, and all the maraes up North. When we got to Te Kao we stayed there for a while and the people brought us beautiful kai moana, crayfish and everything else, and on our second day there one of the elders stood up and said,

'Well, Awatere, take your dead to Te Rerenga Wairua, the leaping-place of the spirits; and while you're there look out to sea – if you see a whale rising that's a good sign, it means that your ancestor is with you!'

Early the next morning we travelled along a rough track right out to the Cape Reinga lighthouse and we could see the beautiful beach below, but when we got there the lighthouse keeper wouldn't let us through. Peta got really wild with him and said,

'Look here, you can't stop us, that's a Maori place down there – I'm going through! I've just come back from the war so you'd better not get in my way!'

The lighthouse keeper let us pass and while I was standing on the cliff I saw a big whale splashing and diving out at sea. He dived once, twice, and then I called out to Peta,

'Hey! Peta – look!'

He looked out to sea and saw the big whale dive for the third time, and then it came to the surface and blew a spout of water high into the air. I said to him,

'Do you remember what the old man said to us at Te Kao? That must be your ancestor greeting you!'

Peta was descended from Amiria's grandfather Wiremu Parata, a well-known man from North, and he had ancestral links to the area. He started to walk down the cliff path to the beach with Kahu and as he went he called out to me,

'Come on, Dick!'

'No, I'm not going down!'

'Why not?'

I could feel the hair *pulling* on my head like that, and I told Peta,

'My ancestor is telling me, "You stay here!" '

I had an idea that it was no good for my mate Kahu to go down there to Spirits Bay because he had no connections with the North, so I called out to him,

'Hey! Kahu – come back!'

Peta took no notice though, he just said 'Oh, come on, Kahu, let's go . . .'

They walked right down the path and looked at that beautiful beach; there was a blow-hole in the rocks that sent the sea roaring up to the sky in a spout, and Peta did a haka on the beach at Spirits Bay with the sea rising and falling around him.

After we left Spirits Bay we travelled on to Kaitaia, Panguru and Whangarei, and when we had visited all the main maraes of Northland we went to Auckland and there was a big reception for Peta in the Town Hall. The Mayor stood up to welcome Colonel Arapeta Awatere, and after his welcome there were 160 people all dressed up on the stage to do the singing. Beautiful!

From Auckland we went on to Ngaruawahia in the Waikato but as we came onto Turangawaewae marae Peta noticed three old women with moko standing in front of Mahinarangi meeting-house, one on the left, one on the right and one in the middle. He turned to me and whispered,

'Oh-h Eruera, something is wrong, there's trouble somewhere. Watch out!'

We went through the customary ceremony of welcome, but when it came time for Peta's speech he *threw* off his coat and started jumping everywhere on the marae, using all these different chants and saying,

'Why are you doing this to us? After all that we've been through in the war, isn't that enough?'

Peta told me later that if you see three old women standing in front of the meeting-house like that it is not a good sign, it means they are preparing a chant of witchcraft for you; he realized something must have come into the minds of those people, some trouble to do with the mixture of tribes in the war or an old ancestral grudge – that was why he started chanting and asked them,

'What have we done to hurt you?'

As soon as Te Puea heard Awatere talking like that she knew what had happened and she got wild with her people, she stood up and *growled* at them and she sent them all away! After that she took Peta and I to the dining-hall to have kai and she was very good to us, but I was glad that Peta knew all those chants . . .

After our visit to Ngaruawahia I went home to look after the farm, and Amiria and Peta and the others completed the job, they went on to Wellington and even to the South Island. At the end of their journey Kahu Puha had some business to do in Gisborne so he came straight back on a taxi from Wellington, and as they were driving over the Wharerata hills the taxi went over the edge. The taxi-driver wasn't hurt and the car wasn't badly damaged, but when they pulled Kahu out he was dead.

They brought him home to Raukokore and we had a big tangi at the marae, and I was very sorry for my mate Kahu. I kept on thinking about that day in Spirits Bay . . .

Within a few months all the soldiers were home from overseas, and that was the end of the Maori people joining up in that big fight against Hitler, in the Second World War.

George Stirling. *Stirling family*

CHAPTER EIGHT
LEAVING THE COAST

At the beginning of the war our son George was a high school boy at St. Stephen's College in Bombay and he won all the records there, he was the Head Prefect and Senior Athletics Champion and Captain of the First XV. When the war had been going for a while they had to close St. Stephen's down and they sent some of the boys to Paerata, and after his time at Paerata George had a year at Feilding Agricultural College. He won the Practical Fieldwork Cup at Feilding and he got through all his subjects, he had a real talent for farming! While George was still at Feilding Apirana came home one day and said to me,

'That boy of yours is going to be one of New Zealand's top farming leaders! We've never had a young man like him before, he gets first class honours everywhere he goes. I've got a place all ready for George, but first he has to go through the diploma course at Massey University . . .'

'But what about the war, Api? George has told me he wants to go away and fight.'

'Look here, Eruera, don't let that boy go! We need somebody like him to help us look after the land. He is one of the first Maoris to learn all the modern ways of farming, and I don't want him killed overseas!'

'All right, Api, if that's what you think.'

So George went on to Massey University and he did very well there, he was Captain of the Massey 1st XV and he got his Diploma of Agriculture, no trouble. Some time in 1945 Dr Barnicoat at Massey wrote to us saying that he and George were going to Australia to do some research, and when Ngata heard about that he rang me up and said,

'No! Stop him. Once he goes off to Australia to do research, he'll never come back to New Zealand!'

'Well, Api, what am I going to tell him? He's set his heart on going away.'

'Tell him that there's a job waiting for him at Ruakura. I want George to give his people just one year, helping to train the returned soldiers to go on to the land – we need a Maori supervisor who can speak the language, someone who knows farming from the bottom to the top, and George is the only man we've got! After that he's free to go – tell him that, Eruera.'

'All right . . .'

Well, when I told George about it, I've never seen that boy so upset! He was all ready to move off to Australia and everything was coming in his life, but we stopped him and he stayed, and he took the job at Ruakura.

While he was working at Ruakura in 1946, he went out one afternoon on his motorbike with one of his mates, and when they came back that night it was very foggy and a truck was parked on the wrong side of the road by a bridge – they didn't see it. There was no light on the trailer of the truck and the motorbike went

under, and George was thrown. He was killed! Well, that was that. George was the
first and only one, and he was getting on top of the world in all his work, but he lost
his life in that accident, and that was the end of it –finish!

There was a big tangi at Wairuru marae for our son, and Dr McMeekan the
Head of Massey College sent us a telegram asking us to hold the burial until he
could get back from England. He flew to New Zealand and came straight to the
marae with Apirana. Ngata was crying when he came on to the marae and he was
really upset, he stood there with Dr McMeekan and then Dr McMeekan put his
hands out like that and burst into tears! The two of them stood there, Ngata and
Dr McMeekan, both crying, and then Ngata turned to me and said,

'Well, Eruera, I am looking at you and I – we are the cause of this! We interfered
with his work and we cut across the pathway that had already been prepared! Yes,
you and I are the cause – no taua te he!'

I looked back at Api and I felt the same too. I felt the same! I was really sorry for
intercepting my son's life. Later Dr McMeekan stood on the marae and told us,

'George was one of the best young men I have ever met. If only he had lived,
he'd have gone to the top of farming work, because he had all the talents!'

And I thought, my son, moumou ra koe, aue . . . You are lost, alas . . . And one
of our relations, George Grace, composed a lament at the tangi for our son:

> Nga iwi karanga ra
> *Call, the tribes!*
> Mo taku mate, taukuri e
> *For my dead, alas*
> Hinga mai nei i runga o
> *Fallen upon*
> Nga mania i Hamutana
> *The plains of Hamilton*
> Toro atu aku ringa
> *I throw out my hands*
> Hei piriti mai ki ahau
> *A bridge for you to come to me*
> Aue! Hori e!
> *Alas! George,*
> Moumou ra koe, i tenei ra
> *You are wasted, this day.*
> Hori e, e tama e
> *George, child,*
> Hoki kino mai ra ki ahau
> *This is a bad home-coming*
> Ki te kore koe i Hamutana
> *If you hadn't gone to Hamilton*
> Ara kei Te Reinga
> *You would not now be dead*
> Toro atu aku ringa
> *I throw out my hands*

Hei piriti mai ki ahau
A bridge for you to come to me
Aue! Hori e!
Alas! George
Moumou ra koe, i tenei ra
You are wasted, this day.*

The death of our son George made a big difference to our lives. We kept thinking about it and Mum went down to the grave every day, the whole family was worried about it and even the people were worried, the pressure got worse and worse and in the finish Amiria and I both got very sick. The doctor in Opotiki told us,

'It's time for you two to get out of here, the place keeps reminding you of your son and if you stay on much longer, your days will be numbered!'

We had a talk about it and we decided to leave the farm and go to Auckland. It took quite a while to settle everything about the property and Amiria went up to Auckland before me, her idea was to get a job and find a place for the family to live. She came to Auckland and got a job cleaning up the Post Office, then she found a flat in Vincent Street, it was a nice flat on the bottom floor with a big living-room and bedrooms and everything, very cheap; the people in the top flat were Samoans and they were good to her. When Amiria had been living in Vincent Street for a while, Lucy and Lilly and Kiwa came to join her and then Kepa and young George, Lucy got a job at Hellaby's and all the other children went to school in Auckland to get a good education.

One day one of her pakeha friends at the Post Office told Amiria about a place in Hobson Street that used to be a pub, and Mum took up the lease of this place and started to run it as a boarding-house. We had a sitting-room and bedrooms all to ourselves and quite a few Maori boarders came to rent the other rooms, but after a while they started to play up with her. They'd spend all their money in the hotel and run away without paying board. After that one of Amiria's friends told her,

'You should get Dalmatian people in your boarding-house, Amy, they're very reliable – you'll find that they're better than all those young people!'

Mum put her advertisement in the paper and three Dalmatian brothers came and took rooms in the place and some of their friends joined them afterwards, they were very nice people and they stayed with Mum for years. By then Lily and Kiwa were working in the Post Office and I was still on the farm trying to sort out all the arrangements, but every now and then I came up to Auckland to stay with my family.

In 1950, the old man Apirana died. He stood for Parliament again and was defeated, and soon after the election he fell sick. In the end they had to send for the doctor and Mere Karaka sent Mum a telegram asking us to come to see him because the doctor told her he would have to shut out all visitors very soon. Mum and I, the Waititi family and Mrs Turei set off to Waiomatatini by bus and when Mere Karaka heard we were on our way she told Api,

---

*This song is adapted from one composed by Tuini Ngawai.

'Kai te haramai a Mihi Kotukutuku – Mihi is coming.'
He opened his eyes and asked her, 'A whea ka tae mai? When?'
'Today.'
He sat up in his bed and he was happy. When we arrived we went straight up to
Api's room and he gave us a big welcome and then he said to Mum,
'E Mihi, I am proud you've come. When I am gone I want you to sit at the head of
my coffin and sing all the old laments, and then I know I'll have a proper tangi!...'
He asked me to say a prayer and we had a short service together, then Api sang
an old Whanau-a-Apanui song, 'Angiangi hau raro whakaeke mai ra', that nobody
else could remember; we shook hands with him and said goodbye, and we all went
back home to Raukokore. The day after that we heard that Apirana had died.
The news of Ngata's death went all over the island, and buses from Kaitaia,
Hastings, Whanganui, Palmerston North, Taranaki, Waikato, Te Arawa, and the
South Island came to Waiomatatini and parked outside the marae. When Te
Whanau-a-Apanui arrived there Renata Ngata, Apirana's brother, came out to us
and said,
'Whanau-a-Apanui, wait here for a while, you can't get through – look at the
people! The place is overflowing!'
There were buses and cars and tents everywhere, the whole of New Zealand was
there and it was one of the biggest tangis I have ever seen, but Mum didn't listen to
him. She stepped out in front of our crowd, calling and crying to Apirana and
singing her chants, and some of the Whanau-a-Apanui men said to Renata,
'No, the people had better make room for us. Give us room!'
When the people on the marae heard my mother chanting those very, very old
songs of the Ngati Porou people all the women started to cry, and as Mum came on
to the marae, singing as she moved, the crowd stepped aside and made way for us.
Mum walked right up to the head of Apirana's coffin, chanting her laments for
him, and all the Ngati Porou women from Waipiro Bay and Te Araroa, the
Marakis and the Peperes stood behind her, and they started to sing. They sang
Apirana's favourite waiata 'Kereruhuahua':

> E hika ma e! I hoki mai au
> *Friends! I have come back*
> I Kereruhuahua
> *From Kereruhuahua*
> Noho tupuhi ana ko au anake
> *I sit here, wasting away*
> I te tamaiti mate
> *For my child is dead.*
> Me te tai hokohoko ki te awa
> *Like the tide rising and falling*
> I Tirau, e i
> *In Tirau river*
> Tangi whakaroro ana ki
> *My wild weeping goes towards*
> Te Houhangapa
> *Te Houhangapa*

The tangi of Sir Apirana Ngata at Porourangi meeting-house, Waiomatatini. *Auckland Weekly News, 1 August 1950*

Tera ia taku mea kei te tau
There is my child, resting
O te marino, e
In a peaceful place
Kei ona whakawiringa i roto
His turbulent spirit
I Te Apiti
In Te Apiti
E taututetute ana, kia puta ia
Strives and struggles
Ki waho ra e i
To get out
Ki te kai tiotio i tiria
To the sea eggs heaped
Ki te mapou
On the Mapou wood
Tera te Rerenga
There the Rerenga
Whakatarawai ana e i
Appears on the horizon
Whakaangi mai ra, e tama
Fly, son

The buses lined up at the unveiling of Sir Apirana's tombstone, 1952. *Alexander Turnbull Library*

> Me he manu
> *Like a bird,*
> Mairatia iho te waha
> *Leave*
> Kai rongorongo e
> *The sound of your voice in the air*
> Hei whakaoho po i ahau
> *To comfort my wakeful nights*
> Ki te whare ra
> *In that house*

The tears of the people came falling down like rain and the whole crowd stood there and wept. That was one of the biggest laments given to Ngata at his tangi on Waiomatatini marae.

Not long after Apirana's tangi I signed all the papers leasing my farm to Percy Barker's sister, and I went up to Auckland to live with my family. That was the end of our life in the Bay of Plenty.

In 1976 when the centennial of the Waiomatatini Maori School was celebrated, the thoughts of all the people at home turned back to Apirana Ngata. Just before the hui Amiria fell sick with rheumatic arthritis and I couldn't go back to pay my last tribute to Api, and my mind was so overcome with memories of all the meetings we had together: Prince of Wales Rotorua 1919, Duke of York Rotorua 1927, Waitangi Meeting-house 1933 and the Te Aute College Jubilee in 1930, that I went into my room and sat down and wrote this memorial to my tipuna papa Apirana:

> Now the Day is over night is
> Drawing nigh, Shadows of the
> evening steal across the skies
> Memories of the Scenes of the Past, The
> memories of old my Dreams have
> warned me, To think Deeply, there with-
> in the House lays Mrs Amiria Manutahi
> Highly strung by the atmosphere
> of Rheumatic Arthritis, that prevented her from
> Joining me in moving Across the
> Pathway of our family History back
> in the Lands of our forefathers . . . The Great
> Centennial of the Waiomatatini Maori School
> brings Back memories of the
> Scenes of the Past, the childhood
> Days of our Great Leader Sir
> Apirana Turupa Ngata, at
> this Waiomatatini School he
> Loved and Directed by the masterly
> teachings of the High Priest of
> the Tapere-nui-a-Whatonga Whare
> Wananga: The Last of the men of
> Te Whare Wananga Bestowed
> all the Secrets of Lore on
> to him, and from the school
>
> He inherited it into his mind
> as Gifted of the Last Mana of the
> great School of Learning, no more
> to be used by the Generations
> after him, His belief in his
> Maori School of Learning the
> Whare Wananga, has assisted him in his
> movement from Waiomatatini
> Maori School to the Otago University
> College, His Humble nest Brought him
> up to the Top of His Education and
> graduated, the first Maori to take
> the High Honours Master of Arts and LLB,

Bachelor of Laws and Dr Literature, I have
been with Apirana Ngata in
all his Life work, I looked after
his Campaigning work on Elections
in the Whanau Apanui, Tuhoe, Ngai Tai
and I have spent the time to visit him,
at Waiomatatini and in 1927, at His
Home, He gave me the first copy of
His Nga Moteatea Copy in Maori
He later translated into English, and
these are the speeches that I
have long to Recall the memory of
one of New Zealand's greatest
statesmen. To Day Hikurangi
Mountain stands without

a Leader to take the Place of Sir
Apirana Ngata, there stand the
four Mountains Hikurangi
and His younger Brothers Whanokao,
Aorangi, Wharekia, Taitai, Standing
all quiet without a Leader in the
atmosphere of Laws to Provide
Great Assistance to the Tribes that
livest Beneath these mountains
when, the Long wide clouds flow
above the Mountain and Silently
Held amidst the air, there falls the
White Snow on the Mountain, the
Early Dawn of the Great Sun
Tama-nui-te-ra cause the Tears
of Love to flow from the
Mountain, and fall far and
near on the plains of Tapuwaeroa,
Kainanga, Waiapu Valley
People, the Tribes called Toi
te ruku-ruku a te Rangitawaea
i ana Rinena: i tenei Ra kua
Ngaro nga tangata
Whakaririka mamau ki nga
Taonga Whakaepaepa o roto i nga

Whare korero o te Whare Wananga o Roto
i Tapere-nui-a-Whatonga, nga kohu
e tatao mai ra i runga o Te Puaha
nui, kei te karanga mai a Tama–

nui-te-ra i te Pua-ao-tanga mai o te ra,
e koro, ma Putaanga whakaaria
mai Ra To Reo Pohiri i te mauri
ara ki roto i nga marae e Tu
Mokemoke mai ra i Te Tai Rawhiti,
Porourangi, Rongomaianiwaniwa
Rauru-nui-a-Toi koutou ko moko –
puna katoa e tu mai ra i nga
marae, kua huri katoa ki nga
Tipuna matua Te Iwinui i tua
o Paerau Tawhiti Pamamao Te
Hono ki Wairua, the Migration
of the Ancestors now are Returning
Spiritually to the Lands of far off
Hawaiki Pamamao, beyond The
Great Sea of Te Moana-nui-a-kiwa, no more to
Return again, forever more
we Mourn the loss of our Great
Leader, Sir Apirana Nohopari Turupa
Ngata.

by Eruera Kawahia Whakatane Stirling, 1978.

I will never forget Apirana, he was the best man I have known.

Ta Apirana Turupa Ngata meeting-house, East Coast. *Hirini Mead, 1970*

CHAPTER NINE
AUCKLAND

When I first came to Auckland I felt lost, but as time went on I got used to the run
of staying in the city. After I had leased the farm to the Barkers, Amiria and I
decided to find a place of our own in Auckland, and one day she saw an
advertisement in the paper for a home in Herne Bay. Mum went straight to Herne
Bay to look at this place and she took a fancy to it, it was a neat little house right by
the harbour, so she went to the real estate office and said to the man,
  'I would like to buy this house – No.1 Mercer Road, Herne Bay.'
  'What is your name, please?'
  'Mrs Stirling – Amiria Stirling.'
  'Oh Mrs Stirling . . . I'm sorry . . . it's sold!'
  Mum was sorry to miss that house and she went away, but the next day when she
looked at the paper the advertisement was still there, No.1 Mercer Road, Herne
Bay is for sale. She rang up the man at the real estate office and said,
  'I would still like to buy that house in Mercer Road, Herne Bay!'
  'Who is this speaking?'
  'Mrs Stirling – I came in to see you yesterday . . .'
  'Oh Mrs Stirling, there must be some mistake, the house has gone, it's been sold!'
  Mum looked at the paper the next night and the advertisement was still there, so
then she knew that it wasn't true, the real estate agent was telling her a lie. He
looked at her and saw that she was Maori, and he told her the place was sold. When
Amiria went to work at the Post Office the next day she was so wild about it that she
told Mr Walker the supervisor the whole story. Mr Walker was a very nice man and
he said,
  'Never mind, Mrs Stirling, I tell you what – the next time that advertisement
comes up, you let me know!'
  That night, sure enough, the advertisement appeared in the paper again, and
Mum got in touch with Mr Walker and he rang the real estate office.
  'This is Mr Walker, Supervisor of the Central Post Office – I want to purchase 1
Mercer Road, Herne Bay, for a member of my staff.'
  'Oh yes, Mr Walker.'
  They made all the arrangements and then the agent asked him,
  'May we have the name of your client?'
  'Mrs Stirling – Amiria Stirling!'
  Well, that shut the man up, he didn't say another word! We had to pay a deposit
of £500 on the house so I transferred the money from the Bank of New Zealand in
Opotiki, and after that we settled down to live in Herne Bay.
  It wasn't easy to find a job in Auckland in those years, but one day I thought of
Mr Thompson, the Stock Manager of Hellaby's, who used to come down to the

Bay of Plenty to buy our fat lambs; the Waititis and I both ran Southdown lambs on our land and Mr Thompson came to Cape Runaway every season to collect them for the killing at Hellaby's. I went straight down to Hellaby's and asked if I could see Mr Thompson, and when he walked in he said to me,

'Hullo, Mr Stirling! What are you doing here?'

'Well, Mr Thompson, I'd like a job. I've left the farm altogether and we're living in Auckland now.'

He looked at me and then he said, 'Yes, Mr Stirling, I can do that for you all right. You're a farmer, so I'll give you a job in the stockyards.'

I started working in the stockyards at Hellaby's and it was a good job, when the stock came into the yards I just had to count them, so many sheep, so many pigs, so many cows, then I signed the invoice and took it to the office and that was the day's work. When tea-time came I collected my wages and went home, and that was all. After a while I got sick of that job so I said to the Manager,

'Oh, I'd like to try something else.'

'All right, Mr Stirling; go and see Mr West, the overseer of the mutton-floor, he might have something for you.'

I went to see Mr West, and as soon as I mentioned my name 'Stirling' he looked at me and asked,

'Are you one of the Stirlings from the South Island?'

'Yes, I am – but my father Duncan shifted to the East Coast.'

'Oh well, you and I are related! My mother is a Maori woman from Bluff, and she is related to your father.'

He was happy and he told me, 'I'll give you a job in the Meat Department – you can please yourself with your work, cutting meat or whatever else you like!'

I worked in the Meat Department for quite a while and then the same thing came to mind, I wanted to try something new. I saw an advertisement in the paper for a job in the Manure Department at Kempthorne's so I talked to my boss at Hellaby's about it, and he gave me a nice leaving reference. When the Manager at Kempthorne's saw my papers he gave me the job and it was very easy, I just sat on top of a box watching stones dropping into the crusher, and when the stones got jammed in the crusher I had to push them through. You could sit down, walk around, have a smoke or do whatever you liked, no trouble. After a while I got used to that job and I was thinking about changing when my son Waha came to Auckland, so I put Waha into that job and I went to the Southdown freezing works, and I had good credentials everywhere I went. Waha stayed in the manure works for quite a time and he was put into a higher position, but one day he came to me and said,

'Well, Dad, I've decided that this is not my job!'

'You're getting good money though, Waha.'

'I know, but I want to follow in my grandfather's footsteps – I'd like to learn the painting and paper-hanging trade.'

Norman Perry helped to arrange a position for Waha in Christchurch under the Returned Servicemen's Scheme, and he was trained with an interior decorating firm down there. When Waha qualified for his certificate Amiria and I went to Christchurch for the presentation, and Mr Williams the supervisor was so pleased with his work that he presented him with a television set worth £70, and Waha went on to become one of the top men in painting and paper-hanging in Christchurch.

Once I had settled down in Auckland I started to think about the work I had been doing with Apirana Ngata, and in 1955 Monty Wickcliffe contacted me about setting up tribal committees in Auckland. I got together with my family and founded Horouta No. 2 Tribal Committee; Bob Mate founded Matatua Tribal Committee and Henry Edmonds founded Ratana Tribal Committee, and we all combined with Henry Graham to form the Auckland District Maori Council in 1956. This was the first district council in Auckland, up until that time they had only the Waitemata Tribal Executive.

Later on that year, in October, I had a big surprise – Tipi Ropiha rang me up from Parliament Buildings in Wellington and asked me to help them with some land business in Parihaka. Tipi was the Undersecretary for Maori Affairs at the time and Mr Corbett was the Minister of Maori Affairs, and they were having trouble over a large block of land at Parihaka in Taranaki; it was a case that had been going on for years, right from the time of the Taranaki wars of 1863 and the days when Te Whiti and Rongomai were the great leaders of Taranaki. Their religion was a Maori belief and they believed in their own spiritual world, but the Government claimed that Te Whiti and Rongomai were trying to bring something against them, and in the end thousands of acres were confiscated from below Taranaki mountain. The people of Parihaka suffered a lot and most of them were killed or put in prison, but the remnants kept on fighting and fighting and fighting and over the years they held on to the sorrows of their ancestors. By 1955 the last lands left to them were 1,500 acres in bush and fern and fifty acres at the marae, and the rates were going up all the time and the Maoris had no money to pay, and in the finish they owed the county council about £4,000. The council ordered the people of Parihaka to pay the money or their land would be confiscated, and the Hawera Council was just on the verge of taking the land when Tipi Ropiha heard about it and said, 'No, we're coming to pay the money!'

He talked to Mr Corbett, the Minister of Maori Affairs, and they decided to visit Parihaka to settle the dispute, but when they got to the marae the people chased them off! The people wouldn't have them there, they said,

'If you Government men come on our ground, we'll kill you both!'

Tipi listened to the voices from the marae and one old woman was calling out, 'Get away! Get out!'

The elders also told them to go, saying, 'We hear the voices of our ancestors calling – our land, you have it!'

So Tipi and Corbett went back to Wellington. About a month after that they came back to Parihaka Pa, and this time the crowd was three times bigger and the people cursed them, saying,

'Go away, you and your Government, the tears of our ancestors still lie upon the land that you stole from us in the days of Te Whiti and Rongomai! Haere atu – get out!!'

Tipi said to Corbett, 'This is useless, we can't do anything. We'll have to go back.'

When they got back to Parliament, Tipi told the Minister,

Parihaka in the days of Te Whiti and Rongomai. *Auckland Star*

'Well, there is one man who might be able to help us. When the Taranaki people went to Waiomatatini to talk with Ngata about their sorrows, Eruera Stirling stood to welcome them at the marae – he has met all those people of Parihaka, and he was close to Ngata in his work on the land. I think those people at Parihaka might listen to him . . .'

Mr Corbett said, 'All right, you make the enquiries about it.'

So Tipi rang me up in Auckland, and after he had explained everything he said to me,

'Well, Eruera, can you help us?'

'Yes.'

'All right, we'll arrange a day for you to go to Parihaka.'

Not long after that the Department of Maori Affairs made all the arrangements, and I went on the plane to Hawera. When I got there Peta Awatere and two other welfare officers from the Department picked me up in a Maori Affairs car, and as we drove to Parihaka Peta asked me,

'What about calling in to some other maraes, Eruera? There are three maraes on our way and they really want to hear what you have to say – they all have the same problems as Parihaka.'

'No! I'm not calling in at any other maraes! My job is at Parihaka, and I want to go straight there!'

While we were driving I looked up at Taranaki mountain, and my mind went back to the days when I was young, and my great-grandfather Pera taught me about the signs of the mountain. We could see Tihirau mountain at Cape Runaway from the hills at home, and one day the old man told me,

'When you are in doubt, e tama, look to the mountains! If the foot of Tihirau is lost in clouds that's a bad sign, and if the clouds come right up and hide the whole mountain it's very bad; but if the clouds go up and down and disappear, and you see the sun shining on top of Tihirau it's a good sign – you'll know that you are safe and your footsteps are on the right pathway.'

It says the same thing in the Bible you know, in Psalm 123,

'Lift up thine eyes to the hills.'

The old people of the Bible had that same belief in them and all these things had been told to me, and as we flew in to Hawera that morning I saw that the day was beautiful, Taranaki mountain was white in the sun, but when I got off the plane I saw a dark cloud coming up from the bottom of the mountain and I knew straight away, oh, something wrong is coming! We drove to Parihaka and the cloud was hanging half-way up the mountain, then I started to pray within myself, saying tribally,

'E koro ma i te po, old men in the world of darkness, I'm not coming here to interfere with you, the spirit of aroha is in me and I'm coming here to help your people!'

Well, when our car landed at Parihaka, boom! The cloud went right up and covered the mountain! I kept on praying, and when we stopped in front of the Parihaka marae it was packed out with people, they were chanting and singing but those were not good songs, and some of the men came out with sticks and yelled at us,

'Why have you people come here? Get out – *get out!* We see the blood of our ancestors upon you! Go, and take those pakehas with you – we don't want them on our marae!'

They were looking at the two welfare officers from the Department, and the next minute one big man dressed up in a cloak and carrying a taiaha walked right out on the marae and started cursing Peta Awatere.

'E Awatere – you are a bloody officer, my colonel when I was overseas! Today, *I'm* the colonel here! If you come in here I'll kill you, the blood of my ancestors and the blood of the wars is still trickling on my hands! You killed my forefathers and stole their land, you and your *bloody* government – get out! and take those pakehas with you!!'

Peta was ready to go and flatten that fellow but I said to him,

'No, Peta – you and I stay here. Let these people talk out their anger, you and I have to be quiet.'

We waited and the people kept on yelling out insults, but after a while they quietened down and the next thing, I heard the voice of an old man calling out from the back of the marae; it was the old Chief Rangihuna, one of the elders I had welcomed at Waiomatatini, standing on a form beside the meeting-house and saying,

'Welcome, Eruera, haere mai! Welcome the kanohi, the representative of our

ancestors, welcome the kanohi of Apirani Ngata! Greetings to the spirits of Ngata
Porou and Te Whanau-a-Apanui resting upon you; welcome, and bring the love
of Timi Kara* and Ngata with you – haere mai, welcome!'

He came out onto the marae and gave me a beautiful whaikorero, and I felt the
warmth moving within me, and as he spoke I saw the clouds rising up the sides of
Taranaki mountain. At the end of his speech the old man sang his song 'Tera te
Haeata' and the clouds went right up and over the mountain. When I stood on the
marae at Parihaka the sun shone on top of Taranaki mountain, and I knew that my
case had been supported. I started my speech with a prayer and returned
Rangihuna's greetings, and the anger of the people passed and everything was
peaceful; the old women opened up the gates and the old man shook hands with
me and took us to the dining-hall for kai. There were about 500 or 600 people
present and no one made a move, and after kai the old man Rangihuna said,

'All the things that were said today are finished – now it is time for love and
peace. The chiefs of Whanau-a-Apanui and Ngati Porou have come here to help
us, and we should listen to them quietly.'

Rangihuna asked me to conduct the service in the meeting-house that night and
as I chanted my prayers, the photos of Timi Kara, Ngata and Pomare looked down
at us from the walls.

*Timi Kara, Sir James Carroll, held the Waiapu seat in Parliament for many years and was a
remarkable figure in both Maori and Parliamentary politics: among other accomplishments he was the
first Maori to hold the portfolio of Native Affairs.

Timi Kara, in Kuramihirangi meeting-house. Painted by Rehu Kereama. *Photographic
Archives, Dept of Anthropology, University of Auckland*

After the service Rangihuna stood and spoke of the days when Te Whiti and Rongomai were alive, and their lands were confiscated by the Government even though their cause was just, then he said to me,

'Well, Eruera, now that you are here I know that our land will be saved, the blessings of our ancestors are upon us and you have come with the love of Ngata, Timi Kara and Pomare to help us. The hui is now open, and the way is clear for you to lay your thoughts before the people.'

I stood inside the meeting-house and said,

'E koro ma, e kui ma, old men and women – I have come from my home with the mauri of the sacred spirit upon me, and I know that I am walking on the right pathway because today, I saw all the signs on your mountain, Taranaki! Now that we have exchanged greetings we can open our minds to each other, and I can give you the messages passed on to me by Tipi Ropiha and the Minister of Maori Affairs. They have invited you people to form a Tribal Committee, a Welfare League and an Incorporation Committee, so that the Government can come and help you to save your land! As soon as these bodies are formed the government will be on a proper footing to pay your debts, and they can stop the county council from confiscating the land at Parihaka.'

The old people listened to me and I told them about incorporations; I told them how Apirana had incorporated our land at Wai-o-rongomai and the Government loaned the owners £30,000 to develop the property. The incorporation worked well and the debt was wiped out, and now the owners were getting dividends every year! I passed around a copy of the Wai-o-rongomai balance sheet and I told those people,

'You can see it is a good thing to incorporate your land! Instead of that land lying idle in scrub and fern it can be developed, and when the time comes and the incorporation pays out money to the owners, that's a big help to the people!'

The people talked about it for a while, then Rangihuna stood up and said,

'All right, Eruera, that is good. I agree with everything you have said – but first let our young men from Te Aute and St. Stephen's have a look at your papers, and they will tell us what they think.'

The educated young men looked at the balance sheet and all the other papers, and they turned to their elders and said, 'Ae – it is good.'

Rangihuna told us, 'Tomorrow we will meet again, and settle all these things.'

The next day after breakfast I laid out the papers in the meeting-house – the forms for the tribal committee, the welfare league and the incorporation committee, and after the people had looked at them one of the elders stood up and said,

'Yes, we agree – Tribal Committee!'

The committee members were chosen and the forms were signed, then another elder said,

'Yes, we agree – Welfare League!'

After the committee for the League was selected and those forms were all signed, another old man stood up and said,

'Yes, we agree – Incorporation Committee!'

We fixed everything up and signed all the papers and 500 people signed the petition to Parliament asking the Government to save their lands. When everything was finished Rangihuna said,

'Tomorrow, our chief will come to confirm the things that we have said.'

The next day their high chieftainess, the great-great-grandaughter of Te Whiti came to the marae, a young person but very well educated, and when she stood up to speak she said,

'I am happy to have my people forming a Tribal Committee, a Welfare League and an Incorporation Committee. But I say to you all, we must now try to follow the ways of the welfare league and the tribal executives and from today and forever more, I want no more drinking on this marae! We will clean up our marae, and nobody can drink here from this day onwards, and that is my last word on it – finish!'

Well, I saw that myself while I was there, the empty crates of beer and whisky were piled up behind the meeting-house and the people were drinking, drinking all the time, but after that day the people of Parihaka started a new life, they cleaned out their marae and they looked after their land, and today their incorporation is one of the wealthiest in New Zealand! Their property pays top dividends and they have even bought back some of their old lands from the pakeha farmers of Taranaki.

When everything was settled I flew to Wellington and delivered the papers to Mr Corbett and Tipi Ropiha; Tipi paid the rates to the Hawera County Council, and Maori Affairs surveyed the Parihaka land. They found that the pakeha farmers had shifted their fences over on to Maori land so they pulled down the fences and shifted them back, and the farmers couldn't say anything about it. Tipi Ropiha and Mr Corbett were really pleased with my work, and not long after I returned to Auckland, John Grace, the Secretary for the Minister of Maori Affairs rang me up,

'Well, Eruera, we've got a job for you. We want you to go as a welfare officer to the farming community around Hawera, and we'll give you a good salary, free house and everything!'

All that was offered to me by John Grace but at the time I couldn't do it, because my family had just settled down in Auckland. I was really thrilled though, and Parihaka was one of the best things I have ever done in my life. It all came through Apirana Ngata – he was always talking about helping other tribes, and he gave me the experience to move on with the work of incorporations and land development, and I took his copies of Hansard to help me when I set off on that trip.

When I first moved to Auckland the Ratana people had a church in Ponsonby not far from the Post Office and one Sunday when I was sitting at 1 Mercer Road feeling lonely with no one to talk to, I heard their bell ringing and I thought, I'm going to go up there! I walked to the church and when I went inside I knew quite a few of the faces; there were people there from the Coast, some from Whanganui and some from North Auckland, and after the service Dobson Paikea stood up and welcomed me.

'Well, Eruera, I'm very pleased to see you here! You are one of the elders that we would always be glad to see at our gatherings – greetings to you, Whanau-a-

Dobson Paikea, M.P. for Northern Maori, 1943–63. *Te Ao Hou*

Apanui and Ngati Porou! I remember when my father visited the Bay of Plenty, you welcomed him at Wairuru marae . . .'

Dobson was the son of Paraire Paikea, the Member for Northern Maori years back, and when Paraire was appointed to the executive position in Maori Affairs, Apirana took him right around all the maraes of the East Coast and told the people,

'He will carry on the work of the Maori people – Paraire Paikea is a good man!'

My mother-in-law Ani saw him at Waiomatatini marae and she cried when they met; afterwards she told Amiria that Paikea was related to her grandfather from North, Wiremu Parata Moihi Ka. The only trouble was, Paraire Paikea didn't live long so Dobson inherited his seat in the House, and he was doing a lot of work in Auckland in those years. That's why he said to me,

'Now that you have come my mind goes back to those leaders of the past, Apirana Ngata from Ngati Porou and your people of Te Whanau-a-Apanui, and my thoughts are directing me to appoint you chairman of the Akarana Marae Society right away! A man from Te Whanau-a-Apanui and Ngati Porou is the right man to take over that position.'

I stood up and thanked him, and then I said, 'Well, Dobbie, I appreciate your offer, but I am not eligible to take over the chairman's job because I'm not a member of your society.'

He said to me, 'You are now! I have just resigned as chairman, and tomorrow I

The 'Hi Fives' at the Maori Community Centre, 1962. *Te Ao Hou*

will send a notice to the Registrar of Friendly Societies nominating you as the new chairman.'

A few days later a letter came from the Registrar of Friendly Societies saying that I had been appointed chairman of the Akarana Marae Society by Dobson Paikea.

While I was chairman of the Akarana Marae Society at the Maori Community Centre we had a busy life because the centre was our marae in Auckland in those years; we had tangis there and socials and concert parties, and the people came in from far and near. On Saturday nights we had dances, and the talented Maori people – Howard Morrison, the Hi-Five Band and Kiri Te Kanawa all performed; the tribal committees, welfare leagues and church groups held their functions at the Centre and we ran a carving school and a tukutuku school there, too. All these activities kept the Maori culture, history and everything going for the people in the city, and a lot of the big guns on the Auckland maraes today picked up their knowledge of Maoritanga at the Maori Community Centre.

The Akarana Marae Society was very strong in those years and we had about 300 members when I was chairman; the Ratana people joined up and although there were no East Coast people in the society the members from North all supported me and they were really good – the Paikeas, the Waipouris, the Harawiras and quite a few others. We were supposed to build a marae at New Lynn because Maharaia Winiata and others had bought six acres there years ago, but the New Lynn Council said that the land was in an industrial zone and they wouldn't let the project go ahead. Not long after I was appointed to the chairman's position a letter came from the council's solicitor, Mr West, saying that our society owed the council £500 in rates and if the money wasn't paid in fourteen days, the land would be put up for auction. When I saw the name 'West' I thought it might be our solicitor Mr West who used to do all our county business in Opotiki, so I went down to his office in town. When I walked into the office it *was* our lawyer sitting there, and he looked at me and started to laugh. He said,

'Well, Mr Stirling, when I saw that you had been appointed chairman of the society I persuaded the council to send a notice to you, because I told them that the Maoris from the Opotiki district always pay their rates. They were going to sell the land but now I know we can fix everything up.'

I pulled out my cheque book and wrote a cheque for £50, and I said to him, 'Here, take £50 for the time being and I'll raise funds for the balance.'

'Don't worry, Mr Stirling, now that you're chairman we won't be pressing the sale.'

When I went home I sent a letter to Hone Heke Rankin, one of the big chiefs up North, and I told him I was coming up to Kaikohe to raise funds for the rates of the Akarana Marae Society. Hone Heke wrote back to say,

'Yes, come and bring your people.'

I went with my group of thirty on a special bus to the marae at Kaikohe, and when we got there Hone Heke Rankin welcomed us and said to me,

'Well, Whanau-a-Apanui and Ngati Porou, I'm proud that you have been appointed chairman of the Akarana Marae Society because I am a Ngati Porou too! I am related to the Ngata family and I went to school at Waiomatatini and stayed with them for years. Tomorrow we are unveiling the monuments of six Nga Puhi chiefs, and I want you to perform the ceremony!'

I stood up and greeted Hone Heke, and then I told him, 'No, it's not right, one of your people should unveil the stones . . .'

Hone Heke said to me, 'We want you to do it, Eruera, and that's that – finish!'

The next morning there was a jubilee for the local school and o-oh! there were about a thousand people present and after that hui we went to the burial ground and I unveiled the tombstones. Each stone was covered with a cloak and according to Nga Puhi custom, when you unveil a tombstone you have to take the cloaks away with you, but Amiria didn't like that and she told me,

'No! We're not going to carry these tapu things around!'

I went to Sue Te Tai, a very prominent old lady from that district and asked her to take the cloaks and she said,

'Yes! The custom of the Nga Puhi is that when the day comes, you return those things to the people.'

When the six tombstones had been unveiled we went to the marae, and after the greetings Hone Heke stood up and said,

'Stirling from Whanau-a-Apanui and Ngati Porou is here with his group to raise funds for the Akarana Marae Society – now Eruera, give your hat to Sue Te Tai!'

I was wearing a big panama hat, and Hone Heke took it and gave it to the old lady, then he called out,

'All you people walking around the marae, if you've got £5 or £10, put it in that hat!'

Sue Te Tai went right around the marae and when she brought my hat back to Hone Heke it had £800 in it and the notes were flying everywhere! I took the money back to Auckland and had a meeting of our society, and we paid the rates to the New Lynn Council. The people from North were so good to me that I formed an association called 'Te Kotahitanga o nga Hapu o te Tai Tokerau' – the Union of

Eruera speaking at Mangere marae, the opening of the Maori Graduates Association Conference, 1968. *Auckland Star*

the Sub-tribes of the North – and we raised a lot of funds for a marae in Auckland in those years.

There was a building on the Society's property at New Lynn and as time went by we stored a lot of carvings for a new meeting-house there, but people were coming in to steal them so I locked the place up and gave the key to the chap who lived next door, and asked him to call the police if anybody tried to break in. The New Lynn Council still refused to let the marae go ahead and in the end the Waikato people at Mangere started to plan their own marae. Tura Hira was a member of the Akarana Marae Society and one day she stood up at one of our meetings and said,

'Since no meeting-house can be built at New Lynn, I am asking for the carvings to be passed over for our marae at Mangere.'

I thought, well it's better to have the carvings out at Mangere than stolen by some thief, so I said,

'Yes!'

Somebody else at the meeting got wild about it and he said,

'No! If these carvings are taken to Ngaruawahia, I will go down there on my truck and bring them straight back!'

I told that chap,

'Look here, if you tried to get those carvings from Ngaruawahia in the old days the people would kill you, but even if you go there today you'll be a dead man; you'll have to cut across the tapu of the Waikato people! No, Tura, you take these carvings away!'

King Koroki sent his people to take the carvings to Ngaruawahia and they were put into Te Puea meeting-house at Mangere and you can see those poupous still standing there today, along one wall of that house. That is why when Tura was alive she always said to me,

'Haramai, Eruera, welcome to your marae . . .'

While I was at the Centre we kept the place in good repair, inside and outside and properly painted, but it was very heavy work and in 1965 I sent in my resignation to Jock McEwen, the Trustee of the Department of Maori Affairs. After that I thought well, I'd better start up something for our own people of the Tai Rawhiti, and that was the beginning of the Tai Rawhiti Association. The idea of our association is to help each other in days to come, and we raise funds in our socials to put aside for bereavements or sickness in hospital, or if some trouble comes to an East Coast family living in Auckland. The Tai Rawhiti Association is very good, it helps to keep the people of the Coast together, and we have two of the outstanding pakehas in Auckland, Stan Gillan and Ted Everton, as our patrons.

I joined up with quite a few societies in Auckland in those years, the Farmers' Society, the Senior Citizens and the Pioneers, and when it came to pension time I finished work and settled down. The people in Auckland were very close to one another when we first came to the city and we had no opposition from anyone; nobody picked on us or said anything funny to us. The Maori people and the pakeha people met anywhere without any trouble – I used to go into the pub and watch them, not to drink but when I wanted to be with people, and you'd see them drinking together, young and old, and they were happy. You'd never hear anybody cursing or fighting, not like today! That was the early life in Auckland.

Even after I came to live in Auckland I still kept thinking about the land back at home, and in 1965 I applied to the Maori Land Court to amalgamate the titles of Tawaroa block, Otaimina, Matangareka and a block at the back, about 10,000 acres all together. Amalgamation brings all the titles into one and it helps the people because everybody has an equal share; in the old way the big shareholders were the only ones to walk about on the land and the people with very small shares got nothing at all. The Minister of Maori Affairs, Mr Hanan, supported my application, and when the case went to court, I laid out the foundations and conditions of the amalgamation, and Judge Acheson put the whole thing through. The only trouble was, when I asked for five trustees the lawyer from Maori Affairs stood up and said,

'No, the Court must leave room for two more trustees to be appointed!'

I didn't want that because it is much easier to run an incorporation with a small committee, it's no use having ten or twelve trustees scattered all over the show, so I said,

'I move that nominations be closed!'

The people supported my resolution and five trustees were appointed; myself, John Waititi, Norman Perry, and two others, and we are now running the incorporation, we are really in control. If we say yes, it means yes! and if we say no, it means no! and even the Maori Affairs can't do anything, it has to go the way we want. Norman Perry and John Waititi are the two men at home who look after the interests of the Whanau-a-Apanui people and watch our programme of land development. We were very lucky with Tawaroa Topu because the lessees returned the land to the owners in good condition when their leases expired; Dr Scott on Orete and the Barkers on Tawaroa Station left the farms in beautiful working order, not like the lessees on some other blocks around our district, and in a few years the owners of Tawaroa Topu will receive good dividends from their land.

The idea of incorporation was the best work Apirana Ngata ever did and if it wasn't for him, I think all the Maori lands would be gone by now. When the Maori owner can't work his land because he has got no money, a pakeha with money will come along and say,

'Your land, Maori.'

'Oh well, all right . . .'

The land goes, eh, hundreds of thousands of acres have gone that way. When the titles are fragmented and the people can't pay their rates, the borough council will come along and sell that land to a man with money, and hundreds of thousands of acres have gone *that* way.† When the land is lying idle and the value is low the Government will come along with the Public Works Act and the Town and Country Planning Act and confiscate it for reserves or something else, and hundreds of thousands of acres have gone that way. If the Maori people have sections on the beach the council will put them under a rural zoning, and the Maori land legislation keeps changing every year and the land keeps sliding away.

I think that there is only one thing to do, the four Maori Members of Parliament must get together and look after the interests of the Maori people throughout New Zealand, and gain control of the millions of pounds held in trust by the Maori Trustee. The rents of people who died years ago are still accumulating in the trust fund, and that money could be put to good use helping Maori owners to develop their land, paying off the rates until the farms are running properly and showing the people how to set up incorporations. When every tribe has its own trust board the Maori Trustee can release their share of the funds to their control, and bring the situation of Maori land to a better understanding.

You can see that the Samoan people in Auckland have organized themselves properly – they started off with nothing but when they came to New Zealand, the chiefs got every Samoan working in Auckland to give $1 from his weekly pay packet, and with 17,000 of them contributing to the fund they soon had a million dollars! They have built their own church and a big flash hall, and last year when I went to the opening of Samoa House in Karangahape Road the Samoan chiefs said to me,

'You Maori people should have a building three times this size in Auckland – there are 70,000 of you and only 17,000 of us living here!'

† The Native Land Rating Act of 1924 allowed the Native Land Court to vest land in the Native Trustee for sale, or to transfer it to the Crown or local authority to meet arrears of rates (Butterworth, *The Politics of Adaptation*, p. 239).

I said, 'Well, you're quite right. If we could only get all of our people to put aside $1 a week we'd soon be wealthy all right!'

The trouble is, the Maori people don't organize and as a result, we've got nothing. The time has come for us to work together and improve our ambitions in this new world of the Maori people, Te Ao Hou.

3
THE BOOK
OF THE RISING
GENERATION

Sir Apirana Turupa Ngata in the 1940s. *Alexander Turnbull Library*

CHAPTER ONE
LIFE IN TE AO HOU

Well, the Maori people are living in a new world now, but I believe that the power of our ancestors is still very strong. The young leaders of today must remain Maori in heart and hold fast to the mana of the ancestors, or they will never find a good pathway for the people and their work will come to nothing. Apirana Ngata said:

> E tipu e rea i nga ra o to ao
> *Grow, child, in the days of your world*
> Ko to ringaringa ki nga rakau a te pakeha
> *Your hand to the weapons of the pakeha*
> Hei oranga mo to tinana
> *As an existence for your body*
> Ko to ngakau ki nga taonga a o tipuna
> *Your heart to the treasures of your ancestors*
> Hei tikitiki mo to mahuna
> *As a topknot for your head*
> Ko to wairua ki te Atua
> *Your spirit to Almighty God*
> Nana nei nga mea katoa
> *Who is the giver of all things!*

That was his message to the young leaders – by all means make a deep study of education and graduate in the ways of moving around in the pakeha world, but always remember your ancestors and the Maori way of life or you'll be nobody! Your mana comes down the descent lines as a gift of power from Io-matua-te-kore, Tane-nui-a-rangi, Tu-matauenga and lesser gods, and as a blessing from our father in heaven; it gives you the power to talk, the power to stand up at the marae, the power to deal with anything. When a man with that blessing upon him stands up to speak he'll be taller than anybody else and his ancestors come to stand beside him – nobody can touch him!

If you don't have that mana or spiritual power, though, it doesn't matter how many degrees you've got, you'll go nowhere. Knowledge or matauranga is a blessing on your mind, it makes everything clear and guides you to do things in the right way, and not a word will be thrown at you by the people. It is the man who goes with his spirit and his mind and heart believing in all these things who can climb to the high summits of leadership.

When the people of Ngati Whatua in Auckland started up a new marae at Bastion Point a few years back, they held a hui and decided to take some of the soil from the old marae up to the new place on the hill, with the blessings of their ancestors. Some of the Orakei people wanted the ceremony performed in broad daylight, but Hapi Pihema stood up in the meeting and said,

'No! I will not allow the soil of my ancestors to be brought up in the day-time, these things should be done at night!'

After the meeting Hapi came to see me about it and he said, 'Well koro, I have a very deep work for you to do, I want you to bring the soil of my great-grandfathers to our new marae.'

He told me about the argument at the hui and I said to him, 'You were quite right, Hapi. I know when my grandfather and my father went to bring the bones of our old people from the caves at the back of Raukokore, they carried out their ceremony at night . . .'

One time when I was young, the elders at Raukokore had decided to take all the bones from the burial caves in the hills behind Raukokore, and rebury them in the graveyard at our marae. The people gathered together on the marae and early that morning before the sun was up the tohunga held his ceremony at the caves, and in the afternoon they carried the bones of their ancestors to the marae graveyard and reburied them, and there was a big celebration. My father brought out the bones of my great-grandfather Poututerangi, and he told me that the ceremony had to be held at night so that the spirits of the old people could come and help with the work, because that was their time for moving around.

Well, I agreed to help Hapi, and early the next morning before the sun was up we went to the old marae, picked up the soil and carried it right up the hill to the new meeting-house, chanting karakia all the way. When we came to the front of the meeting-house I finished off with a special chant for bringing the soil at night, and as the soil was put into the earth of the new marae I looked up and saw lights flashing from the eyes of the tekoteko carvings inside the house, from the top to the bottom! I knew straight away that the ancestors were with me, because that was one thing that Pera Te Kaongahau taught me, when you see different lights coming, yellow, blue and green, well, somebody's there and you're safe, those lights are the signature of your ancestors. It says the same thing in the Bible, the light will come to lead you and Christ will shine upon your pathway, and I believe in all those things. That is why I kept away from the struggles at Bastion Point later on, because my work was over when we blessed the soil of that marae.

In 1975 Whina Cooper started off the Land March to help the Maori people to hang onto their land, and when the marchers came to Auckland Whina contacted me and asked me to join up with the elders at the front of the march. The Land March was coming in the right way so I agreed to go, and early the next morning Ani Salmond came on her car to take us to Hato Petera College. Just as I climbed into the car, hah! something came into my mind, and I remembered a special silver cross that my grandson George had given to me. I told Ani to wait and Mum was *growling* away but I went into the house and got this silver cross and put it in my pocket, then we set off to Hato Petera. There was supposed to be a service that morning for all the marchers, but when we got there and I saw the priest and asked him, 'What time is the service?' he told me, 'Oh, there's no service! Whina and the others have already gone!'

Just then I heard somebody calling out, 'They're on the march!' A big column

Whina Cooper starts the Land March from Te Hapua. *New Zealand Herald*

'The Auckland Harbour Bridge extension lane swayed markedly from side to side as more than 3000 Maori land marchers – many of them terrified by the movement – crossed it today. The sway sent people scrambling back and forth the width of the lane. Unprepared for it, some fell . . .' *Auckland Star, 13 September 1975*

came route marching down the road with Whina Cooper at their head and Whina called to me,

'Come to the head of the march, Eruera!'

'No – I'll come on behind.'

Mum and I joined in with the marchers and we set off for the Auckland Harbour Bridge. The crowd got bigger and bigger, and as we came to the bridge the road was packed out with people, and the next minute, the bridge began to roll! The bridge rolled from side to side and the people started to fall on top of each other, and as the rolling got worse Amiria fell over, I fell over, everybody fell over and women were screaming all around! As I fell down I remembered my silver cross, and I pulled it out and held it up in front of me. The bridge was still swinging but I managed to stand up and after a while the people got to their feet and walked across. When I came to the road on the other side a policeman asked me,

'Why are you carrying that cross, Mr Stirling?'

I told him,

'If it wasn't for that cross today, the bridge would have gone over and I'd have been one of the first to be thrown into the water!'

I had that belief in me because something told me to go back into the house that morning and get that cross; I wasn't thinking about it when I was in a hurry to go to the hui. The people of the Land March were supposed to have a big service that morning but they turned it down, and Almighty God was not with us when the Harbour Bridge rolled and almost threw us into the Waitemata – you have to be blessed to walk across the waters of the ancestors!

The Maoris were the original owners of Auckland and there are still a lot of old burial grounds and pas around the place, and it is no good for people to live on that kind of land because they are walking over the remains of ancestors of many generations. There was a chap farming on the Whangaparaoa peninsula a few years back and he had a beautiful station there with cattle and sheep and a big two-storied house, but there was always something wrong with him and strange things came to him at night. He went to the doctor but there was no change and his wife didn't know what was the matter, and in the end they went to see a psychologist in Auckland about it. They explained the whole thing to him and in the finish the psychologist said,

'Well, I think this might be a Maori trouble, and you should talk to somebody who knows about these things. There is a man in Auckland here, Mr Stirling . . . Why don't you two ask him to come to your farm and see what is happening, he might be able to help you.'

The wife rang me up and I agreed to go to Whangaparaoa, and a few days later they picked me up and took me to their farm. When we drove up the hill to their place I noticed a big stand of bush right next to the house and something came into my mind right away, there was something wrong with that area – I didn't like the look of it at all! I asked,

'What is there behind those trees?'

The husband told me, 'Well, Mr Stirling, I have heard that it used to be a Maori burial ground . . .'

I thought to myself, no wonder! Those people have been walking backwards and forwards over the bones of ancient people and going into their house to eat and sleep and all sorts; no wonder trouble has come to them! I had a big talk to them about it and then the woman asked me,

'Can you help us, Mr Stirling?'

'I am very sorry but I cannot do anything on this land – I came from another district and I can't overstep the local people; if I did, that would be trespassing and I'd only get into trouble myself! We have to find out if some of the local elders can help you . . .'

When I got back to Auckland that night I rang an old kuia from Waikato who was well known for her work on the spiritual side, and asked her if she could help that couple. She said to me,

'Well, Eruera, if you can't do it *I* can't; Whangaparaoa is past the Waikato boundary and we'd both be trespassing! The job has to be done by local people of that standard.'

We couldn't think of anybody from that district, though, and when the farmer's wife rang me again I told her, 'Look, I think you'd better ask a Catholic priest to come out and bless your land – somebody has to do it!'

That's exactly what she did. She got in touch with the Bishop and a priest came out to their property to hold a service and bless the land, and from that day on her husband started to get better. He is quite all right now and he has no more trouble with his worries at night, but today they are very careful with the Maori side of life. The power of these things is still in operation, but if you go in the right way they will never hurt you, your footsteps will automatically follow the right pathway and nothing will touch your mind.

Raglan golf-course is another case of people trampling over ancestral remains, because the golf people of Raglan have been playing their games there over a Maori graveyard for years. The land around the graveyard was taken from the Maori owners during the war for an airstrip, and the Government told them that it would be returned as soon as the war was over; but the airstrip was never built and after the war the Government held on to the land and leased it to the local golf-club. The Maori owners protested, but nobody took any notice until Eva Rickard came along and sat with her people on the land in 1977. Eva came to me and said that she wanted to go to the golf-course and put a blessing back on the graves of her ancestors, and she invited me to take part in the ceremony. Quite a few of us went down to Raglan that day and we started to hold our service of blessing around the graves, then some of the golf people rang up the police and told them to come and arrest us for trespassing! I had a big shock when I saw all these policemen coming, and they moved into the graveyard and started to arrest our people. One Maori policeman stood outside the graveyard and called to the others,
   'Don't arrest those old people! Leave them alone!'
   We were not touched but they took hold of the others and carted them off to gaol. It was not the fault of the police that day, they were only doing their duty and carrying out their orders – it was the golf people who made the big mistake. They had no right to that land in the first place and they were quite wrong to play golf over the graves, and now the courts have returned the land to the Maori owners. The ancestors are still with us and their tapu rests on the land, and they will destroy people who are against them or who show them no respect. It is the same with any of their belongings that have been left behind in this world, those things are tapu and they must be recognized by the people and put in their rightful place. They can cause a lot of trouble.

A few years back one of the doctors from our district rang me up late one night and asked,
   'Mr Stirling, could you go out to see somebody who is sick, not very far from you?'
   I said to him, 'Doctor, why do you want to get me out at this time of night? I'm not a tohunga you know and I don't like to do that kind of work . . .'
   'Oh well, we can't do anything with this chap and I thought you might be able to help – I don't know what else to do with him.'
   I wasn't very happy about it but I went to that man's house, and as soon as I walked in I knew there was something spiritually wrong there, a very strange

The protest marae on the Raglan golf-course – Eruera and Amiria Stirling are sitting in the shelter at right; the police come on to the marae; protesters are arrested. *David Charteris*

'Ka whawhai tonu matou – we will keep on fighting' – outside the Hamilton Magistrate's Court. *David Charteris*

feeling came to me. This chap was married to a Maori woman from Taupo, and for quite a few months they had both been getting sick, going to hospital and all sorts, and the doctors didn't know what was the matter. I talked to the wife and she told me that her father kept coming to her in dreams at night to warn her about something, and in the end I found out that her father had died a while back, but she still had all his belongings in the house. I told that woman,

'You *must* get all those things out of the house at once and bury them, *don't* take them anywhere else – that is our old custom. I will get a minister from your area to come and see you, and after that you'll be right.'

When I went home I rang Reverend Potatau from Taupo and told him,

'E Hemi, there's a sick person from Taupo over here and I think you'd better go and see her tonight.'

He went to that woman's house and held his service, and at midnight he rang me and said, 'Our patient is doing well – kua pai!'

Not long after that the same doctor rang me again and asked me to see another sick person, and I said to him

'Hah, Doctor! You ring me for all your worst cases!'

'No, Mr Stirling, I think you're the only one that can deal with this.'

Well, I went to that chap's place and when I came up the path to the house I could hear him crashing and banging and rattling inside the house, he was moving around from one room to the next. I knocked on the door and nobody answered, but when I called out the wife heard my voice and she came to open the door.

'Quick, Mr Stirling, come in – I'm frightened!'

I walked in and the next moment her husband jumped on me, cursing and crying out, 'Don't kill me! Don't kill me!'

I stood there and listened, and as soon as I heard his voice I knew it was a spirit talking. He said,

'Hey, what are you doing here? Are you coming to kill me? Don't kill me! Don't kill me!'

The man was jumping around and I knew I had to do something, so I asked the wife to bring me a bowl of water and I blessed it, and started to sprinkle it all around the house. The spirit began to cry right then and he said to me,

'Give me back my adze, that's all – it doesn't belong to them! Don't kill me! Just give me back my adze!'

I began to pray, and as I held my service the spirit settled down, and in the finish the man came back into his right mind. I told his wife,

'Now, go and bring me that adze.'

She went into the bedroom and came back carrying a beautiful greenstone adze that her husband had found somewhere in Whanganui, he'd picked it up and brought it home. I rubbed the adze and blessed it and then I said to her,

'I want you to get in touch with some people from Whanganui and ask them to come here and take this adze away – it belongs to their ancestors, not to your husband!'

A few days later she rang and told me that the Whanganui people had taken the stone adze away, and from that time on her husband started to get better. She thanked me but I told her,

'Don't thank me, my dear, it was Almighty God who saved you.'

That is why I say I am not a tohunga and I don't want to be one; I believe in Almighty God and He is the one who carries us through. Remember Apirana's saying, 'Have faith in Almighty God, for He is the giver of all things.'

Apirana Ngata also told the young people to treasure the customs of their ancestors as a top-knot and a plume for their heads, but sometimes I feel very sorry for our young people of today because they are not moving deeply into the Maori way of life. It's not their fault – they don't have the free run of the maraes any more and they don't have a free life in the cities, but my mind is sad when I look back to my young days and remember the unity of the people, and the strength of our tribal groups. The spirit of this new world is very different – the mana and the mauri of the old ways have gone and the young people are wandering about, looking for a pathway to follow. They go back to the maraes and ask the old people,

'E koro ma, me pehea te mea, me pehea te mea – how should this be done, and that?'

They have not been taught their genealogies and most of them can't speak Maori, and when I went back home to Te Kaha not long ago they stood in the meeting-house and asked me,

'E koro, we are seeking our lines of descent, please tell us about our ancestors.'

I started to explain the whakapapas to them and they wrote everything down – all young people! I felt very sad and I thought that these things should be recorded so that our descendants will know them in the years to come. The trouble is, so many of the old people have died before they passed on their knowledge to their children and grandchildren, and the treasures of our ancestors are being lost one by one.

Apirana warned us to hold fast to our Maoritanga no matter how far we move into the pakeha world, because that plume on our heads is the mana, the mauri and the power of the ancestral lines coming down to each new generation; but I think that some of the young have left that plume lying on the ground behind them, and some others cherish it, but do not understand its proper meaning. Very few of our young leaders can bring together the knowledge of the pakeha with the wisdom of their tribal ancestors and yet that is the type of man we need, somebody like Te Rangihiroa or Apirana Ngata to guide us.

I saw this last year when a group of Maori people called 'He Taua' clashed with the Engineering students at Auckland University – they were quite right in their protest but they did not fully understand their Maori background. The Engineering students started off the trouble by performing the haka 'Ka mate ka mate' in the streets of Auckland, dressed in pants and grass skirts and all sorts of attire with rude material written on their bodies and carrying clubs, and when the Maori people saw that they were very upset, because it was not according to custom. A haka party must be properly trained and when they perform in public they must be properly dressed and the leader is the only person to use the mere – nobody should enter the haka field unprepared! The haka is something sacred and treasured, it's not just for show, and 'Ka mate ka mate' is one of the important hakas performed on maraes all over New Zealand; every district has its own tribal haka but they all use 'Ka mate ka mate' to finish a performance.

Some of the Maori people in Auckland formed a group called 'He Taua' and asked the Engineering students to stop mocking the haka, but they refused, and there was a big fight at the University when 'He Taua' came in. When I saw the reports in the newspaper I thought well, the students were degrading the haka and that was the reason that trouble flared up between the two sides; if the students had thought up something of their own, none of this would have happened.

The young people of 'He Taua' were arrested and charged with rioting at the University, and not long after that there was a big meeting at Union Hall in Ponsonby to discuss the whole thing, and John Kaa and I were invited to go. When we arrived they handed over the running of the meeting to us, and after prayers I told the young people about the custom of the taua as I saw it in my young days at home. I told them that the taua was a group organized to control troubles between tribal areas and as far as I know, it was not a case of people fighting one another, but of people getting together to settle a dispute without bloodshed. If they wanted to go under the name 'He Taua' well and good, but they should follow the customary ways and keep away from violence.

In the old days if a match was made between a certain man and a woman and one

A haka correctly performed – Sir Apirana Ngata leads a haka at Waitangi, 1940.
Alexander Turnbull Library

A Maori student remonstrates with Engineering students performing their 'haka', 1978.
Craccum

of them cut across the taumau arrangement, the people on the other side would say,

'Well, so-and-so has refused to marry our child, and his tribe will have to pay for it!'

They'd gather together in one place, and if the other marae was a long way off they'd ride there on horseback, and as they travelled the women composed songs about their grievance – really bad songs talking about the things men and women do together and all sorts! When they came to that marae the women would ride in front of the party, singing:

> Tenei matau te haere mai nei
> *We are coming here*
> Ki te tomotomo i o whare taua-a-a, e-e!
> *To enter your houses of mourning.*
> He nui nga whetu i tiria ki te rangi
> *There are many stars scattered across the sky*
> Ko matau i whakatakirautia e-e!
> *But we stand all together!*

Then they'd let fly with all the rude, insulting songs that came into their minds, and when the people of the marae heard their words they knew exactly what was wrong. The men said nothing, the women sang all the reasons for their visit, and as they came on to the marae they performed a haka in front of the meeting-house where the local people stood in rows. The elders of the marae made speeches of welcome and the visitors replied, and afterwards the two groups came together, because the taua came to settle the divisions between them. When they all went into the meeting-house the chief of the pa stood up and said,

'All right, I can see that we are at fault in this matter. That is my land lying over there – I give it to you to pay for our trouble.'

Land handed over in this manner was placed under a rahui and reserved for all the people, and there were quite a few large blocks in our district that had been gifted to settle a fight between tribal groups.

I saw all the big tauas of Te Whanau-a-Apanui in my young days, and one taua came to our own place when I was still at school. We had an old man staying with us called Te Kiriwai Parakau, who was a chief of our district and a relation of my mother's, and one morning at breakfast-time he knocked the teapot over and burned my older brother's arm. Taikorekore yelled but Mum looked after him and he was all right, and we said nothing more about it. A man from Te Kiriwai's place was passing by our house, though, and he went away and told all the people,

'O – Te Kiriwai has burned Taikorekore! He spilled hot tea all over his arm!'

They decided to send a taua against Te Kiriwai and the next day, hika ma! when we looked out from our house we saw a whole crowd of people riding down the track from Te Kaha, with the women in front singing their songs and calling out,

'E Te Kiriwai! Mo te weranga o ta matau mokopuna, mahau i tahu ki te ahi! Hey Te Kiriwai! We have come here because you burned our grandchild, cooked him in the fire!'

They came in front of our house chanting hakas and all sorts, and when they were finished they came inside and sat down. My mother welcomed them, and then the old man Te Kiriwai stood and said,

'You were right to come!'

He went to his house and fetched clothes, blankets and almost everything he owned, food and money too, and he gave it all to the taua to pay for his mistake. They slept in my mother's house that night and then they all went home.

That was how the taua worked – they came to put things right, not to fight with people, and the women led and the men followed on behind.

Another time a young man from Raukokore was matched with a woman from Oruaiti and when the time came for them to get married she ran away, and the people of Raukokore went on a taua to Oruaiti. My father went with them and he came home with a double-furrow plough, and other people brought back clothes, money and even the Oruaiti whaleboat! In those days people didn't care what they gave away when the taua came, the main thing was to settle the trouble so they handed over land, furniture, clothes, money and everything they owned to put things right again.

I told the young people all these things and after my talk other speakers stood up, and some of them wanted the whole crowd to march to the Town Hall that Friday night to protest about the arresting of 'He Taua.' I said to them,

'My advice to you young people is not to march on Friday night; according to custom, if a group marches at night-time that means bloodshed, and you'll be asking for battle! Our elders at home told us that once the sun sets in the western hills of the world, the turehu people control the hours of darkness, and anything that is started at night will lead to trouble. I have seen people moving onto a marae at night and not welcomed until daylight because of this belief. Anyway I don't like marching, it is not the Maori way – it is pakeha people who are always marching around this town, not Maoris.'

They had a good discussion about it and the young boys and the men supported me, and they decided to go straight to the Town Hall that Friday night without marching. When Friday night came we had a very good meeting in the Town Hall, Maoris and pakehas were gathered together and Rangi Walker explained about 'He Taua', and when I stood up to speak I said,

'I am supporting 'He Taua' but I want them to work between the two peoples and put the differences and the troubles of the past behind us – I don't want these race relations coming in to divide us!'

Later in the evening some pakeha people from the big societies in Auckland gave very nice speeches in support of the Maori group, and one of them said,

'I blame ourselves! We, the pakeha people should not use the Maori haka without understanding it – we are the ones who caused this trouble!'

At the end of the evening the chairman passed around the hat and you could see the spirit of the people that night, $5 and $10 notes were flying! and $600 were donated for the court costs of 'He Taua'.

Not long after our meeting the 'He Taua' case came up in the Magistrate's Court, and during the first days of the trial the judge was not in a very good humour, so the lawyer for 'He Taua' said to me, 'Mr Stirling, we would like you to explain in Maori to the judge about the real meaning of the haka.'

When I gave my evidence Kingi Ihaka translated for me, and I told the judge that the haka has always been one of the most sacred treasures of the Maori people – from the time of our ancestors right down to now. In my young days when my elder brother Taikorekore led the Whanau-a-Apanui haka team we performed in all the big haka competitions, at the visit of the Prince of Wales in 1919, the Duke of York's visit in 1927, the Ahuwhenua Trophy competitions in 1932 and the opening of the carved meeting-house at Waitangi 1935; and every time we trained for months with our teacher the old man Hirini Puha. We had to learn the haka so that the words and actions settled deeply in our minds, and we were taught to dress properly and follow our leader exactly. In those days if somebody came into a haka party dressed in rough clothes and chanting rude words the chief would order his people to take that man away and give him a thrashing – they'd just about kill him for interfering with the mana of the haka! The price of that type of insult could be the life of a man.

Kingi Ihaka translated my speech but some of the hard words were not interpreted, he put it in a softer way, and after I had explained all these things the atmosphere of the judge changed – he began to realize that the Maori people still treasure their hakas. Elizabeth Murchie, the President of the Maori Women's Welfare League also gave evidence in the case and she told the judge, 'If you study the words of a Maori haka, they are as beautiful as the poetry of any Shakespearean play!'

I remember that Apirana said exactly the same thing in 1945 at the Ngarimu Victoria Cross hui in Ruatorea, when the womenfolk of the Whanau-a-Apanui performed a very rare old haka from our district. A male kaea led them and he started off the chant:

> Taka, takahia Taka takahia
> Whakakau he tipua, Hei!
> Whakakau he taniwha, Hei!
> I u nga iwi ki hea,
> I u ki te Kana-nui-a-Tiki, pakia!
> Puhi kura, puhi kura, puhi kaka, puhi reirei
> Ka eke nei hoki kai te umauma, Pakia!
> Kaore nei hoki te tukituki kai taku manawa, Aha ha!
> Nateko, nateko te konunutanga
> O tana pinanauhea meromero iti.
> I whiua ki te taha waitai takoto titaha
> E kaiwhea ia ra o kupu te homai ai
> Hei tuki ake mo taku poho e.
> E hei aha tera.
> I motu te puehu tukawa
> Kanana nei.
> Karariwha nei
> Ka whiti ki Aropango nei
> Me tuku ki te wai whinau me tona hua
> Ka pangò nei.
> Hei, hei, hei!

Apirana judged the haka competitions at the hui and when he announced the results he said,

'The haka of Te Whanau-a-Apanui was so beautiful that I cannot give the decision to any other team! If the words of that haka could be captured in English, it would be as fine as any of Shakespeare's poems!'

The haka of our womenfolks spoke of going into the bush to collect leaves, bringing them home to boil them and mix them to make different colours, red, black and green, and mixing the water with mud and special sorts to dye the fibres for piupius and cloaks – you can still see some old cloaks with these colours woven into them in the Auckland Museum.

Well, the trial of 'He Taua' went on in the Auckland Magistrate's Court for several days and in the finish the judge charged the young people of 'He Taua' with rioting; when he announced his decision the people started shouting out and hooting and I felt very sad. No doubt they were wrong to use violence on a taua but the Engineering students were also quite wrong – they knew nothing about the haka and they treated it with contempt, and that was the whole cause of the trouble – kare i tika, it was not right!

If Maori customs are going to be abused in this way I believe that the Maori and the pakeha people will be forced apart, and I will be very sorry to see that, because when I first came to Auckland we lived peacefully together and walked side by side. The university students should be leading our people on a pathway of peace and understanding, not trampling Maori customs underfoot and belittling the mana of our ancestors.

That is why I worry about the future of our country, I can see the people moving into divisions and clashing with one another – if we are not careful New Zealand will end up like Ireland, with the country divided down the middle and the two sides battling all the time! It is the duty of the Government to bring the Maori and pakeha people together, not to split them, and Maori customs and Maori lands must be treated with respect in the New Zealand courts and elsewhere.

The haka and the taua are both important customs from the past, and the rahui or reserve is another tribal tradition that has come to light in this new world. In 1979 Sid Mead* announced a rahui on Maoris playing football in South Africa; I believe he was trying to do a good thing but his work was not in keeping with the traditions of the ancestors. The old people put rahui on lands, fishing grounds, shellfish rocks or forests but they would never put a rahui on sports; that was an open thing between the tribal groups.

In the old days if two tribes were fighting over land, a broken taumau marriage or some other matter and one side recognized they were wrong, their chief would say to the people of the other group,

'For our fault in this matter I give you this land, to pay for the harm we have caused.'

The land was passed over and put under a rahui, and kept as a papatipu or

---

*Professor Sid Mead of the Maori Department at Victoria University called a rahui, asking Maori rugby players not to join teams going to South Africa as a protest against apartheid.

'growing-ground' for all the people of that tribe, and there are rahui of that type still standing on blocks of land at home.

Another type of rahui was placed on the sea, on fishing grounds or shell-fish rocks, and on the forest where there were places for catching pigeons or collecting berries, and only the local tribe could go to those reserves to collect food. If they saw people from another area coming there without permission, they'd kill them for trespassing – no one would dare to go near a reserved place in my young days at home. Even today there is a rahui still standing on a rock at Omaio below the Tawhais' home; another at Raukokore on a rock called 'Whangai paka', and one at Te Kaha on the mussel rock called 'Toka-a-kuku'. If a stranger went to Whangai paka, he'd be killed, a big wave would come and drown him in the deep waters of Hine Mahuru, 'Te Kopua-a-Hine Mahuru', and people were afraid to go there so those rocks were always covered with mussels. The guardian of Whangai-paka was a stingray and if you saw him coming on a wave you had to rush out of the water – that was a very bad sign!

Toka-a-kuku at Te Kaha is also a dangerous place for strangers; not very long ago a man from Mangakino went there to dive for mussels and the local people warned him,

'Keep away from Toka-a-kuku, its mussels are still tapu to people from outside – don't go there!'

He took no notice and rowed out to Te Toka-a-kuku, and that was the last time anybody saw him alive. Two days later his body was found floating on the sea, with its stomach ripped out by a shark.

The most famous rahui in our district though, was one placed generations ago by Tautuhi-o-rongo,† a high chief in the descent lines of Te Whanau-a-Apanui and Ngati Porou. In the years after the Matatua canoe landed at Whakatane, two of Muriwai's descendants were drowned out at sea, and Tautuhi-o-rongo placed a rahui on the coastline from Nga-kuri-a-Wharei hills at Tauranga to Tihirau mountain at Cape Runaway, 'Mai i Nga Kuri-a-Wharei ki Tihirau', and nobody was allowed to take food from the sea until the rahui was lifted again. The people of our district still remember that rahui and its boundaries, because Tautuhi-o-rongo reserved the territories of the Ngai-te-Rangi of Tauranga and Te Whanau-a-Apanui together, and respected the links between them. Muriwai's great-great-granddaughter Te Kawe-kura-tawhiti had married Taikorekore of the East Coast, and all the great chiefs of Ngati Porou and Te Whanau-a-Apanui, the Houkamaus, the Potaes, the Ngamokis, and the Koopus of Maraenui are descended from that marriage. In my young days the Ngai-te-Rangi people used to come on horseback to tangis at Te Kaha and Raukokore, and people from home went to tangis at Tauranga, and that is why they always respected that saying 'Mai i Nga Kuri-a-Wharei ki Tihirau', from 'The Dogs of Wharei hills to Tihirau mountain'.

If a chief wanted to place a rahui upon a particular area he took a carved totara pole and stuck it into the ground, saying, 'This is my rahui pole posted here – let nobody come in here to interfere with my reserve!'

† See Muriwai genealogy, p. 85; Tautuhi-o-rongo is on the ninth generation from Muriwai.

A campaign poster for Matiu Rata, 1980.

After that if anybody took food from that place or pulled out the pole they were killed for their trouble, and the rahui remained in force until the chief took away his pole and lifted his mana from the land. That is why I say, the rahui is part of the mana motuhake of our ancestors, and it must be treated with respect.

Towards the end of 1979 Matiu Rata, the Member of Parliament for Northern Maori, resigned from the Labour Party and came out as an independent man representing the Mana Motuhake of the Maori people. I think it was good to start a new movement to help the Maori people in Parliament, because as far as I can see there is not much difference between the two parties running the government of New Zealand today, they both pass legislation giving away the rights of the Maori people and they tangle everything up in the house.

Kaea: Ponga ra! Ponga ra!
    The shadows fall! The shadows fall!
Katoa: Ka ta taki mai te Whare o nga ture!
    The House, which makes the laws, is chattering
    Ka whiria ra te Maori! Ka whiria!
    Plaiting the Maori like a rope!
    E ngau nei ona reiti, e ngau nei ona taake!
    Its rates and its taxes are biting!
    A ha ha! Te taea te ueue! I aue! Hei!
    Its teeth cannot be withdrawn – Hei!
    Patua i te whenua!
    The land will be destroyed!
    Hei!
    Hei!
    Whakataua i nga ture!
    The laws will be spread-eagled over it!
    Hei!
    Hei!
    Na nga Mema ra te kohuru
    The Members have betrayed us
    Na te Kawana te koheriheri!
    The Governor has conspired in the evil
    Ka raruraru nga ture
    The laws of the land are confused
    Ka raparapa ki te puatorori! I aue!
    Even the tobacco leaf is singled out – aue!

    Kaore hoki te mate o te whenua e
    We will never
    Te makere atu ki raro ra!
    Forget the loss of our lands
    A ha ha! Iri tonu mai runga
    A ha ha! We always talk of it
    O te kiringutu mau mai ai
    And hold fast to it
    Hei tipare taua mo te hoariri!
    As a warrior's headband against the enemy
    A ha ha! I tahuna mai au
    A ha ha! I was scorched in the fire
    Ki te whakahere toto koa
    In the sacrifice of blood, stripped
    E ki te ngakau o te whenua nei
    To the heart of the land!
    E ki te koura! I aue, taukuri e!
    Bribed with gold – aue, taukiri e!

A ha ha!
A ha ha!
Ko tuhikitia, ko tuhapainga
Shoving up
I raro i te whero o te Maori! Hukiti!
Under the backside of the Maori. He's caught!
A ha ha!
A ha ha!
Na te ngutu o te Maori, pohara, kai kutu
Was it your mission to remove
Na te weri weri ko i homai ki konei?
The tattoo from Maori lips, stop him eating lice,
    take away his disgusting habits?
E, kaore i ara, i haramai tonu koe ki te kai whenua!
No! you came to eat our lands!
Pokokohua! Kauramokai! Hei!
May your heads be boiled! Placed on sticks! Hei!
A ha ha!
A ha ha!
Kei puta atu hoki
How can the prow of our canoe
Te ihu o te waka i nga torouka o Niu Tireni
Pass the headlands of New Zealand
Ka paia pukutia e nga uaua o te ture a te kawana!
When your restrictive, perplexing laws stop us
Te taea te ueue! Au! Au! I aue!
And we cannot bypass them? – aue!

'Te Kiringutu', a men's haka (Ngati Porou)
revised version by Tuta Nihoniho

It is time for a change, and I hope that the other Maori members of Parliament will cooperate with Matiu Rata to do good for their people and bring the Maori people together – Whakakotahi! If they cannot unite into one body, then nothing good will come out of it.

It is not the first time, though, that this kind of movement has been tried; I remember that there was a big fight in Parliament between Apirana Ngata and the Prime Minister Bill Massey in 1913, when Massey tried to bring all the Maori lands in New Zealand under Government control.‡ He put forward his bill in the House but as soon as Ngata saw it he said,

‡In November 1913, Massey's Native Minister W. H. Herries moved the Native Land Amendment Bill, which aimed at speeding up the partition of Maori lands into individual holdings, and its purchase for European settlement. Ngata spoke against the Bill in a heated debate, and said, 'Behind the Minister is the greed of the pakeha, eloquent and aggressive . . . and the honourable gentlemen who sit behind him, and who do not possibly know as well as I do the inner depths of the mind of the Native Minister, say to themselves, "Now this is a splendid Bill, we are going to get hold of the Native Land in the easiest way . . ." ' (*N.Z. Parliamentary Debates*, Vol. 167, pp. 400, 401)

'No! We don't want your Government to take hold of our lands! If you pass this Act, one day the Maori will have nowhere to stay in New Zealand and he'll be swept straight out to sea! I will not agree to your bill – never!'

Massey got really wild with Ngata and in the finish he asked him, 'Are you trying to start a revolution in New Zealand?'

'Yes! If you try to take hold of our lands with this bill, I will start a revolution, and we the Maori people will die under arms, fighting for our land!'

The argument went on and Massey and Ngata 'crossed swords' in the House of Parliament, fighting over this bill – that is what it said in Ngata's Hansard of 1913. Finally W. D. S. McDonald, the East Coast member and Minister of Public Works stood up and said,

'I support Ngata's position, and I move that this session be adjourned.'

The meeting in the House finished and Massey's bill was stopped, and not long after that Apirana Ngata had a talk with Tau Henare, the Member for Northern Maori. He said to him,

'Well, Tau, I want you to turn Independent before the next election comes up, because I think that the fight between the two parties is going to be very close, and you might be able to control the balance.'

Tau Henare turned independent and when election time came, the two parties were tied 80–80, with eighty seats each, and Tau Henare was the only Independent in the House. He supported Massey's Government and Massey stayed in power backed by the vote of one Independent!§ After that Ngata and Tau Henare worked together to set up Incorporations and improve the position of Maori land, and they started some very good schemes for the Maori people. That is why I say, Matiu Rata is following in the footsteps of Tau Henare, the member for Northern Maori who turned Independent all those years ago, and I hope that his movement will come to a good conclusion.‖

Matiu Rata took his thoughts back to the maraes of Northland and discussed them with his old people, and that is the proper way to move in the Maori way of life – quite a few of our young leaders have graduated with degrees, but they don't go home to ask their elders,

'E koro ma, these are my thoughts – will you support me in this matter or not?'

Ngata told us, 'Go back to your maraes! If the old people won't support your work, you can't do anthing – it must be settled on the marae, or it's not worth talking about!'

The way of talking on the marae is to discuss things patiently, letting every man speak without interruption and moving along in a humble manner, and Ngata was a man like that – you would hear the people calling him all sorts at meetings but when he stood up to speak, he never referred back to the insults they had thrown

§ The 1914 election was almost a dead-heat between the Liberals and Massey's Reform party, and Tau Henare as an independent candidate, chose to support Massey. In his eulogy for Tau Henare in the House in 1940, Ngata said: 'There are people who say that the Massey government would not have been possible in 1914 but for Tau Henare's support of the late Mr Massey.' (*N.Z. Parliamentary Debates*, Vol. 257, p. 115)

‖ Matiu Rata was defeated by the Labour candidate for the Northern Maori seat, Dr Bruce Gregory, in the 1980 by-election.

at him. Some of the young people today are very arrogant, they interrupt the elders and they try to control the running of the maraes, they understand nothing of the Maori way of life. We have seen that at Waitangi in past years and at Bastion Point, the young people trampling on the mana of their elders and degrading the customs of their own people and that is not the right way to move about. I do not think that it is proper for the young Maoris of today to call for a boycott of the Treaty of Waitangi – who are they to step over the covenant signed by five hundred chiefs? They're nobody! The men of chiefly line are the right ones to talk about these things; I remember when Apirana told us about the Treaty on the marae at Waiomatatini, he said,

'Well, the worst thing about the Treaty of Waitangi is the third article . . .'

The third article is the one that says, the laws of England shall be the same as the laws of this country, and the laws of this country shall be the same as the laws of England; and that spoiled everything for the Maori people of Aotearoa! I don't think Williams and the other missionaries explained that article to the chiefs, or they would have soon backed out of signing the Treaty of Waitangi! In the old days the chiefs held all their treasures freely, land and cultivations and fishing grounds, and nobody asked them for money, but as soon as the laws of England came here, well . . . the Maoris had to pay taxes, they had to pay rates, their free way of life was ended and the land started slipping away.

The Treaty of Waitangi is not perfect but the young people should remember that when they trample on the work of their ancestors, they are also trampling upon themselves and upon us all.

I must say though that many of the young leaders of today are very nice, the people at John Waititi marae, the members of Nga Tamatoa and the Maori Artists' and Writers' Association all respect their elders and give service to the people, working in their local communities and helping to build up maraes in different parts of the country. I know that Nga Tamatoa did a big job at Tokomaru Bay and they worked on a marae up North, and one day Syd and Hana Jackson came to me and said,

'Well, koro, if you would like some help with your marae, we are ready.'

I said yes, I would like somebody to help paint our marae at home, and Syd and Hana bought all the paint and the young people of Nga Tamatoa came in car-loads to Raukokore, and painted our meeting-house Hine Mahuru and the dining-hall, inside and out! It is very good when the young people work together with their elders, when we are united we can do a lot to help the people.

The future of the Maori people lies with the younger generation but some of our children are not having a good life in the cities today. They hang around at the discos at night and they don't go home to sleep, they get mixed up with the Stormtroopers or Black Power or one of those other gangs and start fighting each other, and the next thing they're in gaol! It is not the fault of the young people, the parents are to blame for not looking after their children. Some of them go off to 'housie' and spend all their money or go to the pub and get drunk, and they leave the children at home with nobody to look after them. The children don't eat properly, they just have a rough kai and go to bed hungry, and they wake up to

Nga Tamatoa on the porch of Hine Mahuru meeting-house, Raukokore, 1973.
John Miller

hear their parents arguing and fighting in the night – that is not a good life for a child! When the parents keep beer and whisky at home the children are bound to have a sip, and in the finish they are drinking spirits when they are still young children, only nine or ten or eleven years old! Then you see them on the streets, picking an argument with old people and swearing and all sorts, and their behaviour is very difficult to mend once it reaches that stage.

Betty Wark and Fred Ellis are two people in Auckland who are working to help our Maori children lost in the city; Betty started up a camp on a council section for them years back, and now she and Fred Ellis are running the Arohanui houses in Ponsonby for homeless young people. Betty is *good* – she finds work for those young people and helps them to get along with each other, and she is doing hard work every day; nobody pays her for it and I think that she deserves a medal! Betty is one woman who should be honoured by the Government for keeping our children out of trouble and helping them to find a better way of life.

When I see our young people hanging about in the streets of Auckland today, looking lost and sad, my mind goes back to the days when I was young, and the elders looked after us on the maraes at home. In those days when we had a hui at Wairuru marae, an old man from Oruaiti called Matiu gathered all the children together and took us aside, and we had our own place on the marae and we had to sit still and listen to the talk of our elders or move to the back of the marae; everything was tapu then and we learned to respect the laws of our old people. When it was time for kai Matiu called out to us,

Stormtroopers organize a marae live-in for handicapped children at Mangatangi, 1979.
Auckland Star

'E tamariki ma, haramai ki te kai! Come on children, come and eat!'

We went into the kauta together and sat in our own area away from the old people, and while we ate Matiu explained to us how the food had been cooked, and about fishing and cultivating the land. At night the older children were allowed to lie down in the meeting-house and listen to the elders telling stories of the past, but one child from each family was chosen especially by his grandparents to take the family whakapapa and to carry on the history of his ancestors.

When I remember that old man Matiu teaching the children of Raukokore how to respect the customary ways of their forefathers, it comes into my mind to help the children of Te Ao Hou in exactly the same way, by saying to them, 'Listen, tamariki ma, and I will explain to you this custom, and that . . .'

CHAPTER TWO
A GIFT AND A GREETING

Apirana Ngata said, 'Go back to the marae . . . the marae is the gathering-place of the people, and everything will be settled there.'

In my young days the tohungas, the last old men of the schools of learning still came to our marae and talked with the people about land, genealogies, boundaries and the works of the ancestors. They were the survivors, the men of senior descent who had been chosen to carry the tribal treasures and pass them down to future generations, heke haere, heke haere, on and down . . .

The Whare Wananga in our district was called Kirieke; it was in Kirieke Pa up on the hills and only the chosen people could go there. Kirieke was a very big pa in its time and it had a whare runanga, a house for all the people, and its own whare wananga, and there were three small pas down on the flats where the people could go fishing or to cultivate their lands. In each generation young men were dedicated in the Kirieke School of Learning to take the history of the ancestors of Te Whanau-a-Maru, and the elders taught them to share their knowledge with others, not to hide it away.

When the people gathered in the whare runanga – grandparents, parents, children and grandchildren – the chosen men came to discuss those things that could rightly be shared with all the tribe, and the work of our ancestors was remembered, and their mana and mauri were passed down. Today our people are forgetting the customs of the old world, and yet the day will come when they will search in every place for their tribal background! That is why I have written some of the teachings of my great-grandpeople in this book, so that future generations can find them and say,

'A, anei te mea nei! Here is what we have been seeking!'

They will marvel at the strength and depth of the works of their forefathers, and the mana and mauri of our ancestors will live on for ever and ever.

In the old days when people came to the marae to sit, to talk, to meet and listen to the speeches and songs, they knew the right ways of moving around, but today even the kawa or etiquette of the maraes is being forgotten. I will tell you about the kawa of Te Whanau-a-Apanui, as it was practised on our maraes at home when my old people were still alive.

When I was a boy our elders were always very careful when they travelled to a hui in another district, because trouble might be waiting for them at the strange marae. On the evening of their departure the tohunga would say to them, 'Tomorrow, you must go to the water.'

At sunrise the next morning they gathered at the sacred water and the tohunga blessed them, and this ceremony was called 'uruuruwhenua' or 'entering the land'. Nobody travelled naked to a strange marae in those times; each sub-tribe had its own prayers to recite as they went on to the marae, and today you rarely hear those prayers in Te Whanau-a-Apanui but their spirit still lives on – whakatupato, beware!

I went with Apirana on many of his journeys and when we sat down to eat in the dining-hall, the old man would take some food from his plate and some tea from his cup and set it aside for the ancestors. This was the 'first food', and it called his ancestors to come and sit beside him, and keep him from all harm.

The ancestors have other ways of coming to you when you are far from home, and one time when I was at Turangawaewae marae on a fine moonlit night, I was just about to go to bed when I heard an owl cry out. I knew straight away that it was my ancestors telling me,

'Everything is all right – we are with you!'

If the owl cries out several times though, that is a warning – 'Look out, trouble is coming!'

You have to move carefully then and look after yourself, and the trouble will pass you by. Soon afterwards, when the news comes to the marae, 'O, so-and-so is very sick,' those men who know the cries of the owl are not surprised.

In our day each district had its own customary proceedings, and the elders of Te Whanau-a-Apanui and Ngati Porou would never allow visitors to come on to a marae once the sun had set at night – it was their sacred law. The old people said,

'E, the turehu people will come on with you because look, the sun has set!'

People who came to a tangihanga after dark were sent away, and they had to wait until the next day to be welcomed.

Once an ope approached the marae at the right time the local women stood in front of the meeting-house and began to karanga or call, and the older women

Hine Mahuru meeting-house, Wairuru marae, with Kirieke Pa in the hills to the right.
Jeremy Salmond, 1976

Coming on to a marae; tangi for Arnold Reedy at Hiruharama, 1971. *Jeremy Salmond*

always took the lead. Sometimes the younger women joined in too, but if the wrong person stood to karanga, watch out! The elders soon got rid of her. The visiting women called back in reply, and as the ope moved slowly on to the marae, ka tangi ka tu, they stopped, stood and then they cried, for all their dead relations.

At a tangi the women of the ope moved forward to the left side of the meeting-house to cry there with the mourners, but if there was no death on the marae they sat behind their menfolks on benches facing the meeting-house. The local women sat at the left side of the meeting-house and the men sat down at the right, and that was when the speech-making began.

First of all the local speakers stood, and they spoke in turn until their chief stood up to settle the home greetings. Once their chief had spoken nobody else could talk, and so he waited until the end. When the local speeches were over (kua pahi) the visitors stood on the marae, and they spoke in turn until their chief ended the greetings from their side. This kawa or 'paeke' has been practised in our district from ancestral times, right down to the present day.

If there was a death on the marae, none of the 'paemate' or mourners were allowed to stand to speak because ill omen was at their side, and they were not freed until a Ringatu tohunga or a Mihinare* minister prayed to lift the tapu from the burial tent, the meeting-house and everywhere around, after the burial was over.

At any hui a son was not supposed to speak on the marae if his father was

*Church of England.

Local orators speak first; Hirini Haig, at Arnold Reedy's tangi, 1971. *Jeremy Salmond*

Visitors farewell the dead – Matiu te Hau, at Arnold Reedy's tangi, 1971. His speech is followed by a waiata (right). *Jeremy Salmond*

present, nor should a younger brother stand to speak if his elder brother was there because the right to talk on the marae passed down the chiefly descent lines from father to eldest son, and on to their descendants. In our district though, the chief often opened up the way for other men to speak, and a father could say to his son or an elder brother to his taina,

'E tu koe! You stand.'

It was like that in my family, because my father was not very fluent in Maori and my elder brother Taikorekore never talked on the marae. He was our 'full-back' for waiatas, patere, and haka and he knew all the tribal songs by heart, but it was not in his mind to give speeches. When the old people called to him,

'Taikorekore . . . e tu ki runga! Stand up, Taikorekore,' he just looked down at the ground and signed to me instead.

After a while they knew, and they called for me every time.

Sometimes when the old men wanted you to speak on the marae they would pass you a special walking stick, and those tokotoko had a very deep history behind them. The tokotoko came from the ancient kawa of the schools of learning in Hawaiki, they were not invented here, and each ancestral tokotoko carried prayers, a mauri or life force and a name of its own. No man possesses a tokotoko of this type, he just carries it for his lifetime and sometimes in the meeting-house the people came to touch the tokotoko of their ancestor. There is talk in a tokotoko and prayers, and it carries the mauri of spiritual treasures to the one who holds it, so you must never interfere with this type of tokotoko unless you are entitled, or you will die.

When our ancestors came on their canoes from Hawaiki their sacred tokotokos guided them to land, and after they had settled in these islands the priests found special woods and carved tokotokos according to the rituals taught to them in the whare wanangas of Hawaiki.

If you were handed a tokotoko by your elders it was an honour and a command to speak, and your ancestors came to stand beside you on the marae. One time when I was with my son Kepa at a tribal meeting on Mangere marae I passed my tokotoko over to him and when he stood up to speak, he moved around and talked and chanted his patere, and he made a great speech on the marae that day. Afterwards he said to me,

'Well Dad, when you gave me your tokotoko that feeling came into my mind, I knew exactly what to say . . .'

All these things came with our ancestors from Hawaiki – the art of shaping canoes, the art of carving and making tokotokos, the art of building houses, and the tohungas of each art were dedicated to carry the proper karakia or rituals, clearing their minds for a single thought and holding fast to the mana from Hawaiki. You can't afford to make a mistake with these things – I know, because I have seen it! One time I went to the opening of a meeting-house in Te Whanau-a-Apanui and the tohunga there was a real expert in all the karakias of house building, but when he stood up on the marae to chant the tomo whare prayers his mind went astray – he broke the ritual, he lost the words and he tried and tried, but he could not carry on! All the people were murmuring,

'O, he aitua! He tohu mate tenei – this is a sign of death!'

We went back to Raukokore and about a week later, sure enough, we heard that the tohunga had died. If you break the ritual in a ceremony of that kind somebody has to pay for it, because the tapu is very strong.

The karakia for carving was taught to me by my grandfather's cousin, Pera Te Kaongahau – he was a master of genealogy and history, but my grandfather was not. The carving karakia came down to us on the descent lines from Apanui, a master carver in his times, and none of the carvers living today know that chant any more. John Taiapa did not know it, Pine Taiapa did not know it right through, and when Roger Duff was planning to return an ancient carved lintel to Tukaki house at Te Kaha he asked me to record it, but I told him, no, it is not right for karakias of this type to be written. Some things can be written down but others should remain secret, passed from the mind of the tohunga to the mind of his tauira according to the ancient laws of tapu. I think that Cliff Whiting is the young carver of today still carrying on the mana of his ancestor Apanui.

It is said that in our district, the women had the right to speak on the marae, but in the old days only a woman of the upoko ariki, the senior line of chiefs, could stand to speak before her menfolk. If any other woman spoke the men would hoot her off, saying,

'E noho koe ki raro – you sit down!'

When a high chieftainess stood on the marae, though, the descent lines of her ancestors came upon her and opened up the pathway for her; the men could not stand without her authority, and they looked to her for the signal to speak on the marae. There were very few women like that, though, and the high chiefs of most tribal groups were men.

My mother's older sister Keita Horowai was the high-born woman of our district and the elders trained her in tribal history and whakapapa, and she spoke on our marae. When Keita died my mother took her place, but although she was a puna (well-spring) of oratory and waiata, she rarely stood to speak in public. Her work was to gather the women together and she led them in singing, and often she would get the old women to speak on the marae and then sang the waiata for them. My mother was a very humble woman and she worked to unite her people.

Every now and then, though, at an important hui the men of Te Whanau-a-Apanui would say,

'E Mihi, our greetings are with you.'

Then my mother would stand on the marae. One time when our people travelled to Te Waimana for a tangi, the old man Te Pairi stood to welcome us, then my mother stood to give her speech of reply. Te Pairi was so wild that he was hopping about all over the place, until somebody told him,

'Hey, that's Mihi Kotukutuku of Te Whanau-a-Apanui you're talking to!'

Te Pairi sat down and the next minute Taua Rakuraku stood up and said,

'E Mihi Kotukutuku, my sister – greetings.'

My mother was closely related to the Rakurakus, the chiefly family of Te Waimana, and after that Te Pairi couldn't say a word.

One East Coast woman who stands to speak on the marae today is Whaia McClutchie of Mangahanea, and a few years back when Te Maraku died in Waikato, Whaia went with a crowd of Ngati Porou people to the tangi at

(Left) A tokotoko, now held in the University Museum, Philadelphia. *Hirini Mead*
Rongomaianiwaniwa, Whaia McClutchie's illustrious ancestress – a poutokomanawa in
Porourangi meeting-house, Waiomatatini. *Cliff Whiting*

Maungatoatoa. I came late to the marae that day and the speeches were just about
over when I arrived, so I joined in with the group from Ngati Porou. Not long
after I sat down a big half-caste fellow from Waikato stood on the marae, and I
heard him saying,

'Ngati Porou! Why did you let that woman stand to return our greetings? She
has trampled on the kawa of Waikato! Meatheads! Slaves! If this was the old days,
she'd be cooked in the hangi – we'd kill her and feed her to the people!'

He was wild because Whaia had cut across their etiquette and made a speech,
but I didn't like to hear that type of talk about Ngati Porou – it was too strong. I
stood up and walked straight to the microphone on the marae, chanting my patere
'To toki e hika' that gives the genealogy from Te Houtina right through to
Apanui, and then I spoke about the tapu of those ancient days, and the talk of
eating people that had been thrown on the marae. I recited a karakia to cut away
those words and kill them, and after that I turned to the people of Waikato and
said,

'Waikato! The king, high chiefs! I do not come to trample on the mana of your
marae; I stand to answer the challenge of that man who said that I, Ngati Porou,

should be eaten! You, friend – you are descended from Tama-te-Kapua and so am I. Tama-te-Kapua begot his eldest son Tuhoromatekaka and then his second son Kahumatamomoe; Tuhoromatekaka begot Ihenga, Ihenga begot Tuariki, Tuariki begot Tuwahiawa, Tuwahiawa begot Turirangi, Turirangi married Rongomaihuatahi and begot Apanui-runga-mutu, my ancestor. You are descended from Tama-te-Kapua's second son, Kahumatamomoe, and you come under the junior line – you are my taina!

'Secondly, let me tell you about the children of Porourangi, the ancestor of Ngati Porou. Hau was the eldest son, Rongomaianiwaniwa was a daughter and Ueroa was the youngest son. Mrs McClutchie, the woman you want to cook and eat, is descended from the ancestress Rongomaianiwaniwa, but you friend, you come down from Ueroa, the youngest son! Ueroa begot Tokerau, Tokerau begot Iwipupu, Iwipupu begot Kahungunu, Kahungunu begot Kahukuranui, Kahukuranui begot Rakaihikuroa, Rakaihikuroa begot Tupurupuru, Tupuru-puru begot Te Rangituehu, Te Rangiteuhu begot Tuaka, and Tuaka begot Mahinarangi who married Turongo, and was the ancestress of the Waikato lines. Mrs McClutchie is descended from Rongomaianiwaniwa but you come under the junior line from Ueroa – you are her taina!

'So now I say this – if these were the old days, I would call out and have *you* killed, cooked in the earth oven and fed to all the people! Who are you to insult your seniors? You threw your challenge on the marae, and now you have been answered – you're nobody!!'

As I sat down I heard the old man Ngakohu Pera from Te Whakatohea asking, 'Who was that who spoke just then?'

Pita Pekama told him, 'E! It was your own mokopuna, Eruera Stirling.'

The old man pulled his coat around him and stood slowly on the marae, and then he pointed his tokotoko at that man from Waikato and said,

'See this, friend? With this weapon I could spear your belly and have you thrown in the oven! I support what my grandson Eruera has said; and if you want to know who is speaking, I will answer you – it is the tribes of Te Whakatohea and Rongowhakaata, who have come to this marae!'

With those words old Ngakohu took his weight of the challenge upon his own shoulders, and when he sat down an elder from Waikato stood and said,

'E tama, Eruera, let me settle this dispute between us. You did not bring anger to this marae, it was my own people who threw it at you. So it was right for you to speak as you did. The man who started all this trouble is the one who should be thrown in the oven. And yet, it is also true that when you visit another marae, you should respect their etiquette and not trample it on the ground. If you treat their procedures lightly, it leads to angry words on the marae . . .'

He was quite right, you know, but I could not leave those insults lying upon the heads of my ancestors – somebody had to answer them back.

When all the speech-making is over, the visitors bring their gifts forward and lay them down on the marae. In my childhood days a visiting party always carried food to a hui, pigs, potatoes, kumaras, dried fish and other special kai, wrapped up in kona baskets or big plaited kits. It was the thought of the people, their love, and

Gifts of food brought to a tangi, 1910. *Alexander Turnbull Library*

people never came empty-handed to the marae. Today people bring money instead, but in my young days it was always food, and sometimes tribal treasures such as cloaks or greenstone for the tangi of a chief. When the koha was placed on the marae the local women called a greeting, and then some of the locals picked up the gift and carried it carefully away – it was never snatched up carelessly, and taken without thanks. It was the same when people visited each other's homes, they always carried kai with them as an awhina (help) and aroha for the people of the house.

After that the visitors came to shake hands with the local people, and as soon as the cooks were ready the ope was called into the dining-hall for kai. The children ate and then their elders, and when the welcome was over the children were free to run around and play on the marae.

In early times, of course, there were no whare kai or dining-halls but they did have kauta, cooksheds made of toetoe and sometimes the guests were fed there. On fine days, though, the tables where taken outside and set up on the grass beside the marae, and everybody ate their kai in the open air. No matter how cold or wet it was, food was never taken into the meeting-house because the house of the ancestors was a tapu place, and that was a sacred law.

Once my mother and I went with all the Whanau-a-Apanui people to a tangi at Rangitukia in the Waiapu district, and when the people had wept and the orators had spoken, a speaker from the local side called out,

'E Te Whanau-a-Apanui! We have wept together – come and shake hands, the kai is ready!'

Mum went at the head of our party to shake hands with the local people, but when she walked into the meeting-house, ha! the dining-table was all set up inside! The next thing we heard a noise like thunder as bowls of sugar, cups and saucers, teapots, plates and kai went crashing to the ground, and my mother dragged the table outside to the back and sent it toppling on its side!

Hariru – shaking hands and greeting with a hongi, as Ngati Porou arrive at Turangawaewae marae for the 1971 coronation. *Jeremy Salmond*

Kai: a feast in the dining-hall at Tikitiki marae, 1971. *Jeremy Salmond*

In earlier times, visitors were fed out in the open. *Alexander Turnbull Library*

One of the old men of Rangitukia called out,

'A-a, where are the cooks? You people have killed us – setting up the table in the meeting-house! There is the dining hall, over there – why did you take the food inside the whare nui? Ana, kua mate tatau!!'

Then my mother came out in front of the meeting-house and she *told* those people off,

'You people are very arrogant – ka whakahihi koutou! Do you want us to come inside your house so you can load food upon our heads? Here is your food . . . eat it! It is not the custom of Te Whanau-a-Apanui to eat the tapu of our ancestors!'

Well, those old people of Rangitukia were ashamed, and one of the elders said, 'Yes, Mihi, you are right . . .'

The cooks had to clean up the meeting-house, and prepare another meal and serve it in the dining-hall and all their plates and sugar basins and cups and saucers were broken. That's why the old people said at my mother's tangi,

'Well, Mihi, you were the first, and you were the last! There will never be another woman like you.'

She held fast to the mana and tapu of her people, and if anybody stepped across her pathway – watch out!

Liquor was also forbidden in the meeting-house, and in our district it was kept right out of the marae. When I was chairman of the Tihirau Tribal Committee I passed a law that no drinks could be taken into the dining-hall, and that notice is still there today,

'No Liquor Allowed in this Hall.'

If a drunken person came into the meeting-house he was threatened and thrown outside, and the next morning he was taken in front of the Maori committee and fined £10 or £20. Anybody who wanted to drink at one of our huis could go down to the beach and you'd hear them on the sand hills singing and laughing away, but they kept off the marae. Liquor is no good at huis because it makes the people fight, and on some maraes today you will hear very nice talk in front of the meeting-house, but around at the back the people are drinking waipiro and scrapping with one another.

The meeting-house is tapu because it is the body of our ancestor and it carries the ancestral name, and the tahuhu or ridgepole is the senior descent line from that ancestor, with all the other lineages coming down below. Our meeting-house at home is called Hine Mahuru, she married Apanui-Waipapa and they had eight children, and that is the tahuhu of our house and of our sub-tribe and the heke, the rafters or descent lines come down from the ridgepole and alight on the poupous, carved figures of the descendants of each line – each poupou has a name. When the people of Roukokore gather within Hine Mahuru all her descendants are together inside, and that is why the house is sometimes called 'Te Poho o Hine Mahuru' or 'Hine Mahuru's belly'; it is a place for her children to shelter. The house is always open and no matter where Hine Mahuru's descendants wander, the house will call to them,

'Anei ahau – here I am!'

Inside the house the poupous hold up the rafters, the rafters hold up the

Within the ancestral house: Porourangi meeting-house at Waiomatatini. *Alexander Turnbull Library*

tahuhu, the tahuhu holds up the house, and that shows the unity of the people. At Tukaki meeting-house in Te Kaha the whakapapa of all the ancestors is written on the wall, so that you can see, yes, that is so-and-so, and this is somebody else . . .

When you went into a meeting-house in the olden days you had to sleep at the feet of your carved ancestor, and late in the evening the tohunga of that place would come in and talk to the visitors, saying,

'A, kia ora, —.'

'A!'

'Are you a descendant of —?'

'Ae . . . Yes.'

If he found out that somebody was sleeping under the wrong ancestor though, he'd get really wild.

'Where are you from?'

'From —.'

'Are you a descendant of —?'

'Kare . . . no.'

'Kia tere to matike mai ki waho! Get up from there at once! Who is your ancestor?'

'Oh – so-and-so . . .'

'Well, you've got a cheek to sleep there – here is the place for you! Don't trample on another man's genealogy!'

Sometimes if that fellow had put his bedding under somebody really important the local people would give him a thrashing and throw him out of the house, yelling,

'Taurekareka – slave! Mongrel! You're nothing!'

When you go inside a meeting-house you should leave your shoes outside at the door, because shoes were never worn in the days of our ancestors. They are a modern invention and they trample upon the mauri of the house.

Visitors sleep on the left side of the meeting-house and the local people go to the right, and the proper place for the chief of an ope to sleep is under the putaauahi or window on the left side of the house. Nobody else can put his bedding there, only the chief, and when the tangata whenua see him lying down they know, 'Hello! Here is the rangatira!'

One time a group of Te Whanau-a-Apanui people went to Tokomaru Bay for the tangi of Henare Potae, and after they had been welcomed on the marae they went inside the meeting-house to rest. After dusk when the local people all came in, they saw this old man called Tata-hare sitting below the window. The real chief of the visitors was a man called Koopu, and after a while an elder from Tokomaru Bay stood up and said,

'I greet our manuhiri tuarangi (distinguished visitor) lying there, and what is your name . . .? Uh, now I remember – hello, Koopu!'

That was a very big insult to Tata-hare, and he had to pick up his bedding and take it to another part of the house.

While a group of manuhuri were in the meeting-house children were not allowed to enter, and men and women could not make love in there at night. It was only when the elders matched a couple, saying 'Here is your woman,' and 'Here is your man,' that those young people were allowed to come together within their ancestral house.

In my young days, when we travelled to a hui, the elders would stay awake all night, singing and telling stories, and after they had exchanged speeches and the visitors had laid down their thoughts, the way was open for all kinds of talk – the two sides were together and everything was noa.

Women could speak inside the meeting-house and younger men, and they talked about tribal history, land, growing kumaras, fishing, making storage pits, gathering crayfish, boundaries, tribal business and the news around the place – you heard all sorts in the meeting-house at night!

Sometimes an old man handed his tokotoko to a champion singer or leader of the haka, and one side of the house would stand to sing and then the other! The walking-stick was passed around and the story-tellers took their turn, joining up the whole crowd with their histories, jokes and pakiwaitara . . . the nights seemed short then and people were still talking when the sun rose in front of the meeting-house, and a new day began.

I have tried to tell you about the power of the ancestors, and the memories of a lifetime. These things must be passed on, so that our descendants will have a spirit to sustain them.

E tamariki ma – study your whakapapa, and learn to trace your descent lines to all your ancestors, tuakana and taina, so that you can join yourselves together. Do not use these treasures to raise yourselves above others – ko mea, ko mea, ko mea, ko 'hau! But if you are challenged, or if somebody throws words at you on the marae, then it is proper to stand up and reply.

The old people said to us, be humble; work amongst the people and they will learn to praise you. That was the wisdom of our ancestors, brought from the ancient houses of learning in Hawaiki, Te Whakaeroero, Rangitane, Aorangi, Tapere-nui-a-Whatonga. The old men told us, study your descent lines, as numerous as the hairs upon your head. When you have gathered them together as a treasure for your mind, you may wear the three plumes 'te iho makawerau', 'te pare raukura' and 'te raukura' on your head. The men of learning said, understand the divisions of your ancestors, so you can talk in the gatherings of the people. Hold fast to the knowledge of your kinship, and unite in the brotherhood of man.

Ana, kua mutu aku korero inaianei – my talk is now finished. I have told you those things which are right, and the blessings of your ancestors will shine upon your pathway.

Na reira e nga iwi katoa e noho mai nei o roto i te rohe o Tamaki-makau-rau, whiti atu ki runga o Te Ika-a-Maui, Te Wai Pounamu, tae atu ki Wharekauri, ka hoki atu enei mihi ki a koutou, ki nga taumata korero, ki nga wananga, ki nga iwi e pupuri mai ana i te mauri o runga i o tatau marae maha katoa.

Ka hoki ake ano nga korero ki a Io-matua-te-kore, ki te mauri o Tane-nui-a-rangi, ki te mauri o Tu-matauenga, ki te mauri hoki o Tangaroa;

engari, apititia ki runga i enei mea katoa, ko to tatau Matua ano i te rangi, ko ia ra te Kai-whakakotahi, te Kai-awhina i a tatau nei mahi katoa. No reira, ko enei nga mihi nui atu ki a koutou i raro i o tatau wairua, a, i raro i o tatau atua o raro i nga wananga e korerotia atu nei e au.

Engari ahakoa, kare e warewaretia nga tangata na ratau i pupuri te mauri, te mana o taua o te iwi Maori. Ka hoki tena ki a Apirana Ngata, ki a Te Rangihiroa, ki a Timi Kara – e koro ma, ahakoa aua atu ki te whenua, engari ko te wairua kai te tangi tonu atu ki a koutou katoa.

Aa, kare hoki e warewaretia i aku matua, Mother and Dad, ahakoa e haere ana nga ra, kare hoki e wareware ki a korua e takoto mai ra, me ta korua mokopuna George Te Ariki-tapu-ki-waho, me a korua tamariki, me nga karangatanga maha e takoto mai na i runga o Moutara.

E mihi atu ana ahau ki nga iwi e noho mai ra i te wa kainga, ko te Whanau-a-Maru, Whanau-a-Pararaki, Te Whanau-a-Kauaetangohia e noho mai na i runga i o tatou marae, nga takahanga waewae o tatau matua tipuna, a me te mihi atu ano hoki ki taku tuahine ki a Mataku-Ariki Waititi, te morehu o te whanau e noho mai na i Raukokore, ko korua ko John, me te whamere katoa – ki a koutou enei mihi nui i raro i nga manaakitanga a to tatau Matua-i-te-rangi.

Kati, ko taku mihi nui ake hoki ki taku mokopuna pakeha i raro i nga mahi, a, ki a Ani Salmond, e mau nei i nga mahi e whakakotahi nei i te wairua i te mauri o nga mahi Maori, kia kaua ai e ngaro. Na reira e Ani, korua ko to rangatira me o tamariki, ko te mihi nui ki a koe i te mea kua whakaarangia mai e koe tenei taonga, hai whakamaharatanga ki a maua ko taku hoa rangatira, a ki a tatau katoa. Ka mau tonu te aroha nui ki a koe.

Ana, ka mutu aku mihi atu ki a koutou; kati, hai whakamutunga mo aku mihi, ki a koutou katoa, ko taku himene:

> Taku nei e koa ai au ko nga whare o te Atua!
> Atahua ana mai enei tohu o te pai
> Kei te ohia atu au ki tou mata e te Atua!
> Whakawhiwhia mai ahau ki au tohu atawhai
> Te Ariki atawhai, tenei arohaina mai
> Tino akona ahau mo nga he e pehi nei
> Okiokitanga mai e-e-e ki tou taha noho ai
> Manu rere takiwa roa tera e koa ia
> Nei ra ia te tino koa mo te ngakau whiwhi nei
> Whiwhi pai nga ora nui mo nga he e pehi nei
> Okiokitanga mai e-e-e ki tou taha noho ai
> A-mi-ne!

Eruera Stirling sings a waiata with his relations, at Pine Taiapa's tangi, Tikitiki, 1971.
Jeremy Salmond

ERUERA
A DISCUSSION

Now the greetings have ended, the chief has spoken and his gift of love lies on the marae. Visitors and hosts shake hands and hongi (press noses), and the guests pass into the dining-hall and are fed. That night all the people gather together in the meeting-house, sheltered by Tane-whakapiripiri, the ancient god of the forest:

Rukutia
Bind
Rukutia nga pou tahuhu
Bind fast the ridge-pole posts
O te whare nei
Of this house
Rukutia nga poupou
Bind the carved slabs
O te whare nei
Of this house
Rukutia nga tukutuku
Bind the reed panels
O te whare nei . . .
Of this house
Rukutia, rukutia
Bind, bind them together
Kia u, kia mau
Make them firm and steadfast
Kai tae mai
Lest
A Te Anu Matao
The cold and stormy elements
Ki roto i a koe – e!
Come inside you!
Kai ninihi atu ai
Keep out the stealthy hailstones
A Ua-whatu, a Ua-nganga
And the sleeting wind
Kai whakamai hoki
Stand up to
A Hau-nui, a Hau-roa
The great wind and the long wind

A Tawhiri-matea
Of Tawhirimatea
Taku hiki i pai ai
This is my charm of blessing
Ma roto i a Tane
Within you, Tane
E tu nei – i
Standing here
Ko Mahana, ko Pumahana
May all be warm and safe inside your walls
Ko Werawera, Ko Kohakoha
May warmth, heaped up warmth, glowing warmth
Nga tangata mo roto
Be the people for this house
I a Tane e tu nei . . .
Standing here!

a house-warming prayer

In the comfort and peace of the ancestral house, the people stand to speak and discussions, dreams, songs and story-telling follow. Now the younger generation, women and the politically unimportant can speak their minds – kua watea, the way is open.

'Where we sleep, you sleep; what we eat, you eat, where we go, you go too.' (Eruera Stirling to Anne Salmond, 1964)

Eruera and Amiria Stirling and I have been friends for about sixteen years now, and this is the third book that we have worked on together. The first was *Hui: A Study of Maori Ceremonial Gatherings*, written in 1971-2 and dedicated to them; the second was *Amiria* (1976), the story of Mrs Stirling's life; and the third is this book, Eruera's gift to a rising generation. They have been friends and grandparents to me, teachers and guides in the Maori world, and my love for them is beyond words.

This book began not long after *Amiria* was published. Eruera rang me at home one day and said that it was time to write his book now, and I agreed. It took us two years to get started though, because I had three small children by then and not many quiet moments to think about the book and write.

Early in 1979 my husband Jeremy gave me the time to begin taping, and that was when the book really began. Eruera and I met for a morning's session about once a week for the next six months, and after that irregularly until the end of the year. We worked mainly at the Stirlings' house in Herne Bay, in a room well away from food and the possibility of interruptions, and our sessions usually began and ended with a karakia or prayer. After a while when I understood more about the tapu of traditional knowledge, it became natural to miss a session if I had a period, and later on to keep this manuscript away from food.

Eruera Stirling and his wife Amiria, outside their home in Herne Bay. *New Zealand Herald*

Our meetings were not interviews, but more like formal classes. I asked questions sometimes but mostly Eruera talked, explaining customs, telling traditions, and recounting the main events of his life. He told me that when I first came to his house in 1964, he had looked to see if I had the 'right spirit', and he wove a metaphor of kinship and apprenticeship between us that made our work together peaceful and unworried. For all that, he always kept this book in mind, and it seemed to me that our conversations were a deliberate and serious passing-on of knowledge, into the tape recorder and out to future generations.

'Maoritanga is not action songs or hakas, it is holding fast to the treasures of your ancestors – lands, marae, pa, the mountains – and returning in spirit to the minds of your forebears. It is not a light and easy thing, but a difficult treasure, and heavy to carry.'
(Eruera Stirling, Maori Artists' and Writers' Conference, 1975)

'Knowledge or matauranga is a blessing on your mind, it makes everything clear and guides you to do things in the right way . . . and not a word will be thrown at you by the people. It is the man who goes with his spirit and his mind and his heart believing in all these things who will climb to the high summits of leadership.'
(Eruera Stirling to Anne Salmond, 1979)

By November 1979 we had completed thirty-seven four-inch tapes of conversation, and Rangi Motu had transcribed most of them with the support of the University Grants Committee. I hid myself away in a small room at the back of one of the old houses at the university, and began to write. I wrote the stories of Captain William Stirling and his South Island descendants from the tape transcripts, but when I came to the East Coast tribal history, I looked into my files and found a collection of written material that Eruera had given me at one time or another – a genealogy tracing his descent from each of the seven main canoes; a story in English entitled *Migration of Tahupotiki the Younger Brother of Porourangi*; an exercise book written cover-to-cover in English when the Waiomatatini School celebrated its centennial in 1978; and a *History of Te Whanau-a-Maru and Ngati Hinekehu of Tapuwaeroa Valley*. Just before Christmas Eruera gave me his whakapapa book for a while so that some of its pages could be photographed, and it held genealogies with stories written above and below them in Maori, decorated with drawings of mountains and buildings and stylized clouds. The written material was quite beautiful and much (although not all) of it has been drawn into this text.

As I wrote on I remembered stories that I had recorded with Eruera as far back as 1970, and accounts that he had given to my class 'Introduction to Maori Society' and to other groups when I was present. Some of these tapes were stored in the Archive of Maori and Pacific Music at the University of Auckland, and others were held in the Maori and Pacific Islands Unit archives of Radio New Zealand. In each case Eruera was talking to a group of young people, sometimes in English and sometimes in Maori, and teaching them about their ancestral past. On one occasion, the Maori Artists' and Writers' Conference of 1975, he held up his genealogy book and talked about each of the illustrated pages in turn. I also found a superb tape of a conversation recorded by Bruce Biggs in 1966, when Eruera Stirling, Arnold Reedy, Matiu Te Hau and a number of other elders gathered at the Anthropology Department in No.13 Symonds Street, and held an uproarious discussion about women's rights to speak on the marae and other traditional topics. A transcript of parts of this tape is given in Appendix 3. Most of the stories in these tapes Eruera had already told me, but the versions given to large audiences were particularly vivid, and they have been used in this text as well.

This book, then, is not strictly oral history since it includes written material, sometimes quoted directly and sometimes woven into the main narrative, and the oral material upon which it is based was spoken to a variety of audiences, sometimes in English and sometimes in Maori. It has been strongly edited, but with close attention to preserving the rhythms and idioms of Eruera Stirling's speech. My one regret is that so little of the final text is in Maori, when so much of our conversation was in that language. I had hoped that some sections of the book might be presented in parallel pages of Maori and English, but after unsuccessful hours of trying to edit the Maori texts, I realized that my command of Maori simply wasn't equal to the task. That is why Eruera's colloquial English is the basic dialect in this narrative.

I should make it clear that apart from the linguistic limits, there are other boundaries set upon this book. It does not try to reveal all of Eruera's traditional knowledge, but only those things that he considered proper to pass on in writing to a younger generation. For this reason many genealogies, karakia (prayers), patere (chants), stories of tribal history and some waiata (songs) have been excluded. There are no doubt many other things that I did not ask Eruera, he did not mention, or that he felt were better left alone, and his silences have been respected here.

'The more important families of a tribe are in the habit of devoting one or more of their members to the study of traditional knowledge . . . Persons so educated are their books of reference, and their lawyers.'
(Edward Shortland in 1851, *The Southern Districts of New Zealand*, p. 95.)

The experience of working with Eruera was quite unlike the sessions I had had with his wife Amiria some years before, hours of women's talk over cups of tea, and I think that their books are also very different. *Amiria* is a collection of domestic stories, based on kinship and family life, robust and personal and without a hint of tapu about them, while Eruera's *Teachings* come out of a chiefly tradition, centred on genealogy and politics and shaped by the powers of the ancestors – mana, ihi, wehi and tapu. They have led me to reflect about knowledge in the European academic tradition and in the Maori world, and to look carefully at my chosen profession of anthropology.

I have learned from Eruera that matauranga in the Maori concept of learning is a difficult and dangerous thing, guarded by sacred restrictions but a blessing to those who approach it in the right spirit. It is tribal and ancestral knowledge, discovered by the gods and passed down the descent lines forever. It is held in the

Amiria Stirling, with god-daughter Amiria Salmond and *Amiria. Auckland Star*

memory and if it is written down, the books are hidden away and often buried with the elder when he dies.

Knowledge in the European tradition of scholarship, on the other hand, is said to be open to all with the intelligence to understand, secular in its nature and created (and continually revised) by man. It is written in books and put on the shelves of libraries for anyone to read. That is what they say, but then I wonder. I think that you could equally describe European knowledge as difficult and dangerous, restricted in its access, and to be approached in a proper spirit. Much of it is written in a language that hardly anyone can understand, and those who speak the dialects of knowledge have power and some prestige. Maori knowledge too, is revised over time and it often passes to apprentices outside the family line. The two systems of learning are indeed different, but perhaps not as irreconcilable in philosophy and practice as at first they might appear.

European and Maori ideas about knowledge have coexisted in New Zealand for the past two hundred years: and, Maori people have done much over that time to bring the two philosophies closer together. Maoris have been interested in European ideas since the early days of contact; they rapidly became literate and read the Bible, newspapers, and anything else that came to hand, and the elders then as now, were intellectually curious and critical. Samuel Marsden, one of the first missionaries who came to this country, described the New Zealanders as 'men of great reflection and observation'† and said,

'The chiefs are in general very sensible men and wish for information upon all subjects. They are accustomed to public discussions from their infancy. The chiefs take their children from their mother's breast to all their public assemblies, where they hear all that is said upon politics, religion, war, etc., by the eldest men. Children will frequently ask questions in public conversation and are answered by the chiefs.'‡

This enquiring frame of mind, founded on traditional patterns of learning, later led to experiments which brought Maori and European ideas together in new and inventive ways. The 'prophetic cults' of Papahurihia in Northland, Pai Marie, of Te Kooti, Te Whiti o Rongomai, and Rua Kenana have often been interpreted as bizarre religious outbreaks, but I think they could be better understood as Maori attempts to bring the two different and sometimes conflicting philosophies into a single working structure.

Maoris have also worked with European methods of storing and passing on knowledge. The writing of tribal history and genealogy into 'whakapapa books' dates back to the early days of Maori literacy, and later on, elders published traditional material in the Journal of the Polynesian Society and sought to use the country's education system to transmit understanding of Maori language and culture. This was despite a considerable mistrust of European knowledge and the uses to which it could be put:

> Te matauranga o te Pakeha
> *The knowledge of the Pakeha*
> He mea whakato hei tinanatanga
> *Is propagated*
> Mo wai ra?
> *For whose benefit?*
> Mo Hatana?
> *For Satan's?*
> Kia tupato i nga whakawai
> *Be wary of its temptations*
> Kia kaha ra, kia kaha ra
> *Be strong, and firm*
>
> Te matauranga o te Pakeha
> *The knowledge of the Pakeha*
> Patipati, a ka muru whenua
> *Engulfs you, then confiscates land*
> Kia kaha ra, e hoa ma
> *Be strong, friends*

---

†*The Letters and Journals of Samuel Marsden* (ed. J. R. Elder), p. 386.
‡Marsden, *op.cit.*, p. 103.

Ka mutu ano
Land is all we have
Te tanga manawa
To rest a beating heart
Oranga, a oranga
And for our livelihood

Te matauranga o te Pakeha
The knowledge of the Pakeha
Ka tuari i te penihana oranga
Gives out social security benefits
Hei aha ra?
Why?
Hei patu tikanga
To kill customs
Patu mahara
To kill memory
Mauri e
To kill our sacred powers§

by Tuini Ngawai (Ngati Porou)

Sir Apirana Ngata, for instance, had strong reservations about European approaches to Maori culture, and yet he helped to establish the Board of Maori Ethnological Research, supported the publication of Elsdon Best's writings, published *Nga Moteatea* (a collection of traditional chants), wrote the *Rauru-nui-a-Toi Lectures*, gave many public addresses on Maori topics and sought to have Maori taught in the universities as far back as 1922. In 1943 he wrote in a letter to his friend Timutimu Tawhai of Te Whanau-a-Apanui:

'The time has long passed, when the heirlooms and treasures of Maori culture can be hidden in the memories of a fond few or in laboriously compiled manuscripts dedicated to descendants, who may never prize them. They can be forgotten, my friend, and lost. And they should not be lost. So you and I and others should have them kept, as the Pakeha keeps his records and knowledge, in print on bookshelves, that those who care may read and learn.'[||]

When Ngata organized the Rauru-nui-a-Toi sessions in 1944 on the East Coast to teach and explore local tribal history, he encouraged pakeha school teachers in the area to join in and he said at that time,

'Our Pakeha members will be given an equal chance with ourselves to learn all they can, and for their benefit I am prepared to give the material in English and if necessary, special lessons.'[¶]

§A song composed by Tuini Ngawai of Ngati Porou, c.1950, quoted by Koro Dewes in *Te Ao Hurihuri* (ed. M. King) pp. 58-9.
||A. T. Ngata, *The Price of Citizenship*, 1943, p. 5.
¶A. T. Ngata, *Rauru-nui-a-Toi Lectures*, introductory address, p. 5.

This was in order that the teachers might 'acquire proficiency in subjects that are assuming greater importance in the schools'.*

Since the 1940s there has been a marked drift of young Maori people from rural districts to the cities, and this has led to further innovations in the passage of traditional knowledge. Urban marae have been established that depart from their rural models, and culture clubs have taken over some of the functions of the tribal society. Some tribes have encouraged their urban descendants to return to the country marae for tribal seminars or 'Whare Wananga', while other groups (the Tai Rawhiti people, for instance) organize 'live-in' sessions on urban marae. Elders are often separated from the young people who might otherwise succeed them, and the education system and the media (particularly radio and television) have played an increasingly important role in the teaching of Maori language and some traditional knowledge. All kinds of experiments are being made by Maoris in New Zealand cities to overcome the breakdown of the tribal group and the disruption of old ways of learning.

I wish I could say that Europeans had been as innovative in their approach to Maori knowledge. The early missionary and settler attitudes to Maori philosophy treated it either as heathenish superstition to be conquered, or as a rudimentary system of thought that would inevitably be displaced by more sophisticated European ideas. These attitudes have remained deep-seated in pakeha thinking, and they help to explain why Maori knowledge has so persistently been either ignored or treated as a subject for European scholarly inquiry and not as a philosophical system in its own right.

The education system in New Zealand has incorporated Maori topics in the curriculum and Maori personnel have been hired to teach them, but so far little has been done to adapt academic structures so that Maori expert knowledge, Maori styles of teaching, Maori methods of evaluation and Maori settings might play their proper role in the search to understand Maori philosophy. It is a deep and difficult study and not likely to be mastered in one or two hours a week; and while talks by elders, marae visits and the employment of native speakers of Maori are steps in the right direction, they are too often seen as extra-curricular or peripheral to the main academic task. For an avowedly bicultural country, we have done very little to give Maori philosophy a proper place in the education system, or to seek for ways in which it can meet with European scholarship in a spirit of mutual respect.

A similar inequity is demonstrated in the literary industry in this country. A great many books on Maori topics have been published over the years, but only a handful of them have been written by Maoris, in Maori or using Maori styles and for a mainly Maori audience. Most of the published works by Maoris (and they are few enough) adopt European styles and address a mainly European audience. Some of the books on Maori topics that are most praised by European critics are held in low esteem by knowledgeable Maoris, and until recently their criticisms have rarely been sought. Maori judgements upon such works of scholarship have

---

* A. T. Ngata, *op.cit.*, p. 1.

not been considered relevant, and that too indicates disrespect and has bred mistrust.

'*When you learn anything Maori, it has to be taken seriously. It involves the laws of tapu: genealogies, history, traditional knowledge, carving, preparing flax, in fact, nature itself. Tapu is something that teaches you to respect the whole of nature . . . I don't think Pakehas are aware of this. They think that because they've been to university and studied the language and the culture, they've mastered it. To me listening, it sounds as if there is no depth there at all . . .*'
(Ngoi Pewhairangi of Ngati Porou, in *Te Ao Hurihuri* (ed. M. King), p. 8.)

The justice of these comments is clear if one reflects that an elder might wait sixty or seventy years before he speaks with authority on matters of traditional knowledge, while a university course might take only three years to complete, and many research projects into Maori topics are even shorter in duration.

I don't believe though, that criticisms such as these imply a wholesale rejection of pakeha knowledge and culture; indeed, they often come from people who have been closely involved in the pakeha world and who understand it better than most. They arise in defence of Maori knowledge from casual and incautious approaches, and they call for a proper recognition of Maori philosophy as a system with its own values and standards of expertise.

I want now to reflect briefly upon the implications of such arguments for anthropology, and particularly for anthropology in New Zealand.

> Ki te tuohu koe
> *If you bow your head*
> Me maunga teitei
> *Let it be to a lofty mountain*
>
> (proverb)
>
> Ko Whanokao te maunga
> *Whanokao is the mountain*
> Ko Motu te awa
> *Motu is the river*
> Ko Apanui te tangata
> *Apanui is the man.*
>
> (Whanau-a-Apanui proverb)

I take anthropology to be not a science, but a humanity in the true sense of that term. Its proper task, I think, is to seek to understand and communicate cultural differences, and in its finest moments to bridge them. At this level anthropology is rooted both in our common humanity and our construction of different worlds of meaning, and whenever people find themselves living side by side (as Maori and pakeha do in New Zealand) and yet cultural worlds apart, some such attempt at talking out our differences seems to me inevitable.

The question in my mind is, how can this discussion best be carried out? What kind of style and structure most suits our situation, Maori and pakeha, living together in New Zealand? I am not at all sure, for instance, that the established style of anthropology, the writing of monographs and scientific papers, is particularly apt or helpful. First, the style that dominates international anthropology owes nothing to local styles of discussion (Maori or pakeha): it evolved in Europe or America and irresistibly tends to discuss Maori (or pakeha) topics in a European or American way. I agree with Maoris who say there is little which is recognizably Maori which survives in such descriptions. Second, this style is too often founded upon a scientism that turns people into objects or positions in a structure, a philosophy that I reject. Third, the style is that of a monologue spoken to an anthropological audience, where the anthropologist proposes, sets the rules, makes the analyses and the interpretations. Fourth and worst, the style is not very successful in communicating cultural differences: it communicates *about* them, at the same time domesticating them and robbing them of their inherent power (mana, mauri, wairua).

I dream of an anthropology for New Zealand that celebrates both our common humanity and our cultural differences, drawing strength from one without detracting from the other. I think of a conversation shared between Maori and Pakeha in which each side has its chance to talk, in its own way and on its own topics, to a genuinely attentive audience. I try to imagine an approach that draws upon both Maori and Pakeha styles, and reaches out to Maori as well as Pakeha audiences. I look for an anthropology with heart as well as mind, that can learn to talk to people in a way that lets them understand.

One condition for this kind of conversation is, I think, that both sides should have their positions of strength. 'Maori' and 'pakeha' are categories that define each other in New Zealand, if you accept that Europeans became 'pakeha' in this country and largely within their dealings with Maoris, and tribal groups came to think of themselves as 'Maori' largely within their encounters with pakehas. The interaction between us is our strongest source of national identity. At the same time there are many 'pakehas' who despise that label, and who would like to wipe out everything labelled 'Maori' as well – the four Maori seats in Parliament, Maori schools, Maori synods, Maori scholarships, the Department of Maori Affairs, Maori housing and so on. It is ironic, for these positions of strength are not very strong in fact, being European in concept and construction, and bounded on every side by European controls. Every conceivable Maori avenue to power is rigidly constrained, and European styles of communication are imposed, from the bureaucracy to the mass media. If there is ever to be proper conversation between Maori and Pakeha in this country, I think that this stylistic and structural domination must stop. If it can be stopped in anthropology, that is at least a beginning.

A second condition for proper conversation is, on the other hand, that there must be some common ground, some basis for respect and understanding. I have spoken quite scathingly of a Western style of ethnographic description, particularly the mode that sees people as objects or displaces them with structures; and I hold to my view that the kind of 'social scientist' who thinks of the Pacific as a laboratory and practises a thwarted parody of experimental procedures will contribute little to a local anthropology. There are, however, other kinds of thinkers within the Western tradition. One image is that of the scholar, trying to understand the human condition, intolerant of carelessness and fired with some sort of vocation; and of humane scholarship, the art of constructing knowledge without forgetting its human consequences. This image seems in some deep harmony with the tradition of matauranga, with its long apprenticeships, veneration of knowledge, awareness of its dangers and intolerance of mistakes. I think of elders who treasure learning in a way that is all too uncommon in our universities, who spend long years in its pursuit and who begin to be attributed wisdom round about the time our academics begin to retire. They and our most dedicated scholars are brothers of the mind, and in that kinship lies the possibility of dialogue.

'Ko te kai a te rangatira he korero.

Talk is the food of chiefs.'

Maybe one day, anthropology in New Zealand will be like that.

E koro Eruera, kua ea pea nga wawata inaianei. Engari ko taku aroha ki a korua, kei te mau mo ake tonu . . .

                                                                    Naku, na
                                                                    Ani

                                                                    ANNE SALMOND

NOTES

[1]Appendix I, A and B, discusses Eruera's great-grandfather Captain William Stirling.

[2]The Battle of Trafalgar was in 1805.

[3]Appendix I, A and B, talks about Eruera's grandfather John Stirling.

[4]Other stories of Paikea can be found in Nepia Pohuhu, *AJHR* 1880, Vol II, G-L; *Te Ao Hou*, No. 40, Sept 1962, p. 6; A. T. Ngata, *Rauru-nui-a-Toi Lectures* No. 2, pp. 5, 10-11; P. Harrison, *Traditions of the Ngati Porou Tribe*, p. 5; and David Simmons, *The Great New Zealand Myth*, Ch. 8.

[5]For stories of Hau and Ueroa see A. T. Ngata, *Rauru-nui-a-Toi Lectures*, Lecture 2.

[6]From A. T. Ngata, *Ngarimu V.C. Hui Souvenir Programme*, p. 22.

[7]For stories of Hingangaroa see A. T. Ngata, *Rauru-nui-a-Toi Lectures*, Lecture 4, pp. 10-12; and *Te Wananga*, Vol. II, No. 1 'He Tangi Na Rangiuia,' pp. 21-35.

[8]Apirana Ngata discusses the three sons of Hingangaroa – Taua, Mahaki and Hauiti, in *Rauru-nui-a-Toi Lectures*, Lectures 4 and 5.

[9]For another account of the killing of Apanui, see A. T. Ngata, *Rauru-nui-a-Toi Lectures*, Lecture 5, p. 16.

[10]Muturangi is mentioned in Rongo Halbert, *Te Tini o Toi*, p. 82. Halbert says that this ancestor married a descendant of Toi called Rangitapu.

[11]For other accounts of the deeds of Tamahae, see *Te Kaha District High School Centennial Publication*, pp. 7-8; John Waititi, *The Story of Tamahae*, University of Auckland mimeo; Leo Fowler, 'The Knight Errantry of Tamahae', *Te Ao Hou* No. 24, Oct 1958; and Apirana Mahuika, *Nga Wahine Kai Hautu o Ngati Porou*, Appendix H.

[12]For more detailed accounts of the siege of Toka-a-Kuku pa, see MacKay, J. A., *Historic East Coast and Poverty Bay*, pp. 91-2; *Te Kaha District High School Centennial Publication*, p. 24; and Peta Wairua, 'The Siege of Toka-a-Kuku Pa', *Te Ao Hou* No. 25, Dec. 1958.

[13]For Makahuri's descent, see A. T. Ngata, *Rauru-nui-a-Toi Lectures*, p. 47a.

[14]Apirana Mahuika has written about Hinekehu in *Nga Wahine-Kai-Hautu o Ngati Porou*, pp. 148-50.

[15]For more detail about Toi see Wi Tahata's evidence in the Tapuwaeroa No. 1 Case, Waiapu Minute Book No. 10, and Rongo Halbert, *Te Tini o Toi*.

[16]A whakapapa of Mahu-tai-te-rangi is given on the endpapers of the first printing of Amiria Stirling, *Amiria: The Life Story of a Maori Woman*.

[17]Detailed accounts of the siege of Te Whetumatarau Pa are given in T. Wirepa, *Te Whetumatarau*; and MacKay, J., *Historic East Coast and Poverty Bay*, p. 76.

[18]Another important source for Eruera Stirling's knowledge of tribal history is Apirana Mahuika, *Nga Wahine-Kai-Hautu o Ngati Porou*, particularly Appendix E, 'A Letter from Eruera Stirling 26.2.72.'

GLOSSARY

Anei! –here!

Ao Hou –new world

Aroha – love, pity

E kai –eat!

E tau! – sit!

E tu! – stand!

Haere mai – welcome

Haka – war chant, with actions

Hangi – earth oven

Hapu – sub-tribe

Hapuku – a species of fish, groper

Hika! – a term of address

Houama – a tree with light wood (for floats, etc.)

Hui – gathering

Iho makawerau – lit. 'strength of a hundred hairs'; a plume

Kai – food

Kai moana – sea food

Kaka – native parrot

Kanohi – face, representative

Karaka – a tree with yellow berries, *Corynocarpus laevigata*

Karakia – prayer

Karanga – call, ceremonial call

Kaumatua – elder

Kawa – marae protocol

Kawakawa – a shrub, *Macropiper excelsum*

Kiekie – a climbing plant, *Freycinetia banskii*

Kina – sea egg

Koha – gift

Koro – old man

Kotukutuku – a tree, *Fuchsia excorticata*

Kuia – old woman

Kumara – sweet potato

Makutu – witchcraft, a curse

Mana – spiritual power

Mana motuhake – separate spiritual power

Manuhiri – visitor

Manuka – a shrub or tree, *Leptospermum scoparium*

Maomao –a fish, *Diretmus argenteus*

Marae – ceremonial meeting-place

Matamua – first born child

Matauranga – knowledge, understanding

Mauri – life force.

Mere – a stone club

Mihi – greeting

Moki – a fish, *Latridopsis ciliaris*

Mokihi – a raft made of bundles of rushes

Moko – facial tattoo

Mokopuna – grandchild

Nikau – New Zealand palm, *Rhopalostylis sapida*

Ope – party

Pa – fortified site

Pai – good, well

Pakeha – European

Papatipu – lit. 'growing earth'; ancestral rights to land

Parengo – edible seaweed, *Pophyra columbina*

Pare raukura – feathered head ornament

Patere – chant

Patete – a tree with hollow-stemmed twigs, *Schefflera digitata*

Patu – hand weapon

Paua – shellfish, *haliotis*

Piupiu – a flax kirtle or waist garment

Ponga – treefern, *Cyathea dealbata*

Pupu – winkle

Puriri – a tree, *Vitex lucens*

Rahui – reserve
Rangatira – chief
Rarauhe – bracken, *Pteridium aquilinum*
Rata – a tree, in the East Coast district = a
pohutukawa or *Metrosideros excelsa*

Taharua – lit. 'two sides', a person with
descent from two different tribes
Tahuhu – lit. 'ridge-pole'; senior line of
descent
Taiaha – a long wooden fighting staff
Taina – relative in a junior line of descent
Takapau wharanui – birth mat
Tama – child
Taniwha – a water monster
Tangi – funeral
Tapu – sacred restriction, sacred
Tatai – descent line
Taua – hostile expedition
Tauira – student
Taumau – arranged marriage
Taurekareka – slave
Tiko – defecate
Tipuna – ancestor, grandfather

Toetoe – sedge, *Arunda kakao*
Tohunga – priestly expert
Tokotoko – talking stick
Tuakana – relative in a senior line of
descent
Turehu – fairy people
Tutu – a shrub, *Coriaria arborea*

Upoko ariki – head of chiefly family
Upokokohua – lit. 'your head in my belly' –
a great insult

Wai – water
Waiata – chant, song
Wai tapu – sacred water
Whaikorero – oration, speech
Whakakotahi – unite
Whakapapa – genealogy
Whakatane – to make into a man
Whare puni – sleeping-house
Whare runanga – council house
Whare wananga – house of learning
Whariki – woven floor mats

[Long vowels are not marked in the main text of this book, in deference to Eruera Stirling's
wishes.]

APPENDICES

1. Some notes on Eruera's forebears

A. JOHN STIRLING speaking to Herries Beattie about his father WILLIAM STIRLING and his grandfather MAKERE TE WHANAWHANA in 1911:

John Stirling on Old Maori Days

John Stirling, of Riverton, speaking to me in 1911 said that his father before coming to start the whaling station at the Bluff at the end of 1836 was whaling at Otago Heads about the 1833-35 period. During that time the Maoris left to fight Te Rauparaha. The narrator's grandfather, Makere, led the taua (war party). He died in 1839 and narrator is the sole surviving descendant. The first crowd to go after Te Rauparaha had been led in the Taua-nui (Big Raid) by Whakataupuka and Makere; and the second lot were led by Makere with Bloody Jack and Taiaroa under him as under-chiefs. The first lot fought at Cloudy Bay, and the second expedition fought at the same place. The southerners had been warned to be careful and leave no signs as enemy were unaware of their presence but one young man rashly left traces on the shore and Te Rauparaha noticed the human dung just in time to become really suspicious and rush for the sea, escaping by a narrow margin indeed.

The narrator's father had various marital ventures. He was first married to a sister of Tuhawaiki, but she died childless. When she died the Native custom of finding another wife from the same family was observed, and Tuhawaiki and Haereroa (who was Makere's brother) picked a daughter of Makere, Hiwikau by name, and brought her to Stirling as his wife. Narrator was first male child born at Bluff. His mother bore Stirling two children but one died young. Narrator did not remember his mother. After her death his father married Miss Parker, a halfcaste, and she only had one child and it was stillborn. While I was waiting to see him Mrs Stirling gave me the name of creek nearby as Te Rere and the lagoon as Waihauka ('stinking water'). I asked Stirling the meaning of Pouripourikino and he said as far as he knew it meant 'dark water'.

(Herries Beattie MS 582, E/18 p. 12; courtesy HOCKEN LIBRARY)

B. An obituary for JOHN STIRLING after his death in 1920 (author unknown):

The recent death of Mr John Stirling brings back old memories of the past connected with the early settlement of Southland when the names of those sturdy pioneers loom up before our mind's eye. Let us refer to one in particular and the part played by him, viz., Captain William Stirling, father of the late Mr John Stirling. William Stirling was born in the year 1812 at Broadstairs, Crow Hill, England.* At the age of 14 years he ran away from home,

*There is some dispute over William Stirling's birthplace. When Bishop Selwyn married Stirling to Mary Parker in 1844, he recorded the marriage, 'William Stirling of Brookland, in Kent, to Mary, daughter of John Parker, of Ilfracombe, Devonshire, by a native woman since dead' (F. G. Hall-Jones, *Kelly of Inverkelly*, p. 148). The family say that Stirling was Scottish, however, and some years ago I saw a letter addressed to Eruera Stirling from Scotland, making enquiries about his entitlement through William Stirling to an estate there.

leaving England by a brig bound for New South Wales, his mother arriving at the dock too late to recover her young hopeful. He sailed in this and other vessels, in the Australian waters for some years. In 1830 he, with others, arrived from Sydney to work for Captain Peter Williams at his whaling station at Cuttle Cove, Preservation Inlet (the first whaling station in the south). In 1833 he moved to Otago Heads, being appointed to a responsible position at a fishery owned by a Sydney firm. Whilst here he saw the departure of the two great expeditions made by the Southern Maoris against the North Islanders, the fighting ground being Marlborough. The first expedition, or 'taua nui', was led by chiefs Te Whakataupuka and Makere te Whanawhana. The second expedition or 'taua iti', was led again by the chief Makere te Whanawhana,† with Tuhawaiki and Taiaroa. Later William Stirling left Otago and came to the Bluff, and started the shore station near the site of the present jetty, it remaining there for about two years. Owing to sands getting into the oil, which turned it black, a shift was made to Stirling Point, where, by piling rocks as a breakwater, he made a splendid boat harbour. Evidence of his handywork remain to this day in the shape of rocks near the point which bears his name. Dr Shortland, who visited the Bluff in 1843, paid a high tribute to the conduct and general organization of the community of those days. His remarks especially are a flattering testimonial to the ability of Captain Stirling, who appears to have been not only successful in managing his fellow countrymen but also in dealing with the Maoris. Indeed, the Chief Topi many years after, in speaking of the whaling days, paid a high mead of praise to Stirling in regard to his treatment of the natives. Captain Stirling was the first to introduce cattle into Southland, about the year 1840.‡ When Captain Smith surveyed the Bluff harbour in 1842 he mentioned the cattle station near the 'neck', and subsequent visitors also speak of the cattle. Some of these animals, which got away, formed the bands of wild cattle, which afterwards roamed over the site of Invercargill. The origin of the Bluff herd was five cows and one bull brought over from Twofold Bay by Captain Stirling. The honour of being the first to introduce a horse into Southland is also given to Stirling, as he brought one down from Waikouaiti in his vessel the Frolic. The name of 'Blucher' was given to the horse. The horse was afterwards sold to George Printz. We have been calling our pioneer as Stirling, which name was given him by Captain Peter Williams. The story runs that Williams was writing down the names of the men, and when he came to Pankhirst (which is Stirling's real name) he said 'Oh, that's too hard to spell, I'll stick it down as Stirling'. The name stuck to him.§ The hardships and vicissitudes of whaling life were too much for Stirling's constitution, and he died about the year 1851 at the comparatively early age of 39 years,‖ leaving one son, the late Mr J. Stirling, who is said to be the first male child born and baptised at the Bluff, the year of his nativity being 1840. His mother, Te Huikau, was the daughter of the great fighting chief, Makere te Whanawhana, referred to above as leading the two expeditions of the Southern Maoris against the North Islanders. Te Huikau died a year or two after giving birth to her son, Mr John Stirling. Captain Stirling later married Miss Parker, the wedding

---

†F. G. Hall-Jones, in *The Life and Times of Tuhawaiki* said of this taua, 'A Bluff version describes it as Makere's expedition. Makere, an elder brother of Haereroa, is stated to have sought vengeance for his half-brother Tu-matauenga, who had been enticed ashore from a whaler at Kapiti and slain.' (p. 26).

‡F. G. Hall-Jones in *Kelly of Inverkelly* disputes this, and says that 'it is clear now that Spencer had imported cattle long before Stirling's arrival' (p. 149).

§This story seems improbable.

‖Rev. Wohler's Register No. 11 states 'William Stirling – Bluff; aged 41 years, European. Master of Whaling Vessel, died of consumption 9.12.1851.' (courtesy Ulva Belsham)

being solemnised by Bishop Selwyn. There were no children to this marriage. The late Mr John Stirling was a well-known figure in the district, and especially in Riverton. Previous to coming to Riverton he resided with his father-in-law, Mr Davis, and family on his farm at Waimatuku. After about 14 years residence there he removed to Riverton erecting his homestead upon the portion of the Native Reserve allotted to his wife,¶ and finally ending his days there. The late Mr John Stirling was noted for his kindly, lovable, Christian disposition, and always tried to be just in anything that was submitted for his consideration; this was much seen in matters pertaining to native lands, etc. His definite Christian experience began at Waimatuku, where he came into contact with members of the Primitive Brethren Body, whom he joined, but on coming to Riverton he joined the Salvation Army, becoming an active member of it up to the end, which came at 2 a.m. on Friday morning last. He died peacefully, humming hymns up to within half-an-hour of his actual passing over the vale which divides, possessing that full assurance of rest and peace in Him, whom he called his Lord and Saviour.

Mr John Stirling leaves a widow and grown up family of three sons and two daughters – Mr W. J. Stirling, Invercargill; Mr R. J. Stirling, Auckland; D. Stirling, Bay of Plenty; Mrs E. Murphy, Waipukurau; Mrs Rev. H. Munro, Rotorua – to rejoice in the departure of their father in the faith of Him who truly declared himself to be the Day, the Truth, and the Life.

Western Star, 5 October 1920

For other accounts of William Stirling, see F. G. Hall-Jones, *Kelly of Inverkelly,* pp. 148-9, *Historical Southland,* p. 50; John Hall-Jones, *Bluff Harbour,* pp. 2-3, 21, 22, 24, 26-8, 43; *Records of Early Riverton and District,* pp. 7, 47; *The Bluff Centenary Booklet,* p. 26; and Robert McNab *Old Whaling Days,* pp. 240, 281. Some original documents are held in National Archives Old Land Claims File 1023, and in the Department of Lands and Survey, Invercargill.

C. SOME GENEALOGICAL MATERIAL FROM THE SOUTH ISLAND

Herries Beattie Whakapapa Book   No. 40

Paikea	i moe i a	Te Mahoruatea
Tahupotiki	,, ,,	Hemo
Iratahu	,, ,,	Iwi
Rakatehurumanu	,, ,,	Matiheiraki
Tahumuri	,, ,,	Marutai

¶In an obituary dated 23.1.1921, an unknown writer says, 'The late Mrs J. Stirling of Riverton was a daughter of George Davis, a whaler from Paisley in Scotland; her mother was Kutamamae (Ngati Mamoe – Ngai Tahu). Kutamamae was a first cousin to Paroro. Mr and Mrs Stirling were married at Ruapuke by Rev. Wohlers. There were five children.' (courtesy Ulva Belsham)

And in a Herries Beattie manuscript, Mrs Wixon of Clifton described a fight over mutton-birding rights and said 'an influential woman Kutamaimai who had married Big George the whaler, appeared on the scene and her word was law and the affair was settled.' (courtesy June Starke)

Rakawahakura	i moe i a		Irakehu
Rakaiwhakaata	,,	,,	Manawatakitu
Tuhaitara (f)	,,	,,	Marukore
Tamamaeroa	,,	,,	Te Rahuanui
Te Aohikuraki	,,	,,	Rakai te Kura
Tuahuriri	,,	,,	Hine Te Wai
Turakautahi	,,	,,	Hine Kakai
Kawariri	,,	,,	Ritoka
Te Rere rakau	,,	,,	Tatua
Te Mohene	,,	,,	Hine nui a Te Kawa
Tihope	,,	,,	Te Haki

Haereroa(m)   Makere(m)   Kawa(f)   Tuatara(f)

from Emily Bates Whakapapa:

Makere   =   Teoweka

Te Huakau   =   Capt Stirling

Writing by Rose Clark/Taylor:

'Their cousin Awika married Makuru [sic?], their issue Te Huikau who married Captain
Stirling, and the issue is Jack Stirling who married Betsy Davis and their issue the present
Stirling family Hera and her brothers.'

Wallace Early Settlers' Association, Riverton. *(Courtesy Ulva Belsham)*

D. MIHI KOTUKUTUKU: A report of the unveiling of her gravestone in 1958:

There was a large gathering of people at Raukokore on Saturday for the unveiling of a
gravestone in memory of the late Mrs Mihi Kotukutuku Stirling who died on the 15th
November, 1956. The unveiling ceremony was performed in the church yard of the
Raukokore Church of England by Bishop W. N. Panapa. The actual unveiling was
performed by a grand-daughter of the later Mrs Stirling, Miss Peace Stirling. Mr A. H.
Reedy spoke at the ceremony.

The late Mrs Stirling was a great leader amongst her people and could trace her descent
from most of the canoes. She had lived her 86 years of useful life at Raukokore and her
good work was well known not only on the Coast but throughout the Dominion. When the
Coronation of King George V took place she was presented with a medal with a certificate of
the occasion, from Buckingham Palace, for the work she had done and in recognition of the
work of her father, Maaka Tehutu, who in the early days joined the Government in the
Maori Wars. Mrs Stirling assisted many good causes and all the maraes on the coast
benefitted from her generosity. She was responsible for fostering Maori crafts and she
assisted greatly with patriotic causes during the war. The large holdings of land were leased
to assist Sir Apirana Ngata in his work in Maori development, and in assisting local Maori
causes, the land acting as security for loans. She helped in breaking down prejudice against
land development schemes, and all matters of importance were referred to her.

There were many notable visitors to the ceremony, including the Mayors of Gisborne and
Opotiki, Messrs P. Barker and Mr S. N. Chatfield. Proceedings opened when Mr Chatfield
stepped onto the Marae and was challenged, and respects were paid. He was escorted by Mr

Edwards of Rotorua, Mr Eruera Stirling and Mr C. Anaru. After this welcome the party went to the church where the unveiling took place, and then returned to the Marae. Mr Sonny Smith acted as master of ceremonies.

The first speaker was Mr Eruera Stirling, who gave a short genealogy and then extended a welcome to all present. He welcomed the registrar representing the Maori Affairs, Mr Barber of Rotorua. He also extended a welcome to the Pakeha friends present. He said that during her lifetime his mother had helped in many parts of the East Coast district, and by her good will had brought the people together. A particular welcome was extended to Mr N. V. Hodgson and Mr G. S. Moody.

Mr W. Maxwell joined in the welcome to the visitors. One of the great leaders had gone, he said, and it was up to the young generation to follow in the footsteps of Mrs Stirling. She had been a chief, a mother and a friend and had always told her people to preserve that friendship.

Two other Maori visitors to speak were Mr Tu Mahue, of Te Arawa and Mr Tohi Koopu of Maraenui.

Mr Claude Anaru, Rotorua paid a fitting tribute to the memory of Mrs Stirling as one of the great benefactors of the district. She had always been one of the great leaders of her people and he hoped that the young people would live up to the foundations laid by Mrs Stirling. She had upheld the arts and crafts of her people.

Another speaker was Mr Peta Awatere of Rotorua.

Mr Barber, representing the Maori Affairs Department, thanked speakers for their kind words of welcome, and he brought greetings from the Minister of Maori Affairs and departmental officials. Mrs Stirling was well respected and did beneficial work for which she was known right around New Zealand.

Both Maori and Pakeha should strive to live up to the standards which she had set. He was particularly pleased to see the Mayors of Gisborne and Opotiki there as it was in cooperation with local bodies that the Maori people were likly to succeed. He expressed pleasure at the homecraft he had seen right down the Coast. The department was going on building houses and at present had 10 to 12 plans ready to go ahead with.

Mr P. Barker, Mayor of Gisborne joined with other speakers in paying a tribute for a very old friend. They remembered and revered what she had done for her people.

Mr Hodgson said that he was grateful for the invitation to be present. He had known Mrs Stirling for over eight years and always regarded her as a great Rangatira. Her loss was greatly felt by the whole of the Maori people and by all Pakehas who had known her.

After tributes had been paid by Mr Tane Tukaki, Te Kaha and Mr Wi Campbell, Hicks Bay, the gathering partook of a sumptuous meal which upheld amply the traditions of the Maori people for hospitality.

(*Opotiki News*, 8 November 1958)

2. Raukokore: early history of the district

EXTRACTS FROM THE JUBILEE PUBLICATION OF THE RAUKOKORE MAORI SCHOOL, 1962

He Pitopito Korero no nga ra ki muri:

(Na Moana Waititi)
Ko tenei iwi, mai, i Taumata-o-Apanui ki Tihirau hi iwi kotahi tonu e karangatia nei ko te Whanau Apanui. Na nga karangatanga hapu i roto i a te Whanau Apanui nana i wehe mai enei hapu a te Whanau-a-Pararaki, a te Whanau-a-Maruhaeremuri me te Whanau-a-Kauetangohia, mai i Otiki ki Whangaparaoa (Tikirau).

Ko te Whanau-a-Maruhaeremuri i noho ki Raukokore mai i Otiki ki Ngutuone.

Ko tona marae ko Wairuru, te whare ko Hinemahuru, te pa me te urupa ko Kirieke, te wai ko Wairuru, te rangatira ko Maaka te Ehutu.

Ka noho ano tetahi wahanga o te Whanau-a-Maru ki Moutara. Ko tona whare ko te Haukitikirau, te whare kai, ko te Whareroa, tona taumata ko Urutana, tona wai he puna, ko Ngakititaha, te rangitira ko te Hata Moutara.

Ka waihangatia te whare karakia ki k'onei, ka tapaia te ingoa ko te Karaiti.

Te Whanau-a-Pararaki e noho ki Orete, mai i Ngutuone ki Mangatoetoe, te Whanau-a-Kauaetangohia i Mangatoetoe ki Whangaparaoa (Tihirau), enei hapu i nohotahi ki Orete. Ko te marae ko te Maru-o-Hinemaka. Nga whare i waihangatia ki tenei marae, tuatahi ko te Tepoho-o-Hinetera, murimai ko Ruamanawahonu, tua toru Pararaki. Ko te whare tenei o tenei marae i naianei. Ko Tawhitinui te pa me te urupa, ko Tauranga te wai, ko te Aopururangi te rangatira.

Early History of the District
The location of the Raukokore Maori School is on the lower western side of Orete, facing the sea and the island of Whakaari or White Island, so named by Captain Cook, as it appeared to him on November 1, 1769.

Let us go back twenty years before the school was opened in 1887. At the time of the Hauhau hostilities in Opotiki in 1865, there were two important tribes here, the same as today. Whanau-a-Maru at Raukokore and Whanau-a-Pararaki at Orete. At the head of these tribes * was the chief, Te Hata Moutara, by whose intervention the lives of four pakehas had been saved from the Hauhau. The following year in 1866, Captain W. Allison, Master Mariner of the brig, Stella, rescued these Pakehas who were at Maruohinemaka, a pa on Orete. Captain Allison returned after the hostilities in 1880 to Cape Runaway to manage Mr Cartwright Brown's property, and ten years later started a store at Tataramoa, Raukokore. He was appointed postmaster, a position he retained for thirty years until the time of his death. In addition he was the first Justice of Peace for the district.

Since there is no record of any other European, prior to 1878, it can be assumed that Mr Thomas Secombe, known as 'Hekama', was the first white man to settle and commence agricultural and pastoral development on Orete. In 1870 he made a horseback trip down the coast to Orete Point, in which area he was particularly interested for farming. With the help of Captain Gilbert Mair, who was at Lake Rotomahana at the time, he obtained the signatures of the landowners for the lease of 1030 acres of property for 21 years.

---

*Note though, that in the Maori text by Moana Waititi, he said that there were three sub-tribes living around Raukokore, Te Whanau-a-Maruhaeremuri, Te Whanau-a-Pararaki and Te Whanau-a-Kauaetangohia. Te Whanau-a-Maru had two sections, one living at Raukokore from Otiki to Ngutuone under Maaka Te Ehutu, and the other living at Moutara under Te Hata Moutara.

All livestock, farm equipment and machinery were shipped to Waihau Bay by schooner. Landing animals was a difficult operation, as they were dropped overboard and expected to swim ashore, but occasionally some headed out to sea. Blackberry and boxthorn, locals claim, were also brought into the district by Hekama, as several can remember the original blackberry hedge on his farm. Farm labourers were employed from Auckland at 5/- a week and found.

On the property were a hundred cows, a cowshed, a cheese factory and a substantial homestead of weatherboards with a shingle roof. In what was known as the Waipatiki paddock were a hydraulic ram, pump and a concrete dam, 20 feet by 10 feet, the remains of which can still be seen. With the Secombes lived the Kerr family, also in Mr Secombe's employ. Miss Kerr was the elder sister of Mr Jack Kerr, builder of the present Raukokore Bridge.

Sir George Grey's 'sugar and flour' policy commenced in 1857 from Taupo to Cape Runaway. An attempt at wheat growing must have taken place, as mention is made of a flour mill existing at Maruohinemaka. Before Mr Secombe left the district in 1897, ten years after the school opened, maize growing had already started on a large scale. The people here were among the most industrious in the Dominion. Every acre of land was under close cultivation. Their kaingas were well kept, houses substantial and evidence was shown of a progressive and energetic community.

'Moni kaanga', meaning paying in corn, appeared on invoices of a shop at the pa of Wairuru, Raukokore, in 1892. There were also marae or iwi shops at Maruohinemaka, Orete, called the Tangari store, later shifted to a kainga or settlement at Taheke, Waihau Bay, by Mr Frank McDonald (who did contract work with his team of bullocks), and at a settlement at Peria, Orete. These places also had a 'wharewaea' or telephone house. There was telephone communication along the coast from one pa to another before the Government line was put through. The cost of a call from Wairuru Pa to Ruatoki in those days was only tenpence.

The main items purchased were men's and women's hosiery at 2/6 and 3/- a pair respectively, men's tweed coats (koti hipi) at £1/10/- each, men's cotton shirts (haate katene) at 6/- each, men's tweed trousers (tarau hipi) at £1 a pair, blue and white print material (kaone puuru and kaone ma) at 9d and 1/6 a yard respectively, a coloured blanket (paraikete kara) at £1/5/- and reels of cotton and boxes of matches at 3d.

It was not until 1894-95 that foodstuffs, such as bags of flour at 6/- a bag and sugar at 16/8 for 70 lbs, appeared on pa invoices.

Pastoral farming had commenced, but had not followed along scientific lines, as the soil had become exhausted. The necessity of providing for a large extent of pastoral land back in from the coast, had compelled Maori farmers to direct more attention to cleaning and grassing their bush and scrub lands. Seven small sheep flocks had started, and much of the land was cleaned, sown in grass and fenced.

Labour was sought locally when Waikura Station was opened in 1895 by Mr Cartwright Brown, as the fencers were old identities at Wairuru Pa. After the turn of the century, Tawaroa Station was opened, first by Mr Baker, then by Mr Rutledge who sold out to Mr Neilson in association with the Barker family. Orete Station was opened by Mr Rutledge and Dr Scott, and later still Pohueroro Station by Mr J. Kemp. Mr Neilson was on the top of Mt. Hikurangi when he gazed in this direction and noticed the rolling country of Tawaroa and made a horseback trip to its location where bushfelling had already commenced. The early sheep stations had their own station shop for the labourers.

The early schooners were the Kaeo and the Aotea run by Captain Skinner. A resident recalls getting off at Moutara on her way from Hukarere College, Napier, from a kaipuke or schooner, to the opening of the Anglican Church at Raukokore. At the time of the

Tarawera eruption she was ten years old. Fifty years ago when the road down the coast was just a horse track, the waterways provided a thriving business for the early launches, scows and steamers, transporting produce, such as wool and maize, general merchandise and passengers.

Before 1915 mail from Opotiki was delivered by pack horse and riders once a fortnight, after which date it was brought together with meat and bread orders and merchandise for stores along the coast by the launches, first the Olive and later the Waihau, twice a week weather permitting. Before the coast road was completely formed in 1931 and after the Te Kaha Dairy Factory had opened in 1925 there was a cream service by the launch Royal Irish, operated by Mr Moana Waititi for five or six years. Cream was conveyed direct to the factory on pack horses in specially made cream cans when the weather was unsuitable.

Early launches plying between Opotiki and Cape Runaway were the Olive, Waihau, and Aio. Steamers from Auckland called into Waihau Bay, taking away produce and occasionally one or two pupils who received their secondary education in Auckland. They were the Mako, Awahou, Parere (Richardson and Co., Napier), Tiroa (Gisborne Sheep Farmers) and Fingall. Operating between Auckland and Cape Runaway were the scows, Tamahae and Horouta.

Whaling was carried out in the district but not to the extent that it was at Te Kaha, the centre of whaling on the coast. This is evident from the number of tripots in the district. In the early days, from Moutara, where there was a large settlement, the boats Te Aparangi, Horowai, Hariata and Kiri o te Wai set out chasing whales which had been sighted from the taumata or look-out point called Urutana. The carcases were taken to the boat landing at Waikoukou where they were boiled down.

Into the boat landings at Wairuru, Awarahi and Peria in later times sailed the Whanau-a-Pararaki whaleboats. A look-out was stationed at Pukeahunoa, giving the signal to the boats, Te Aparangi, Tauira and Kamupene. Boiling down the blubber took place at Otamataari. There were also recollections of a whale either washed up or caught at Waihau Bay and the use of a tripot for boiling down the blubber near the present Guest House.

Besides the early Pakeha settlers already mentioned were W. Swinton, a publican at a hotel built at Tataramoa in 1886; J. Callaghan, a blacksmith and later a farmer who also lived at Tataramoa; J. Quinton, who in later years was a cobbler and billiard marker at Waihau Bay, and who formerly lived at Te Karaka, Orete; C. D. Walker, a farmer who lived above Maruohinemaka; Mr F. McDonald, a teamster, also a settler on a part of Orete; E. Richardson, a labourer; and J. Walker, a storekeeper at Waihau Bay.

Here are some of the old Maori Kaingas and some of the people who lived there.

(N.B. The editors apologise for any omissions in this list, and would welcome any corrections and additions).

Oruaiti – Waiariki Matiu, Hunia Pako and their mother Ramari
Matapapa – Tumau Kori, Ikinihi Karapaina
Taheke – Hoani Retimana
Uruparapara – Honana Haare Maioha
Otutehapara – Herewini Te Moana
Te Kohai – Te Rere Paipa Waititi
Te-Ara-a-te-kuri – Paratene Hiia, Tiweka Anaru
Upoko-o-rete – Kenana Ihaka, Hohua Te Arokapa
Te Karaka – Harete Waititi
Peria – Parekoihu Te Kani
Moutara – Te Hata Moutara (chief)
Kaimakawe – Te Kiriwai

Waikoukou – Pekama Ngatai, Mihi Kotukutuku
Pahiko – Hirini Puha
Waitaia – Eruera
Te pa o Maruhinemaka – Hirini Te Aopururangi, Wikuki Waititi, Pene Ponia, Kawariki, Timi Mekerapata, Eria, Noho Apiata, Hamiora Taitua, Te Weeti Katae
Te pa o Wairuru – Taitoko, Pita Tautuhi, Pohoi Mihaere, Hoani Puihi, Timora, Te Whare Moana, Hoani Tiki, Pihi Hei, Maaka Te Ehutu, Heremai Kaurori, Hunia Piahu, Wiropi.

Not only are many of the present generation in the district able to trace their descent from ancestral canoes, but also they are able to claim origins in the Shetland Islands, England, Scotland, Ireland, Sweden, Denmark, French Canada and America from whose many shores the early settlers came.

Reprinted with the kind permission of the Headmaster of the Raukokore School and the local community – ka nui nga mihi ki a koutou katoa!

3. He Koorero Moo Te Kawa Waahine

naa Eruera Stirling, Arnold Reedy, Matiu Te Hau, me eetahi atu (1966) (naa Ata Pedersen i kapo ngaa koorero nei)*

Eruera Stirling: Ka mate te kaumaatua o Te Kotahitangi nei – a Te Maraku. Ka tae mai te koorero ki a maatau, kua mate a Te Maraku. Ka mea mai a Peta ki a au, 'E hoa, me haere taatau ki te tangihanga.'

Aa, ka huihui maatau – too maatau roopuu, aa, ka tau te koorero; kii mai ra, 'Kauaka noa taatau e haere.'

Aa, ka piki au ki runga i te waka, ka haere maaua – tokorua – no Taranaki taku hoa i haere ai. Aa, ka tae maatau ki te marae. Engari tae rawa atu au ki te marae nei! Whakarongo au ki ngaa whai-koorero o te marae nei! oo – ko aahua pau kee ngaa mihimihi i te tangata whenua.

Kaati, ka titiro atu au i te 'mike' e tuu mai ana i te whanga. Whakaaro au, mutu tonu te mea e puta ai o aku koorero – me haere tika kee au ki reira. Kua pau kee ngaa mihi o te marae mo Maraku – te hura koohatu. E tae ana ki ngaa mihimihi whakamutunga kua riro i a Ngaati Porou te whakautu, ka tae atu au, Well, kuhu atu awau, aa, e noho mai ana, aa . . . katoa.

Naa, te koorero i mau atu i a au, taku taetanga atu ki te marae, teetahi tangata i tuu mai i te marae. Aao! he tangata kaitaa, naa, nei tona koorero. Whakarongo atu au, aa, anei te koorero na,

'Na ko taku whakahee; e whakahee ana a au ki te wahine o Ngaati Porou ki tuu mai nei ki te whakautu i ngaa koorero i te marae i te raa nei. Kua takatakahia e ia i te kawa o Waikato. Pookokoohua!'

Arnold Reedy ('Nehe'): Ko taua tangata ko McKinnon, he tangata haawhe-kaahe. Naa, ko te wahine e whakahee ra a ia, ko te tamaahine a Tuwaka, e moe ra i a Taawhai McClutchie, aa, ko wai ana te ingoa? Aa, ko, Whaea.

---

* Double vowels are marked in this text in deference to Bruce Biggs, who taped the discussion.

Eruera Stirling: Naa, koiraa te tangata i tuu mai.

'Aa, e whakahee ana au. Ngaati Porou, mehemea ko ngaa raa o neheraa, kua taona atu te wahine nei i teenei raa, ka patua hai kai mo te hui.'

I reina ka rongo atu au, aa-ii, kua aahua pakari rawa te koorero nei. Kaatahi anoo au ka haramai. Haere tika atu au ki te 'microphone' i te marae. Aa, kua titiro mai ngaa taangata, haa-ii! Haere tika atu au. Taku taenga atu ki te microphone, ka koorerotia e au te waahi waahanga oo taku paatere i koorerorero au;

> Too toki e Hika ko Hui-te-Rangi-Ora
> Too toki e Hika ko Te Atua – Haemata
> Too toki e Hika ko te Rakuraku-a-Taawhaki!
> Teenei hoki te Manawa-ka-ue!
> Teenei hoki te Manawa-ka-pore
> Ko taku manawa ra a ia i hoake moohou
> Ko Hou-tiinaa, ko Hou-maaota, ko Te Aahutu
> Koo-ee, ko Horo-te-poo ee.
> Ko Marua-nuku, ko Marua-rangi.
> Ko Hau-whaka-tuuria, ko Te Whaka-hotu-nuku
> Me ko Tuu anoo raa, ko Te Ao Maarama, Aue!
> Me ko Taatai-aro-Rangi
> Me ko Te Hua-o-Paeraa
> Me ko Hine-huhuritai
> Me ko Manutangirua
> Ko Hingaangaroa
> Ka tuu toona whare ki Uuawa-e o Te Raawheoro
> Ka tipu te whaihanga, te Ngai-o-Tuu ki Rarotonga
> Ka taka, i raro ra, i a Apanui, ee
> Kia whakarongo mai e too tipuna paapaa, a Te Maatorohanga.

Ka mutu taku karakia nei, kua koorero hoki au mo te tapu i teeraa waa. Kua koorero au mo te kupu, kaitangata kua makaia i te marae. Naa reira, me karakia atu au i ngaa karakia o neheraa, hai wete i teeraa mea i te kupu, kia mate – patu – i eeraa koorero, kia mate.

Ka mutu, kaatahi anoo au ka haere atu, 'Waikato, e te Kiingi, e ngaa Ariki, kaare au i te takatakahi i te mana o too marae. Engari, e haramai ana au ki te whakautu i te koorero, kia kainga au, a Ngaati Porou, hai utu i te marae i teenei raa. Kaati, e hoa, a koe e tuu mai naa, he uri koe na Tama-te-Kapua. Ko au hoki, he uri au na Tama-te-Kapua.

'Na Tama-te-Kapua, ko Tuuhoro-mate-kakaa, ko Wahiawa ko Tuu-rii-Rangi, ko Apanui, ko ahau e koorero atu nei. Ko ahau too tuakana.'

Katoa Ha-a! (*e kata ana raatou katoa*)

'Ki raro iho i a Tuuhoro-mate-kakaa, ko Kahumatamomoe, naana ko Taawake – moe – tahanga, naana ko Uenuku-mai-i-Rarotonga, ko Rangitihi, anaa kua taurua oo raatau katoa, kua pakaru koe a Te Arawa. E hoa, ko au too tuakana.'

Arnold Reedy: Ka moe ra a Rangitihi i a Papawharanui, kia puta ki waho, ko Tuuhourangi, ka moe i a Rongomai-Paapaa, ka puta mai ngaa Arawa na ki waho.

Eruera Stirling: 'Naa reira, ka mutu toou taku koorero. Na te maataamua a au, naa, o ngaa uri a Tama-te-Kapua, na Tuuhoro-mate-kakaa. Naa reira, Ae! maaku e whakautu too koorero.

'Tuarua, taku koorero ki a koe, E toru ngaa tamariki a Porourangi; me waiho ngaa koorero i runga i a Porourangi. Ko Hau too mua, raro iho ko Rongomai-aniwaniwa, raro iho, ko Ueroa.' Kaatahi ka whakapapangia e au te raaina mai i ahau, ka puta ki te wahine e kiia ra, kia kainga. Ka whakaheketia mai e au, a Rongomai-aniwaniwa kia puta, a Mrs McClutchie. Whakaheketia mai e au i runga i a Ueroa, i a Kahungunu, i a Iranui i te sister, te tuahine o Kahungunu, i a Iranui, ka eke te wahine nei ki runga.

Anei aku koorero, mehemea ko neheraa teenei, ka riro koe maaku e karanga atu kia tahuna, kia kainga koe, hai kai mo te hui nei i teenei raa. Naa reira, naahau i whiu te koorero ki runga i te marae. E kore hoki au e pai kia puta mai ki runga i tooku maahunga teenaa koorero, kia kainga a au mo taku tapu i te marae i teenei rangi.'

Aa, ka puta aaku koorero, ka mutu.

Mutu atu ana taku koorero, kaare au i kite, kai reira a Te Whakatoohea, kai reira a Ngaati Awa, kai reira a Ngaati Porou. Te mutunga o aku koorero, ka rongo au i te paatere ra, kua paatai a Ngaakohu, 'Ko wai teeraa e koorero ra?'

Ka kii atu a Pita Pekama,

'Ee! Too mokopuna tonu teeraa, ko Eruera e koorero mai ra.'

Tahi te koroua ra ka whiitiki i a ia, ka tango i oona kaakahu, tahi anoo ka haramai ki te marae me te tokotoko.

'E hoa, anei toou te tokotoko hai wero atu – naa! – kia werohia atu e au too puku na naa, kia riro toou koe maaku e maka ki runga i te umu hai kai mo te mea nei. Noo reira e tautoko ana au i te koorero a taku mokopuna. Naahau te kupu nei i maka ki te marae, e, me aha hoki e au a Ngaati Porou? Ee, me whakautu ra. Awau a Te Whakatoohea e tau nei i te marae, anaa, anei a Rongowhakaata e tau nei i te marae.'

Naa reira, aa, ka tuu a Ngaakohu aa, naa te koroua kee ra, e Nehe, i whakaneke atu te taumaha o ngaa koorero, i taaku. Ka mutu ngaa koorero ka noho te koroua ra ki raro, ka tuu mai te kaumaatua o roto o Waikato. Kaatahi anoo ka karanga mai,

'E hoa, e tama, Ngaati Porou, kai te whakaae au ki a koe. Ehara i a koe i tono te riri i te marae, engari naaku na te tangata whenua i hoatu. Mea a au, ee, me patu ra, me utu. Ka tika hoki too koorero, me mea ko ngaa raa o neheraa, naa, ko wai te mea o maaua e tau ki roto i te umu? Ee, ko ia ra te mea kai te hee! Ko taaku, me whakangaawari kee au i runga i te kupu i makaia mai ki runga i te aahuatanga o te kai-koorero ra, a Mrs McClutchie, eh!'

Naa, ka kite ai taatau he mea tika toou eenei mea kia tohutohungia ki a taatau. Ki te haere koe ki teenaa marae, ee mauria te kawa o teenaa marae! Kaua hai takatakahia. Kai aha? Kai puta he koorero peenei i teenei i pakaru nei i a au i te hui i Mangatoatoa.

Arnold Reedy: He mea aata wero marika ra i peenaa ai. He kupu makere.

Eruera Stirling: Naa, ka tuu hoki a ia, ko te waa teenaa i rere ai te koorero. Tika tonu, e Nehe! Me aha hoki teeraa iwi i te mauri i te mana o oo raatau na tiipuna, kia takatakahia hoki e teenei mea e te waahine.

Reo: Engari kai te kupu. He kaha rawa te taumaha!

Eruera Stirling: Ae! ko te kupu kee. He ngaawari noa te koorero mai i teetahi koorero peenei na, 'Ei, e tau koe ki raro Ngaati Porou, kai a au te marae.'

Teeraa, makaia mai, naa, me maka te tangata ki roto i te haangi kia kainga hai kai mo te hui. Naa, koiraa te koorero whaanui i puta i a au nei i roto i te huihuinga . . .

Matiu Te Hau: Anei kee ra te koorero i koorero mai ai koe ki a au mo taua mea. I whangawhanga rawa koe. Aa, kei a koe!

Eruera Stirling: Aae! i whangawhanga a au. Kai te moohio atu hoki awau ki eetahi o taatau. E moohio atu ana a au, kai reira aaku taaina, aa mea Maara, a Te Retimana Maara. I reira raatau. Kai reira ngaa mea o roto i a Rongowhakaata hai whakautu i te koorero. Kore he mea i tuu mai ki te whakautu.

Matiu Te Hau: Aa, he kore moohio tonu hoki ra.

Eruera Stirling: Aa, i kite atu a au; kaatahi ka nohohoho mai, e nohonoho mai ana, kaatahi, no te mutunga ka kii atu au, 'E tama maa, he aha koutou te tuu noa ai ki te whakangaawari i te mea nei? Waiho rawa ai e koutou kia taakirihia, peenei te taumaha o te koorero i te marae-aatea, ee! Naa reira au, ka tangi taku ngaakau, ka whakautua e au ngaa koorero i te marae ra i teenei raa.'

Naa, me whakamaaroo toou taku koorero mo teenei mea mo te waahine e tuu i te marae.

Matiu Te Hau: Aa, koinaa aa taatau koorero. Aa, koorero, koorero!

Eruera Stirling: I te tekau maa whitu te tau, 1917, ka mate te pootiki a Tiiweka Aamaru, ee, he taina no Karauria maa. Aa, ka haramai maatau ki te tangihanga i te marae o Ohinemutu. Tae mai maatau ki te tangihanga i te marae o Ohinemutu; Te Whaanau-a-Apanui – aa, teetahi haere nui teenaa na maatau, ee, ki te tangihanga. Naa, too maatau taenga mai ki te marae, naa, ka tiimata te whaikoorero mai a Te Arawa. I reira katoa a Koopuu maa; i reira katoa, katoa ngaa rangatira katoa.

Naa tuu mai te tangata kotahi. Kaati, kaare hoki Te Whaanau-a-Apanui e tuu, me mea kai reira taku kookaa. Kaare e tuu a Koopuu, kaare e tuu teetahi atu, teetahi atu, teetahi atu.

Naa, ka mea ngaa taangata nei, mo te whakautu i te koorero. Kaati, kaare hoki e tuu ngaa kaumaatua o Te Whaanau-a-Apanui, aa tae atu ki teeraa pito katoa, aa, kai reira taku maamaa, taku kookaa . . .

Kaare tahi he tangata e tuu. Engari maana te koorero ake. Kaati, kua whai atu Te Whaanau-a-Apanui, ngaa kaumaatua, kaare e pai maa wai e whakautu, engari ma taku kookaa toou e whakautu ngaa whai-koorero a Te Arawa.

Aa, ka tuu taku maamaa ki runga. Tona tuuranga ki runga – ka tuu taku maamaa ki runga – tuu ana ki runga taku kookaa, kua karanga mai a Mita Taupopoki, 'E tau! E tau! E tau! E tau! Kaare i tika, tooku kawa, tooku marae kia riro ma te iwi ma te wahine e takatahi. E tau! E tau!'

Tuu tonu taku maamaa ki runga.

Te mutunga o te koorero a Mita Taupopoki, kaatahi anoo taku maamaa ka karanga atu, 'E Mita, kaare koe i tau hai koorero mai ki a au. Kaare koe i tau hai koorero mai ki a au. Kai te tuu au i runga i taku marae, i roto i taku tipuna i a Tama-te-Kapua. He uri au na Tuuhoro-mate-kakaa, he uri au na Apanui. Kaare koe hai tika – e tau! – hai koorero mai ki a au. Noho atu ki raro! Na te taina koe na Taawake-moe-tahanga. Na te tuakana au, na Tuuhoro-mate-kakaa. Naa reira, kaare he tangata i konei hai koorero mai ki a au. E tau koe ki raro! Aa kaati, naahau i koorero, i te wahine. E tama a ia, anei te waahi i puta atu ai koe, i aku kuuhaa nei, (*Katakata ana ngaa kaumaatua*). I puta mai koe i whea? Ee – i tomo mai too uupoko na i roto i a au, te wahine. Anei! Anei te waahi, te ara i puta ai koe ki waho, ko koe e koorero mai na ki a au i teenei raa. Naa reira e Mita, kaare au e tau i a koe ki raro.'

Noo reira ka koorero te kuia ra, ka mutu, te mutunga, kati katoa ngaa whai-koorero!

Naa, ka tuu ake hoki a mea – a Kiingi nee! te brother o Dan King. Ka tuu a Wiremu Kiingi ki runga, ka kii a ia, 'Te Arawa, kaare e taea e taatau te koorero a taku tuahine e tuu nei. E koorero ana a ia i runga i toona kawa, i toona marae tonu. Ma wai oo taatau e whakautu tona koorero? Ko wai? Naa reira, teenaa koorero, e takoto mai ra.'

Naa, e Nehe, i rongo koe i teetahi koorero miiharo i te matenga o taku maamaa. Na, ka whakaaro a Te Arawa, kua mate a Mihi Kootukutuku, kaatahi anoo a Te Arawa ka huihui.

Ka mea ngaa taangata kia taapukena te kuia ra, ka tae atu au. Ka mea mai aku taaina ki a au, me taapuke. Ka kii atu au,

'Kaare! Kaare anoo kia tae mai tona iwi a Te Arawa. Kia tae mai a Te Arawa, ma Te Arawa e tuku.'

Kaare au e whakaae. Kua koorero a Ngaati Porou ma Ngaati Porou – a Nehe maa nei. I koorero hoki a Nehe, me tanu – kia tanungia te kuia ra, kia hoki ai raatau. Ka kii atu au,

'Kaare! Waiho kia tae mai a Te Arawa. Ma Te Arawa e tuku taku kookaa ki te koopuu o te whenua.'

Naa, ka mahia te pahi mo te haere. Kohikohia ngaa taangata, aa full bus. Kaatahi ka raakai mai a Te Arawa i a ia, oo-oo! (Ko Nehe maa anake) Naa kaatahi raatau ka haramai. Ka tae, kii ana a Karauria, ka tae mai raatau ki Oopootiki, ka kii atu a ia ki a Kepa Ehau, 'E Kepa, haere taatau ki te unu.'

Ko te korooria ra hoki teeraa o Kepa Ehau, he unu. Ka kii atu a Karauria, 'Ee Kepa, me peka taatau ki te unu?'

Aa, karanga atu a Kepa, 'This is one tangi – kore au e paa ki teenei mea ki te waipiro, kia tae rangatira ai au ki te marae, kia pakaru aku koorero mo teenei wahine!'

Kaare rawa atu a Kepa Ehau i unu. Kai te mahi atu a Karauria maa – kii atu a Kepa, 'Kaare! Kia tae rangatira ai au ki te marae, aa rongo koutou – ka rongo nei ki aku koorero.'

Naa, taenga ki te marae, i reira maatau, aa, tuu a Nehe nei i te manaaki i a Te Arawa. Mutu ana, peke mai a Kepa Ehau me tona tokotoko, me ana – peke haere ana i te marae, 'Pokokoohua, Mihi Kootukutuku! Kaitoa noa atu koe kia hemo atu! Te wahine naana i takatakahi te mauri o Te Arawa mai i ngaa tipuna, tae mai ki teenei raa, kore teetahi wahine i tuu i te marae. Kaitoa koe, kia mate atu.' (*Ka umere te kata a te tangata*).

Arnold Reedy: Me te tangi tonu!

Eruera Stirling: Tangi toou a Kepa, 'Kaitoa! Pokokoohua! Kaitoa koe kia mate noa atu. Naahau i takatakahi te mauri o ngaa tipuna, mai i a Tama-te-Kapua, aa . . . . naahau! takahia e koe te marae o Ohinemutu. E kore teetahi Mihi Kootukutuku e tuu i teenei marae, e ara mai i muri mai, kia tuu ki runga i ooku marae, takahi ai i ooku tapu.'

Ka mutu ngaa koorero a Kepa, kua mea mai aku taaina ki a au, 'Ee, Bad!'

Kua piirangi taku taina ki te tutuu nee! Aa he rite taku taina ki a Peta, aa, ki a Koro nei! (*Ka pahuu te kata*).

Kua tuu taku taina a Maaka, 'Ee, by golly! That fella, got a cheek, te koorero peeraa mai!'

Kaati, ko te aahua waiwai pea, kua karanga mai ki a au, 'Oo, kaare koe e whakautu i te koorero ra?'

Ka kii atu au, 'Waiho te koorero rangatira kia takoto ana i te marae. Kua rangatira too taaua maamaa. Ko koe, kaua koe hai tuu ki runga. Me noho koe ki raro.' (*Ka menemene raatau ki te kata*).

Aa, ka mutu ra, ka tangi ra kaatahi anoo au ka kii atu, 'Te Arawa, tanungia taa koutou tuupaapaku.'

Naa, teetahi tangi nui teenaa na Te Arawa.

Arnold Reedy: You know Dick, that was the most impressive tangi I have ever been to . . . especially with Kepa, eh . . . 'Purari paka! Pokokohua! Kaitoa a koe kia mate noa atu! . . . .'

Reo: 'He aha te taki i tuu ai te wahine, ki te koorero whaanui tonu i runga i ngaa marae o Ngaati Porou? No hea te tiimatanga mai?'

Eruera Stirling: Naa, maaku e whakautu teenaa. Ee, ko te wahine e pupuri i ngaa koorero, ee, i kurangia i tohia e ngaa kaumaatua, ko te tuakana oo taku kookaa, o Horowai. Koiraa te wahine i uuhia ngaa koorero, ngaa whakapapa ngaa mea katoa, ki runga i a ia. Koiraa te wahine pupuri i ngaa koorero katoa o te rohe o too maatau nei takiwaa. Naa reira, me te whakatakoto, peenei ana, maahau e waahi ngaa koororo i roto i ngaa marae. Kauaa teetahi tangata e tuu. Te take i peeraa ai, kai runga i te kaawai tonu. Te take, ka tuu koe, ka heke i runga i te kaawai o ngaa whakapapa. Ka aahei te wahine ki te tuu. Ka aahei. Koiraa te wahine tuatahi ki te tuu ki roto ki te rohe, right throughout, ko taku Aunty ko Keita Horowai.

Reo: E Eru, mahara au-ee, he tika tonu teenaa koorero i heke iho i runga i ngaa kaawai.

Naahau toou teenei whakamaarama ki a au i heke iho i runga i ngaa kaawai. He koorero hou teenei ki a au, engari i tooku rongo, kua tiimata noa mai i muaatu i te waa i a Hine Matioro.

Eruera Stirling: Aa, taihoa! Aakuni au te hoki ai ki te koorero na. Naa, ka tae mai ra ki te waa i ngaa koroua ra, ka tohia taku kookaa ki ngaa koorero katoa, oo te Ao Maaori. Na ko teena wahine, te tuakana oo taku kookaa i mate atu, kaare ana uri. Haere katoa atu i a ia ngaa taonga katoa. Naa, kaatahi taatau ka hoki mai, ka hoki mai taatau, ka hoki mai ki runga ki too taatau karangatanga, o Maataatua. Kai te moohio katoa taatau, te uunga o te waka ki Whakataane. Ka tae ki reira, i reira ngaa taane, i reira ngaa – e kiia ana ra ngaa koorero, ee koiraa ngaa tuaakana ko Toroa maa. Engari ka waiho au i aku koorero, engari ma ngaa whakamaarama. Koinei toou taku koorero whaanui i ngaa koorero i Whakataane, te waa e ora ana a Te Hurinui, i koorerotia,

'Ko wai te tuakana o roto i ngaa uri o Maataatua?' Naa, ka tae mai i te waa i te uunga mai o te waka, ka raruraru te waka o Maataatua. Naa, kaare e tuu ana te wahine i roto i ngaa raa o neheraa. Engari no te waa o te raruraru, kaare a Toroa maa i runga i te waka. Kaatahi a Muriwai ka tirotiro, aa, kai whea ra ngaa taangata nei. Ma raatau kee te kupu koorero ki te iwi, Ee, me peenei taatau. Aa kaati, ko te tuunga teeraa o Muriwai, anaa ka whakahaua ra e ia ngaa taangata, te uunga mai o te waka ra, na reira i pupuri te mauri.

Ka riro te tiimatanga teeraa o te tuu o te waahine, teenei mea i te koorero, i tuku iho i runga i a Muriwai. Na Muriwai, Koteroau, ko Puaitekaraka, ko Rau-o-te-ake, ko Te Kawekuratawhiti – eh Mat!

Ka moe a Te Kawekuratawhiti, ka moe i a Tai-kore-kore pakaru ki waho, ko koe ko Te Whakatoohea, ko Ngaati Porou tae noa atu ki roto ki a Rongowhakaata. Naa, koinei te kawa. He kawa waahine, he kawa waahine. Kua tiimata noa mai, engari, no te heke haeretanga ki roto ki ngaa raa o muri nei, aa, kua kii ngaa taane, ee, me tau ngaa waahine ki raro!

Arnold Reedy: Ko taku paatai e whakahoki atu ana i a taatou whakapapa, nei . . ., kia hoomai na e koe eetahi o ngaa taahuhu, I rongo au i te takiwaa kua whakatata haere, kua moohio tonu a Waikato kaaore e kore ka whawhai a Waikato ki te paakehaa mo te whenua te take. Na ka whakaaro a Te Wherowhero – naaraa he koorero teenei i rongo au, engari kaare tonu au i te tino moohio mehemea he tika raanei, peewhea raanei. Engari, maahau maana e whakamaarama ki a taatau. I te moohio tonu o Te Wherowhero, kaatahi a ia ka koorero a ia i teenei koorero na,

'Ee, ka hanatu au ki Te Tairaawhiti ki taku tuakana ki a Te Kani-a-Takirau hai Kiingi.' Naa, koiraa taaku e paatai nei ki a koe, me mea ka taea e koe te taakiri mai ki a taatau. Ee, te whakapapa, ngaa whakapapa raanei e eke ai te koorero a Pootatau, "Ka hanatu au ki Te Tairaawhiti ki taku tuakana ki a Te Kani, hai Kiingi."

Eruera Stirling: Aa, te kaupapa i huri mai ai a Waikato ki runga i teenei koorero, kai runga i ngaa tamariki tokotoru a Porourangi. Ka heke a Waikato i runga i a Ueroa, te pootiki a Porourangi. Na Porourangi, ko Hau, ko Raakaipoo, ko Manutangirua, ko Hingaangaroa, anaa Tauaa. Naa ko Hinga-angaroa, ko Hauiti nee! Aa ko Hingaangaroa, na Hingaangaroa ko Maahaki. Aa kaati teenaa weheweheanga.

Aa ka hoki ki runga, ki aa . . . na Porourangi ko Ueroa, ko te pootiki teeraa, the third. Na Ueroa ko Tokerau, ko Iwipuupuu anaa ko Kahungunu, ko Kahukuranui ko Raakaihikuroa ko Tuupurupuru ko Te Rangituehu, ko Mahina-aa-rangi ko Waikato katoa.

Reo: Aa, kua taina. Kai te moohio tonu a ia ki tona whakapapa!

Eruera Stirling: Koianei te take i kiia ai a Te Kani-aa-Takirau, 'Ee, haere ra! Tiikina ki Hikurangi ki te taatai Too-Ihu-Mai a te poo, koinaa hai Kiingi mo taatau.'

Arnold Reedy: Aa teenaa. Ka tae ra te koorero ki a Te Kani, anei te whakahoki a Te Kani ki taku whakaaro araa ki taaku nei rongo, engari kaare tonu au i te moohio mehemea he tika teenei koorero. Naa, ko te whakahoki a Te Kani, aa i peenei te whakahoki a Te Kani, 'Ee kai te pai too haramai. Engari haramai, e hoki. E ko taku mauna ko Hikurangi, engari inaa ra, ko tooku kiingitanga i heke iho no ooku tiipuna, he Ihu-too-mai no te poo. Ko taku mauna ko Hikurangi, he mauna tuu. Ehara i te mauna haere.'
Engari, he tika anoo eeraa koorero?

Eruera Stirling: Aa, he tika teenaa koorero. Koinaa hoki te take i whakaaro ai a Pootatau; ee, i tae mai a Taiaroa ki konei; I tae mai katoa ki konei ki te hui i konei. Naa kaatahi ka koorerotia te mea nei. Naa kaatahi ka kii te motu katoa; naa Tuuwharetoa te koorero tuatahi, 'Ee, me hoki taatau ki a Te Kani-aa-Takirau, kia noho koia hai Kiingi mo taatau,' i runga tonu i ngaa taatai nei.

Naa, ka haere atu te koorero ki a Te Arawa, ee, anei te koorero. Ee, te koorero teenei a Tuuwharetoa, 'Me hoki taatau ki a Te Kani-aa-Takirau, ki Te Tairaawhiti, aa, hai mau i te tuunga mo te tuunga Kiingi o te motu.'

Koiraa anoo taa Ngaati Kahungunu, koiraa anoo hoki taa – ngaa mea e moohio ana ki te taatai i runga i kaarawarawa e koorero ake ra au. E whaa ngaa uri a Porourangi, e toru, ka eke katoa taatau o te motu katoa ki runga. Kaare he mea o te motu nei e hapa. Ka maarenarenatia ngaa tukutuku i runga i a Ueroa, ka pakaru iho a Te Tai-Tokerau katoa. Tai-Tokerau a Tuwharetoa, a Wanganui, ka uru katoa ki roto i te mea nei, i runga i a Rongomai-Aaniwaniwa, aa, koiraa te mea i kiia i te whiuwhiu kupu a Tamahae raaua ko Putaanga, karanga ake ra a Tamahae,

'Ee, te kino tangata, te tangata e wero iho nei!'

Ka whakahokia ra e Putaanga, 'Ee, he kino tangata ra, no Tau-o-te-Wai no roto i te maara kootipuu a Tuumoana-kootore.'

Karanga ake ra a Tamahae, 'Ee, taaua tonu ia taaua.'

Karanga mai ra a Putaanga, 'Ee, kore noa atu koe o te waa tauware noa atu.'

Engari, ki te whakapapangia, araa kee. Ka moe a Tuumoana-Kootore, ka moe i a Rongomai-Tauarau, i a Ruatau – kia puta ki waho naa ko Hine-maahuru. Ka moe i a Rongomai-tauarau ka puta ki waho, naa ko teeraa hanga – he married two sisters.

Ka moe a Tuu-moana-kootore ka moe i ngaa waahine tokorua i a Rongomai-tauarau raaua ko Ruutanga. Ka moe a Tuu-moana-kootore ka moe i a Rongomai-tauarau kia puta ki waho ko Ngaati-Hau naana ko Taataakura naana ko Tuuwhakairiora. Ka pakaru teenei i a Ngaati Porou katoa. Na ka moe i a Ruutanga ka puta ki waho ko Hine-maahuru. Na ka moe i a Apanui-Waipapa, ka puta ki waho ko Te Whaanau-a-Apanui. Ehara i te mea ko Te Whaanau-a-Apanui anake, ko Ngaati Porou katoa.

E waru ngaa tamariki a Apanui-Waipapa. Koiraa te koorero i too maatau taenga atu ki Rotorua, tuu mai a Kepa ki te whai-koorero i te marae, 'Haramai koutou a Te Whaanau-a-Apanui, kia kite koutou te waru puu-manawa o Te Arawa!'

Te waru puu-manawa e waru ngaa tamariki a Tama-te-Kapua. Noo reira, koinei anake te iwi peenei, e waru ngaa tamariki, e waru puu-manawa.

Reo: 'E ko ngaa tamariki a Rangitihi?'

Eruera Stirling: Koiraa te koorero, te waru puumanawa o roto i ngaa uri o Tama-te-Kapua. Ngaa uri nei! Ngaa uri o waru-puu-manawa. Naa, kaatahi ka whakautua e au te marae o Ohinemutu, 'E Kepa, kai te pai ra. Teenaa i roto i te waru puu-manawa o Te Arawa, kaarangarangatia mai e koe ki a au; e hia ngaa rangatira o te motu, ka pakaru i roto?'

I roto i te waru, kia puta te waru puu-manawa. Koina taku kii atu. Karangarangatia mai e koe, te waru puumanawa na, kia puta ngaa rangatira o te Arawa. Anaa, muri iho, ka kiia atu au, 'Kaati! Whakapapatia atu e au te whakapapa nei. Ka moe a Apanui-Waipapa ka moe i a

Hine-maahuru, ka puta ki waho, e waru ngaa tamariki. Ka whakahekeheketia e au ngaa
rangatira katoa o te motu, ka uru ki roto. Engari au, te waru puu-manawa o roto i a Apanui
pau katoa te motu. Ka whakahekengia e au a Tuupaea, ka whakahekengia e au ngaa mea o
Ngaati Kahungunu, a Maku Ellison maa, a Turi Kara maa, ka whakahekeheketia e au!'

Ka tuu a Timutimu Taawhai, kaatahi a Timutimu Taawhai ka karanga atu, 'E Kepa,
naahau anoo i tono kia koorerotia. Anei, anei to pou-koorero o maatau o Te
Whaanau-a-Apanui e koorero nei.'

Naa, koiraa taku koorero ki a Te Arawa. Aa, ka rite ki te koorero a te Maaori i koorero ra i
roto i te waa . . . – he maangai waha nui. Maangai nui, aa, e koorero tonu ra a ia i te mea ra
raa, aa, kai te kata mai au ki taua koorero . . .

Reo: 'Aa, he tika toou teenaa. I kite atu hoki a ia, i a koe i teenaa kokonga na, naa reira i puta
ai i a ia teeraa koorero.'

Eruera Stirling: Noo reira nee, kua whakautungia e au a Te Arawa mo ngaa mea peenaa; mo
ngaa koorero whaanui. I kii atu au, engari te waru puu-manawa o roto i a Apanui, pakaru
ngaa rangatira o Tuuwharetoa a Te Heuheu ra. Ka pakaru a Te Haapuku-Niha ki roto o
Wairarapa, ka pakaru a Tuupaea ki roto o Heretaunga. Ka pakaru hoki a MeteKiingi, ka
pakaru hoki ngaa roto – a Tuupaea, aa, whiti atu ki Wharekauri, Te Waipounamu. Naa
reira . . .

Matiu Te Hau: E a Tuupaea na no roto o Tauranga

Arnold Reedy: E rua ngaa Tuupaea na – E ko te Tuupaea o Hawke's Bay

Reo: E mahara ana au kotahi tonu te Tuupaea –

Eetahi atu reo:
Oh! no, no!

Eruera Stirling: Ee, ko teenei Tuupaea, Te Tuupaea o Ngati Kahungunu, aa, i tuku atu i Te
Tuupaea o Tauranga. Te Tuupaea tamariki nee! Well, they are descended from the
Tuupaea from Tauranga, aa, taha ki roto i a Kahungunu. No teenei koorero o aaku, ka tuu
mai a Kepa Ehau, 'E hoa, me mutu too hoki mai ki konei!'

Kepa give me a lot of jokes!

Arnold Reedy: Aa taihoa! taihoa! Ko wau hai aarahi atu i a koe. Ee ka tae maatau ki Rotorua,
ko Neepia Mahuika, Wii Peewhairangi taku taina, ko Tuuhoro Kershaw, me au. Manaakitia
maatau e Kepa. Aa, ka pai te manaaki a Kepa Ehau i a maatau i roto o Tuunohopuu. Te
whaangai i a maatau ki te kai me ngaa koorero, me ngaa manaaki. Kaatahi a Kepa ka
koorero mai, 'E Nehe, moohio anoo koe ki teenei tipuna ki a Koroingo?'

Kii atu au, 'No Ngaati Porou te tipuna na?'

'Aae!'

Ka kii mai a ia ki a au, 'Aa teenaa, kaare e taea e koe te hoomai i te whakapapa o
Koroingo?'

Kaati maahau te mea nei – anei taku whakahoki ki a Kepa.

E Kepa, he nui ngaa waahine a Tuuwhakairiora – he nui ona waahine. Na tona wahine
tuatahi ko tana tama tonu, ko Tuu-te-Rangi-Whiu. Naa, ka moe te koroua ra i teetahi o
oona wahine, ka puta mai ko eeraa, o oona tamariki. Ka moe i teenaa o oona wahine, ka puta
mai ko eenaa. Naa wai ra i taea, kua kore noa iho e taea te kaute i te nui o ngaa tamariki a te
koroua ra.

Naa ka tae kei tona kaumaatuatanga, ka whakahokia a ia ma tana tama, maana e tiaki.
Naa, a kaati! koinei ngaa koorero, me te mea nei i teenei takiwaa kua tino kaumaatua rawa
atu. Aa, e kiia ana, a ka mahia he whare motuhake tonu moona, hai nohoanga moona i roto.
He wharau! He wharau!

Aa kaati, ko ngaa koorero o teenei tangata o Tuuwhakairiora e kiia ana, koiraa te tangata kaare tahi i paa oona ringaringa ki teenei mea ki te kai, aa, tae noa ki toona matenga. Kaare tahi i paa ngaa ringaringa ki te kai. His hands never touched food right throughout his whole life. Even in war. Ahakoa i ngaa waa o te whawhai, kaare tahi oona ringaringa i paa ki te kai.

Naa, ka mauria mai ra a ia ki reira, na raa peenei te aahua, e Koro, ki reira, aa, whakahemohemo ai. Naa, ko ngaa waahine a te koroua ra, a tana paapaa, ki te mau kai atu maana. Engari, ki ngaa koorero ki a au e Eru, ko Whiri-tuaa-Rangi te wahine. Aakuni pea ai aakuni, ko teetahi kee noa atu. Otiraa mo teenei waa ko Whiri-tuaa-Rangi te wahine. Engari maahau maana, e whakatikatika mai.

Naa, he raa ana, kua haere te – a-Whiri-tuaa-Rangi, ko te wahine tonu teenei a Tuu-te-Rangi-Whiu, ko teetahi o ngaa waahine a Tuu-te-Rangi-Whiu. Naa, kia mau mai koutou ki teeraa, Ray! Naa, he raa ana- ko tona hunaonga toou. Ka haere a ia ki te kawe kai i roto i te koona. Heoi anoo hoki aa, ka whaangai atu i te mea; ma te raakau e hoatu te kai. He tapu ra hoki. Kaare hoki e – he tapu. Ahakoa i te whawhai he peeraa tonu. Kaare tahi e paa ana ngaa ringaringa ki te kai.

Engari, kai teetahi rangi ka haere atu a Whiri-tuaa-Rangi ki te whooatu koonaa, kaare tahi i rere mai ngaa ringaringa ki te koonaa ra, i whaawhaa kee ake – i rarau kee.

Reo: He kai kee noa atu taana e rarau ra.

Arnold Reedy: Kaatahi te wahine ra ka whakaaro, me koorero raanei a ia ki tana taane, ki te tama tonu a te kaumaatua ra, i a Tuu-te-Rangi-Whiu. Aa, ka whakaaro a ia, pai kee atu me koorero a ia.

Kaatahi ka mea atu, 'Ei! Haere atu nei au ki te mau kai atu ma te koroua nei, ka rarau kee mai a ia ki a au.'

Kua kii atu a Tuu-te-Rangi-Whiu, 'I nee! Aa kaati ra, me mea ki te rarau mai anoo koe ki a ia, me takoto koe ki tona taha.'

'Oo! Kore rawa e taea e au teenaa!'

I teetahi rangi ka whakahau a Tuu-te-Rangi-Whiu, haere tahi. Ka haere atu a ia. Na haere atu ana a Whiri-tuaa-Rangi ki te mau atu, aa tahi, koia kai muri e whakakiko atu ana nee! Koia e titiro atu ana. Aa, no tona kitenga atu, aa, kua kiia atu ra hoki e ia a Whiri-tuaa-Rangi, me takoto ka tika. Me hoatu! Me hoatu, ka tika!

Kaatahi a ia ka karanga atu, 'E Tuu! E Tuu! Ka heke ra anoo koe i te poo, kai te koroingo toou. He aha, kai te kaha tonu koe?'

'E tama, he mahi tuu rawa ai oti ki runga!'

Naa, ka whaanau mai te tamaiti, ka whaanau mai te tamaiti ko Koroingo, ko Koroingo.

Naa ko te koorero teenei a Kepa ki a maatau i reira. Ko ana manaaki teenei i a maatau, a Kepa. E kii ana a Kepa, ko Te Koroingo nei, i haere atu Te Koroingo nei, ka noho peeraka atu ki teeraa takiwaa i Murupara ra, ki a Ngaati Manawa. Ka mate te wahine a teetahi rangatira i reira, ka moea e te Koroingo nei. Aa, i te koorero mai a Kepa ki a maatau ko Ngaati Whakaaue, te uri. Aa, koiraa ngaa whai-koorero a Kepa ki a maatau. Na maahau maana e too haere te mea nei.

Eruera Stirling: Naa, e koorero ana au mo Koroingo. Haere hoki te waa i mua o te matenga o te koroua ra aa - -

Arnold Reedy: Just a moment Dick. I wonder if a Paakehaa has the heart big enough to do that. Eh! Nee! For the son to say to - -

*Matiu Te Hau:*Ee, i taea ra hoki e Charlie Chaplin! (Laughter.)

Arnold Reedy: Kaare! Inaa kee taaku! Inaa kee taaku. Ko teetahi toou o oona waahine ka hoatu tonungia e ia, ma tona paapaa.

Reo: Kao! Kao! Mo te kaha tangata kee taaku e koorero ra.

Matiu Te Hau: E Nehe! E Nehe! There's a Paakehaa saying 'Nought for his comfort!' (Laughter.)

Reo: Koinei kee ki aau! Koinei kee ki aau. Naaraa, he whakatoi kee. He whakatoi kee, te maataamua ra; tana tuku i tana wahine kia – He aha ra – kia moea e tana paapaa. Na ko teeraa tangata hoki e whakamatemate ana. Na te kaha o tona paapaa, ka puta a Koroingo ki waho.

Eruera Stirling: Aa, he tika teenaa e Nehe. Anaa i te whakawaatanga, o te i nga whakawaa o Te Araroa ra, ka haere 'Te Keehi' a Koroingo nee! Naaraa ko oo taaua maatua toou ra, ko Heenare Te Ahuriri ka tuku mai, on Koroingo. Well, ka mahia ra te township i Te Araroa. Well, haere ngaa tukutuku. Naa, i runga i te whakaaro o Tuu-whakairiora, ka tukuna eetahi o ngaa tekihana tonu o ngaa papa-kaainga tonu i te marae ra. Ka tukuna ki a Koroingo. Naa, no te haeretanga o ngaa whakawaa, kaatahi ka tirohia, ha! he uri toou ia Koroingo na Tuu-whaka-iri-ora. Aa, no teehea taha?

    I mua i te matenga o Tuuwhakairiora nee! Kaatahi a Tuuwhakairiora ka kii, 'Naa moohou, i whakatuutuki i ngaa koorero o toou hinengaro. Naa kaati! ka tukua e au teetahi whenua.'

    E kai te taaone ra nee! Ka tukuna atu, koiraa teetahi o ngaa tekihana o te taaone, ka tukuna ki a Koroingo.

    Naa, kaatahi ka hopu atu eetahi; ngaa mea o maatau nei o Te Whaanau-a-Apanui, a Hoohepa Karapaena maa, they disputed the mea ra, te tuku ra. Aa, te whakawaatanga a te kooti, ka riro i ngaa uri a Koroingo. He mea tuku iho na Tuuwhakairiora. Araa a Heenare Te Ahiriri maa. Yes! kai reira a Te Ahuriri maa. Well they derived the interest – and they got the interest from Koroingo. Tika tonu! Tika tonu te koorero ra.

Reo: I hea teenaa? I Rotorua! I hea teenaa taaone?

Ngaa reo: I Te Araroa. I Te Araroa tonu naa. I mua o tona haerenga nee!

Eruera Stirling: Naa ka riro ki ngaa – koiraa ngaa uri a Koroingo ko Heenare Te Ahuriri maa ra. Well, ka riro i a raatau ngaa tekihana o Te Araroa ra, i runga i a Koroingo.

Reo: Aa, ko wau ra teeraa!

Eruera Stirling: Aa, koutou ra hoki!

Arnold Reedy: Aa, kaare tonu au i moohio i karaati whenua a ia!

Eruera Stirling: Oh, yes! I karaati whenua a ia. I mahara tonutia a ia. I karaati whenua tonu a ia.

Arnold Reedy: Kaati, me waiata a taatau koorero!

Eruera Stirling: A tenaa! Ko teenei te waiata e tika ana, 'He ue ake ra . . .!'

(Waiata) Eruera Stirling: Ue ake ra ka hee too manawa,
                             Ka titiro ki waho ra . . .
Arnold Reedy: Ka titiro ki uta ra . . .

Eruera Stirling: Ki waho ra! Kai tiko mai koe ki Hikurangi! *(Ka mate raatau i te katanga . . . kia ora! kia ora!)*

(Waiata) Eruera Stirling anake.
Paatai: Ee, mea kee ana hoki au ki te paatai atu ki a koorua, kia koorerotia mai e koe, e koorua te whakaheketanga o Te Whaanau-a-Apanui, anaa, o Mihi Kootukutuku, i te waa e

takoto ana te koroura ra i te marae. Ooku rongo, kua koorero mai koe i eenei koorero ki a au, heoi anoo ee, kia rongo ai te whaanau.

Eruera Stirling: Aa, naa! tae mai te waea mai ki a maatau, ki a Te Whaanau-a-Apanui, ki a maatau ko aku maatua – taku kookaa, ki a Mihi Kootukutuku, ki ngaa Waititi, ka nui te taumaha o Apirana. Anoo ka whiriwhiri maatau, aa, kia haere maatau kia kite i te koroua. Whakariteritengia e maatau, ka haere too maatau pahi. Ka tae maatau ki Wai-o-mata-tini. Tae atu maatau ki reira, ki te marae, aa, ka mihi mai ngaa koroua a Hoone Ngata maa ki a maatau, aa i too maatau haerenga atu kia kite i te koroua.

Kaati, ka tae atu maatau ki reira ka kiia mai, kaare e whakaaeangia e te taakuta kia haere atu kia kite i a Aapirana i te mea kua taumaha. Kua tae ki a ia ki te waa, kua huri. Kaatahi, a Mere Karaka ka puta mai ki waho, ka paatai atu taku maamaa, taku kookaa, a Mihi, mehemea kai te peehea te koroua. Kii mai a Mere, 'Kua hee! Kua kiia e te taakuta, kauaa he tangata e haere kia kite.'

Kaatahi taku maamaa ka kii atu ki a Mere Karaka, 'E me kii atu koe, ko maatau ko aku tungaane kua tae mai.'

Ko Moana Waititi maa, ko Haariata maa. Haere a Mere Karaka. Te taenga atu o Mere Karaka ki roto, naa tatari. Ohonga ake o te koroua ra, ka kii atu a Mere Karaka, 'Oo kai waho nei a Mihi Kootukutuku, raatau ko oona tungaane.'

Aa, tere tonu to ohonga mai o te koroua ra.

Ka karanga atu te koroua ra, 'Aa, kai whea?'

'Aa, kai waho nei.'

'Kiia atu kia haramai!'

Ka puta mai a Mere Karaka, kaatahi ka karanga mai a Mere Karaka, 'Oo, kai piirangi mai te koroua nei, kia haere atu koutou.'

Ka kuhu atu maatau ki roto, aa, tae atu maatau, aa! Tona takoto anoo ka moohio tonu atu, ka tiro tonu atu ki te aahua, aa, kai te haere, e whakatata ana ki te waa o eeraa – tuuiwi, mo te mate. Tau atu maatau ki roto, ka haere atu ki te ringaringa ki a ia, ka mutu te ringaringa kaatahi anoo a ia ka karanga mai ki a au.

'Eruera, me karakia koe i a taatau. Kia mutu too karakia i a taatau, ka whai-koorero ai au ki a koutou.' Aa, karakia tonu hoki au. Anei taku hiimene i karakia ai au:

'Taaku nei e koa ai au ko ngaa whare o Te Atua,
Aataahua ana mai eenei tohu o te pai, ee
Kai te oohia atu au ki toou mata e Te Atua
Whakawhiwhia mai ahau, ki a au tohu atawhai
Manu rere takiwaa roa tera e koa nei
Nei ra ia te tino koa mo te ngakau whiwhi nei
Hei aarahi ake, ki te uma o te Atua i.'

Teenei hiimene, e hiimenetia ana teenei e ngaa kaumaatua. Tino hiimene teenei i ngaa huihuinga o roto i ngaa tau i tooku tamarikitanga, aa, i roto i ngaa tau te iwa rau maa iwa te tau, huri atu. Koinei teetahi hiimene, hiimenetia ana mo ngaa mea, e tata ana te whakawhiti ki tua o te aarai. Hiimenetia e au taku hiimene nei aa, ka mutu. Mutu atu ana taku hiimene, maranga haere mai te koroua ki runga.

Ka mutu taku hiimene, ka whakatau au i taku karakia, whakamutu, ka waiatangia mai e ia te waiata nei na, 'Angiangi hau raro whakaeke mai ra.'

Teenei waiata na Te Whaanau-a-Apanui. Naa kai te pupuhi ngaa hauaauru o taua raa. Koiraa te tangi a te koroua, 'Angiangi hau-raro.'

Naa, ka mihimihi maatau ki a ia. Kaatahi a ia ka huri mai ki taku maamaa. Kaatahi a ia ka kii mai taku maamaa, 'E Mihi, ka hoki atu koe, ka tae ki te waa e hinga ai au, e mate ai au, me haramai koe kia tangihia ngaa tangi a oo tiipuna i konei. Kia riro ahau maahau e tangi, ma oo koutou ko o taaina e noho nei. Me tae tonu mai koe. Kia aha? Kia tangihia ai au.'

Reo: Naa, me tona whakatuupato anoo. Aahua hee manawa ana te kuia ra.

Eruera Stirling: Aa, me tona kii tonu mai, 'Ahakoa tonu, kia kaha tonu koe e Mihi. Kia ora tonu koe. Kia tuutuki teenaa hui. Maahau ngaa waiata e tangi ki a au. Kia aha ai? Kia tangi ai – kai konei o taaina. Kai konei te Whaanau-o-Raakairoa, hai tuu, hai tangi i te marae nei.'

Aa, ka mutu oona mihi mai, Te koroua, ka mihimihi mai ka hokihoki maatau. Tae atu maatau ki te kaainga, ao ake the next day, i teetahi rangi mai, aa, ka, tae mai te waea, kua mate te koroua ra.

Anaa, ka hoki mai maatau. Tae mai maatau ki te marae, i reira a Ngaapuhi e tuu ana. E tuu ana a Ngaapuhi katoa, e tuu ana i te marae. Kai te karanga mai, aa, te tangata whenua, 'Ei, taihoa koutou e haere. Taihoa koutou e haramai, Te Whaanau-a-Apanui!'

Kaatahi anoo taku maamaa ka haere atu, 'Kaare! Ko ngaa mea kai runga i te marae na, whakawaatea ake te whanga! Whakawaatea ake! Kai te haere atu au. Maaku e tangi inaianei ma Te Whaanau-a-Apanui!'

Naa, ka rongo hoki a Whina maa i te koorero ra, karanga ana te kuia ta.

'Kaare! E kii me tatari au ki a raatau. Ko raatau anoo me huri ki te whanga.'

Reo: Naa, anaa kee tana koorero, 'E kii me puru au i aku roimata mo raatau te take.'

Eruera Stirling: 'Me puru au i aku roimata mo raatau te take. Me whakawaatea!'

Anaa, kaatahi ka haere atu ki te marae. Tona taenga atu hoki, tangihia e ia ngaa waiata. Anaa, teetahi tangihanga whakamiiharo teenaa. Maringi ai te roimata, katoa, i ngaa manuhiri katoa i te tuunga o taku maamaa.

Arnold Reedy: Naaraa te tangi a Ngaati Porou. Ka rongo i te kuia ra, i tona tangi, i aana Aue! ka tangi tuaruangia nei.

Eruera Stirling: Aa, ka tangi tuaruangia. Aa, te mutunga iho – ko teenei waiata, ahakoa peehea waa maatau haere i roto i a maatau tangi mate, i ngaa mahi e haere ana au i te taha o te koroua, tana waiata, karanga mai ana a ia ahakoa mutu ana ngaa koorero, ka karanga mai, 'Eruera, hai wareware ra ki too waiata!'

Aa, ka moohio au ko 'Kereruu-huahua' teeraa.

Naa, ka tangi ra maatau, ka mutu. Anaa, ko taku waiata teenei. I mau ai au i teenei waiata, kai runga i te aahua tonu o ngaa koorero a te koroua nei ki a au. Aa ka waiatangia e au:

'E hika maa ee, I hoki mai au i Kereruuhuahua, ee. Noho tuupuhi ana ko au anake i te tamaiti mate . . .' (Nga Moteatea 40)

Teenei waiata naana ra teenei waiata tonu i koorero mai ki a au nei i au e haere ana i a maatau haere nui. Ahakoa haere maatau ki whea, koinei taana, 'Eruera!' kua waiata. Kaati koinei te take au nei e mau nei ki teenei waiata, he mea, he taonga i mahue iho na te iwi kua huri ki tua o te aarai. Ka pau ra eenei whakamaarama eenei koorero inaianei.

BIBLIOGRAPHY

TAPES

—— *John Waititi interviews Eruera and Amiria Stirling about Wharerakau's lament for Poututerangi, and Rangiuia's lament for Tuterangiwhaitiri;* taped Bruce Biggs; Archive of Maori and Pacific Music, University of Auckland (ref. no. 036).

1965   *Eruera Stirling gives mihi to Tai Tokerau at opening ceremony of Tamawahine Community Centre, Te Puea Marae, Mangere 13.11.65;* Archive of aori and Pacific Music, University of Auckland (ref. no. 189).

1966   *Eruera Stiring and Arnold Reedy discuss women on the marae and related topics at University of Auckland, 1966;* taped Bruce Biggs; Archive of Maori and Pacific Music, University of Auckland (ref. no. 0233).

1968   *Eruera Stirling gives whaikorero at Mangahanea Marae, 5.1.68;* Archive of Maori and Pacific Music, University of Auckland (ref. no. 297).

1968   *Eruera Stirling gives whaikorero at Waikato visit to Mangahanea Marae, 7.1.68;* Archive of Maori and Pacific Music, University of Auckland (ref. no. 309).

1968   *A programme made on the 50th wedding anniversary of Mr and Mrs Eruera Stirling, May 1968;* Maori and Pacific Islands Programme Unit Archives, Radio New Zealand.

1970   *Eruera Stirling talks to Anne Salmond, records waiata and tauparapara, 29.11.70;* Archive of Maori and Pacific Music, University of Auckland (ref. no. 72/054).

1971   *Eruera Stirling speaks at Wairuru, Raukokore, and talks of Apanui Waipapa, Hine Mahuru and Apanui Ringamutu, 24.1.71;* taped Anne Salmond; Archive of Maori and Pacific Music, University of Auckland (ref. no. 72/061).

1971   *Eruera Stirling speaks at welcome to Duncan McIntyre, Mangahanea Marae 19.1.71;* taped Anne Salmond; Archive of Maori and Pacific Music, University of Auckland (ref. nos. 72/068, 72/069).

1971   *Eruera and Tama Stirling speak at Tom Kirkwood's tangi, Mangere Marae 31.5.71;* taped Anne Salmond; Archive of Maori and Pacific Music, University of Auckland (ref. no. 72/092).

1971   *Eruera Stirling gives whaikorero at Turangawaewae Marae Golden Jubilee, 15.8.71;* Archive of Maori and Pacific Music, University of Auckland (ref. no. 72/110).

1971   *Eruera Stirling gives whaikorero at Bishop Panapa's unveiling, Mangere Marae, August 1971;* taped Anne Salmond; Archive of Maori and Pacific Music, University of Auckland (ref. no. 72/095).

1972   *Eruera Stirling at Waiata School 1972;* Archive of Maori and Pacific Music, University of Auckland (ref. no. 72/194).

1973   *Eruera Stirling gives karakia and hymn at ritual for opening the Wharepuni at Orakei Marae, NZBC Maori Programme, 3.6.73;* Archive of Maori and Pacific Music, University of Auckland (ref. no. 73/119).

1973   *Eruera Stirling talks about Sir Apirana Ngata to Stage I Class 'Introduction to Maori Society' at Auckland University 1.8.73;* Archive of Maori and Pacific Music, University of Auckland (ref. no. 74/136).

1975   *Eruera Stirling speaks at the opening of a dining-hall in Whareroa, Tauranga, 28.5.75;* Maori and Pacific Island Programme Unit Archives, Radio New Zealand.

1975   *Eruera Stirling addresses Maori Artists' and Writers' Conference in Papakura, 10.8.75;* taped Haare Williams; Maori and Pacific Islands Programme Unit Achives, Radio New Zealand.

1975   *Eruera Stirling gives a tribute to Norman Kirk, 29.8.75;* Maori and Pacific Islands Programme Unit Archives, Radio New Zealand.

1975   *Eruera Stirling speaks on 'The Land' in a programme on the Maori Land March, 18.9.75;* Maori and Pacific Islands Programme Unit Archives, Radio New Zealand.

1978   *Eruera Stirling addresses Tai Rawhiti Association at Holy Sepulchre Marae, Khyber Pass, Auckland, 1978;* taped Whai Ngata; Maori and Pacific Islands Programme Unit Archives, Radio New Zealand.

1979   *Eruera Stirling speaks to Anne Salmond, February-December 1979;* Tapes 1-35; Archive of Maori and Pacific Music, University of Auckland (ref. nos. 79/086 – 79/118C).

1980   *Eruera Stirling interviewed by TV 1 for 'Koha' programme, March 1980; Archive of Maori and Pacific Music, University of Auckland (ref. no. C80/005).*

NEWSPAPERS
Gisborne Herald 'Sterling Record, Mr William G. Sherratt', 16.11.43
Gisborne Times 'Mr T. S. Williams: Passing of a Sterling Pioneer', 26.5.28
   'Maori History of the East Coast', W. E. Goffe, 12.5.31, 19.5.31
Opotiki News 'Canon H. Pahewa', 22.10.48.
   A report on the unveiling of Mrs Mihi Kotukutuku Stirling's gravestone, 8.11.58.
Poverty Bay Herald 'Dean of Sportsmen: Mr R. Sherratt passes', 14.12.38.
Western Star 'A Link with the Past—Mr John Stirling', 5.10.20.
Southland Times 'Captain Stirling's Remains found at Tiwai', 11.5.71.
   'Burial Area Wanted at Tiwai', 16.6.71.

THESES
Butterworth, G.V., 'The Politics of Adaptation. The Career of Sir Apirana Ngata 1874-1928', M.A. thesis in History, Victoria University 1969.

Drummond, R. J. H., 'The Origins and Early History of Ngati Porou', M.A. thesis in History, Alexander Turnbull Library.

Mahuika, Apirana, 'Nga Wahine-Kai-Hautu o Ngati Porou', M.A. thesis, University of Sydney 1973.

McClean, Sheila, 'Maori Representation 1905-1948', M.A. thesis in History, University of Auckland, 1950.

MANUSCRIPTS
Army Department Files, AD1/70 1548, 1057, National Archives.
Army Department Nominal Index 1869, 1870-71, National Archives.
Army Department Register 1870, National Archives.
Awatere, Peta and Dewes, Koro. 'Te Kawa o Te Marae', mimeo, Department of Anthropology, University of Auckland.
Beattie, Herries, Whakapapa Book, M 1 S82, E/18, Hocken Library.
Best, Elsdon. Maori material contributed by Mohi Ruatapu and Henare Potae, c.1880, Alexander Turnbull Library.
Garvie, Alex. Sketch books 1856, Lands and Survey Department, Invercargill.
Green, Pinky Laureston. 'A History of Northern Waiapu', a collection of material as a research project, 1960 Alexander Turnbull Library.

Harris, F. 'Maori Genealogies, East Coast' (annotated by Elsdon Best), Alexander Turnbull Library.

Harrison, P. R. 'The Traditions of the Ngati Porou Tribe', mimeo, Department of Maori Studies, University of Auckland 1967.

Historical Atlas papers, Alexander Turnbull Library.

Horouta Maori Council, Minute Book 1909-1935, Alexander Turnbull Library.

Kapiti, Pita, Book of East Coast Legends, Waiata and Whakapapa, dictated to Rev. Mohi Turei, Alexander Turnbull Library.

'Ko nga Waiata a nga tangata Maori', some written at Tuparoa, September 1868; incl. waiata from Mohi Turei, Alexander Turnbull Library.

Old Land Claims File 1023, National Archives.

Opotiki Minute Books 1-24, Rotorua Maori Land Court Office.

Potae, Henare. 'Genealogies and traditions, East Coast, by Henare Potae of Tokomaru Bay, 1884', Alexander Turnbull Library.

Shortland, Edward, papers, Hocken Library.

South Island Whakapapa, papers, Wallace Early Settlers' Association, Riverton (courtesy Ulva Belsham).

Stirling, Eruera, 'The Centennial of the Waiamatatini School' (notebook) 1978.

'A History of Te Whanau-a-Maru and Ngati Hinekehu of the Tapuwaeroa Valley' (pages from exercise book).

'Migration of Tahupotiki the Younger Brother of Porourangi' (handwritten blue pages).

Whakapapa book (large artist's sketch book).

'Whakapapa from the Seven Canoes', drawn by Anne Salmond at his dictation, c.1968.

Waiapu Minute Books 10-11, Gisborne Maori Land Court Office.

Williams, William, 'Journal 1869-1871', Alexander Turnbull Library.

PUBLISHED WORKS

Anderson, Len, *Throughout the East Coast: The Story of Williams and Kettle Ltd*, Pictoria Publications, Hastings, 1974.

Anonymous, 'Rev. Mohi Turei—A Biography', in *Te Ao Hou*, Vol. 2 no. 1, 1953.

Anonymous, 'The Story of Paikea and Ruatapu', in *Te Ao Hou*, no. 40, September 1962, p. 6.

Begg, A.C. and N.C., *Port Preservation*, Whitcombe and Tombs, 1973.

Best, Elsdon, *The Maori Division of Time*, Dominion Museum Monograph No. 1, 1922.

Blanc, Arapera, 'Ko Taku Kumara', in *Te Ao Hou*, no. 24, October 1958, pp. 6-8.

The Bluff 1836-1936 Centenary Souvenir Programme, 1936.

Colenso, William, *Excursion in the Northern Island of New Zealand*, Launceston Examiner, 1844.

Cyclopaedia of New Zealand, 1897-1908, Vol. 4: Otago and Southland, The Cyclopaedia Co. Ltd.

Dewes, Koro, 'The Growing of Kumara', in *Te Ao Hou*, no. 25, December 1958, pp. 41-5.

Fowler, Leo, 'The Knight Errantry of Tamahae' in *Te Ao Hou*, no. 24, October 1958.

Gudgeon, W. E., 'The Maori Tribes of the East Coast of New Zealand', in *Journal of the Polynesian Society*, Vol. 3, 1894, pp. 208-219.

Halbert, Rongo, *Te Tini o Toi*, Whakatane and District Historical Society Inc., Memoir No. 1, 1961.

Hall-Jones, F. G., 'Kelly of Inverkelly', *Otago Daily Times*, 1944.

'King of the Bluff', *Otago Daily Times*, 1943.

'Historical Southland', *Otago Daily Times*, 1945.

Hall-Jones, John, *Bluff Harbour*, Southland Harbour Board, Bluff, 1976.

Hiruharama Maori School, *67th Jubilee 1895-1961*, 1961.

History of the East Coast Native Schools, 'East Coast Watch' Print, Tokomaru Bay, 1924.

Kapiti, Pita, 'History of the Horouta Canoe', dictated to Rev. Mohi Turei, in *Journal of the Polynesian Society,* Vol. 21, no. 84, December 1912, pp. 152-63.

    'Kumara Lore', dictated to Rev. Mohi Turei, in *Journal of the Polynesian Society,* Vol. 22, no. 85, March 1913, pp. 36-41.

King, Michael (ed.), *Te Ao Hurihuri: The World Moves On,* Hicks, Smith and Sons, Wellington, 1975.

McCallion, A. J., Bennett, E. D. and Gardner, A. L., *Their Greatness: Tales of the Pioneers of the Eastern Bay of Plenty,* Rotorua Printers, 1956.

Mackay, J. A., *Historic Poverty Bay and East Coast,* J. A. Mackay, 57 Centennial Crescent, Gisborne, 1966.

McNab, Robert, *The Old Whaling Days,* Whitcombe and Tombs Ltd, 1913.

Marsden, Samuel, *The Letters and Journals of Samuel Marsden, 1765-1838,* ed. by J. R. Elder, Coulls Somerville Wilkie Ltd, 1932.

Ngata, A. T., 'He Tangi Na Rangiuia', in *Te Wananga,* Vol. II, no. I, March 1930, pp. 21-35.

    Nga Moteatea, Part I, The Polynesian Society Inc., Wellington 1959.

    Nga Moteatea, Part II, The Polynesian Society Inc., Wellington, 1961.

    Ngarimu V.C. Hui Souvenir Programme, Wellington, 1943.

    The Past, Present and Future of the Maori, Christchurch, 1893.

    The Price of Citizenship, Whitcombe and Tombs, Wellington, 1943.

    Rauru-Nui-a-Toi Lectures and Ngati Kahungunu Origins, Victoria University, Wellington, 1972.

    The Treaty of Waitangi: An Explanation, Maori Purposes Fund Board, 1922.

Okawhare, Paratene, 'History of the Horouta Migration', in *Appendices to the Journals of the House of Representatives 1880,* Vol. 11, G-L.

Omaio Maori School Ninety-Second Anniversary, Booklet, 13 April 1963.

Omarumutu War Memorial Hall, Booklet, Official Opening, printed Opotiki News, 1961.

Owen, Lynne, *School at Cape Runaway,* A. H. and A. W. Reed, Wellington, 1964.

Palgrave, F. T., *The Golden Treasury,* Collins, London and Glasgow, 1946.

Piripi Taumata-A-Kura Celebrations, Booklet, 1834-1964, Waiapu Pastorate, at Rangitukia, 1964.

Pohuhu, Nepia, 'History of the Horouta Migration', in *Appendices to the Journals of the House of Representatives 1880,* Vol. 11, G-L.

Porter, Lieutenant-Colonel, *History of the Early Days of Poverty Bay,* Poverty Bay Herald, Gisborne, 1923.

Raukokore Maori School Jubilee Booklet, Gisborne Herald, 1962.

Records of Early Riverton and District, Southland Times Co. Ltd, 1937.

Rickard, L. S., *The Whaling Trade in Old New Zealand,* Minerva, Auckland, 1965.

Riverton Presbyterian Church, Booklet, Jubilee 1861-1936, Southland Times Print, 1936.

Rosevear, Watson, *Waiapu: Story of a Diocese,* Pauls Book Arcade, MCMLX.

Salmond, Anne, *Hui: A Study of Maori Ceremonial Gatherings,* A. H. and A.W. Reed, Wellington, 1975.

Sansom, Olga, *The Stewart Islanders* A. H. and A. W. Reed, 1970.

Sewell, Ralph, *Waihau: One of New Zealand's Last Trading Coasters,* Endeavour Press, 1978.

Shortland, Edward, *The Southern Districts of New Zealand,* Longman, Brown, Green and Longmans, London, MDCCCLI.

Simmons, David, *The Great New Zealand Myth: A study of the discovery and origin traditions of the Maori,* Reed, Wellington, 1976.

Stirling, Amiria, as told to Anne Salmond, *Amiria: The Life Story of a Maori Woman,* A. H. and A. W. Reed, Wellington, 1976.

The Story of Te Hono-Ki-Rarotonga Carved Meeting-House, Booklet (held in Gisborne Public
        Library), 1969.

Taiapa, Pine, 'How the Kumara Came to New Zealand', in *Te Ao Hou,* no. 23, July 1958, pp.
        13-15.

    Tuwhakairiora Souvenir Booklet, Te Rau Press, Gisborne, 1959.

Te Kaha Maori District High School Anniversary Booklet, 1875-1955, printed by Gisborne
        Herald, 1955.

Te Whanau-A-Apanui Centennial Booklet, 1875-1975, 1975.

Turei, Rev. Mohi, 'Tuwhakairiora', in *Journal of the Polynesian Society,* Vol. 20, no. 77, March
        1911, pp. 17-34, translated by Archdeacon Williams.

Torere Maori School Booklet, 85th Jubilee 1878-1963, 1963.

Wairua, Peta, '*The Siege of Toka-a-kuku Pa', in Te Ao Hou,* no. 25, December 1958.

Waititi, Moana, 'Na Te Take o Tihirau-Whangaparaoa-mai-Tawhiti', in *Te Ao Hou,* no. 30,
        March 1960.

Whangaparaoa Maori School Golden Jubilee, Booklet, 1914-64, 1964.

Wilson, Eva, *Hakoro Ki Te Iwi,* Times Printing Service, 1976.

INDEX